CHARLEY'S WAR

THE GREAT MUTINY

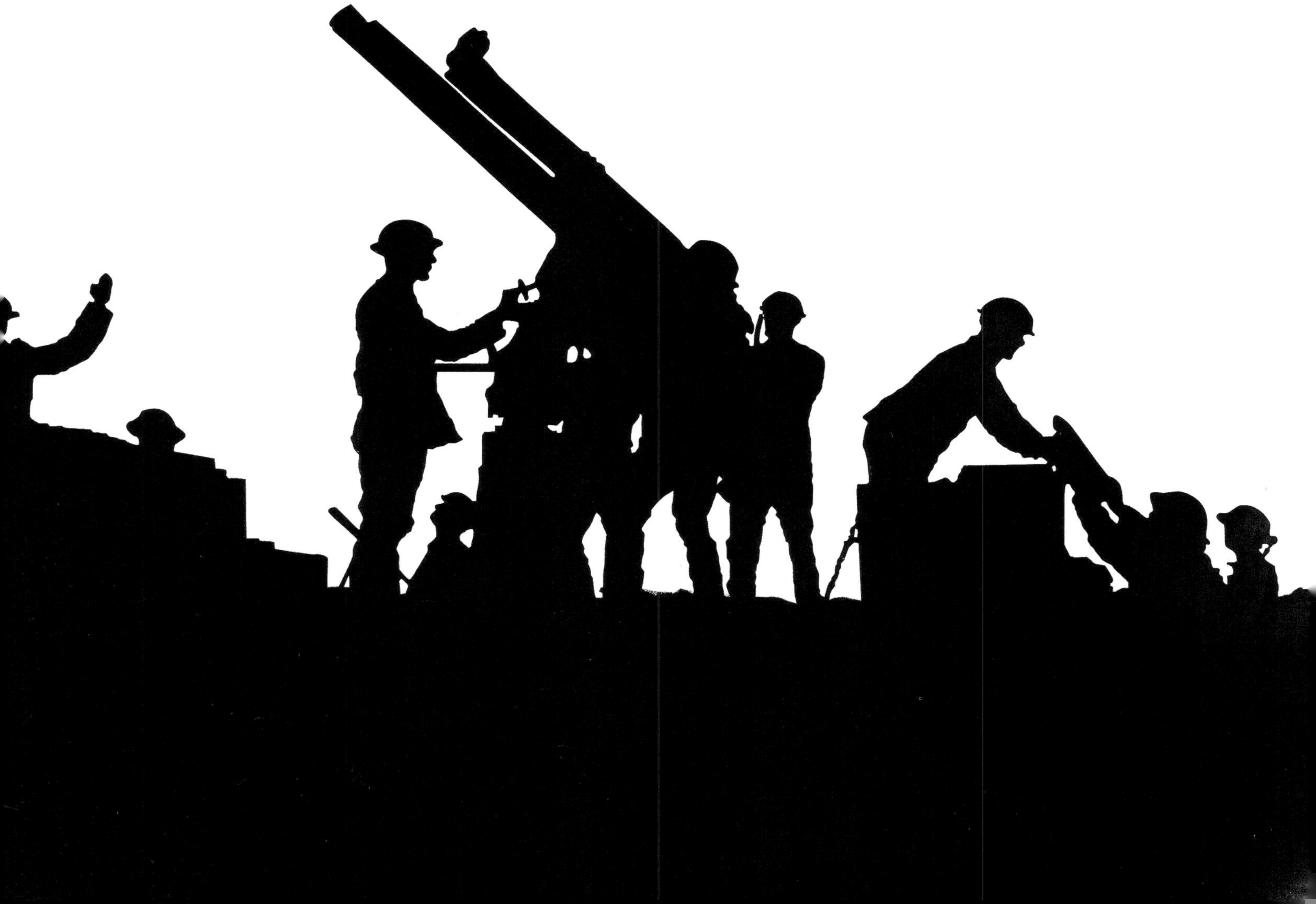

CHARLEY'S WAR: The Great Mutiny
ISBN: 9781848567412

Published by
Titan Books
A division of Titan Publishing Group Ltd.
144 Southwark St.
London SE1 0UP

A CIP catalogue record for this title is available from the British Library.

This edition first published: October 2010
2 4 6 8 10 9 7 5 3 1

Printed in Spain.

Also available from Titan Books:
Charley's War: 2 June 1916 – 1 August 1916 (ISBN: 9781840236279)
Charley's War: 1 August 1916 – 17 October 1916 (ISBN: 9781840239294)
Charley's War: 17 October 1916 – 21 February 1917 (ISBN: 9781845762704)
Charley's War: Blue's Story – 21 February 1917 (ISBN: 9781845763237)
Charley's War: Return to The Front – April 1917 (ISBN: 9781845767969)
Charley's War: Underground and Over the Top – May 1917 (ISBN: 9781845767976)

Grateful thanks to Pat Mills, Trucie Henderson, Moose Harris and Steve
White for their help and support in the production of this book.

For Neil Emery, whose dedication to *Charley's War* helped
bring it back into print – ghost soldier in the sky.

...py artwork © 2005 Trucie Henderson.

...hoto by James Francis Hurley, taken from:
 cas.awm.gov.au/photograph/E00825

...n the Western Front' feature © 2010 Steve White.
...Strip commentary © 2010 Pat Mills.

...rom the public domain except where indicated, archived
...partment of Photos and Film. Other photographs from
...Primary Document Archive: *www.gwpda.org/photos*

What did you think of this book? We love to hear from our readers. Please email
us at: readerfeedback@titanemail.com, or write to us at the above address.

To receive advance information, news, competitions, and exclusive offers
online, please sign up for the Titan newsletter on our website:
www.titanbooks.com

CHARLEY'S WAR

THE GREAT MUTINY

PAT MILLS
JOE COLQUHOUN

Titan Books

ALL DISQUIET ON THE WESTERN FRONT

The French Army Mutinies of 1917

by Steve White

There can be few more seminal movies about the First World War than Stanley Kubrick's classic, *Paths of Glory*. Released in October 1957, it held at its heart the disparity between the troops fighting at the front and the men who commanded them between dinner courses at French chateaus.

Unstinting in its portrayal of trench warfare, it focuses on the trial of three French soldiers accused of cowardice by senior officers after an ill-conceived, disastrous attack on a fortified German position. Defending the soldiers is their colonel; war-weary and disenchanted with his so-called superiors, he makes a career-destroying decision to protect his men, knowing full well the outcome of the trial is already a foregone conclusion.

In France, reaction to the film is perhaps best exemplified by the fact that, while never officially banned, it was not shown there until 1975. It could be argued that the film's powerfully anti-war sentiments did not sit well with a nation mired in a guerrilla war in Algeria. However, more likely is that Kubrick's masterpiece highlighted an episode that the French establishment had long tried to keep secret.

'COLLECTIVE INDISCIPLINE'

The French High Command could never bring itself to use the word 'mutiny'; instead, the disturbances that rippled through the French Army facing the Germans on the Western front were dressed up rather euphemistically as 'collective indiscipline'.

The trigger for such unmilitary behaviour can be traced back to the Second Battle of the Aisne, which began on 16 April 1917. With the war now almost four years old, the French army had suffered over a million fatalities – 121,000 in 1917 alone. Conditions in the trenches remained atrocious whilst the continued failure of the French military commanders to effect any kind of breakthrough in the war caused increasing consternation amongst the men they were leading.

The offensive, involving some 1.2 million troops, was conceived by the French Army commander-in chief General Robert Nivelle, who wrongly believed his new attack would break the German lines in forty-eight hours. Instead, the assaulting French infantry found themselves caught on barbed wire in a hail of machine gun fire from well-protected German positions that French artillery had singularly failed to destroy. Casualties were over 40,000 on the first day alone; some divisions suffered 60% losses.

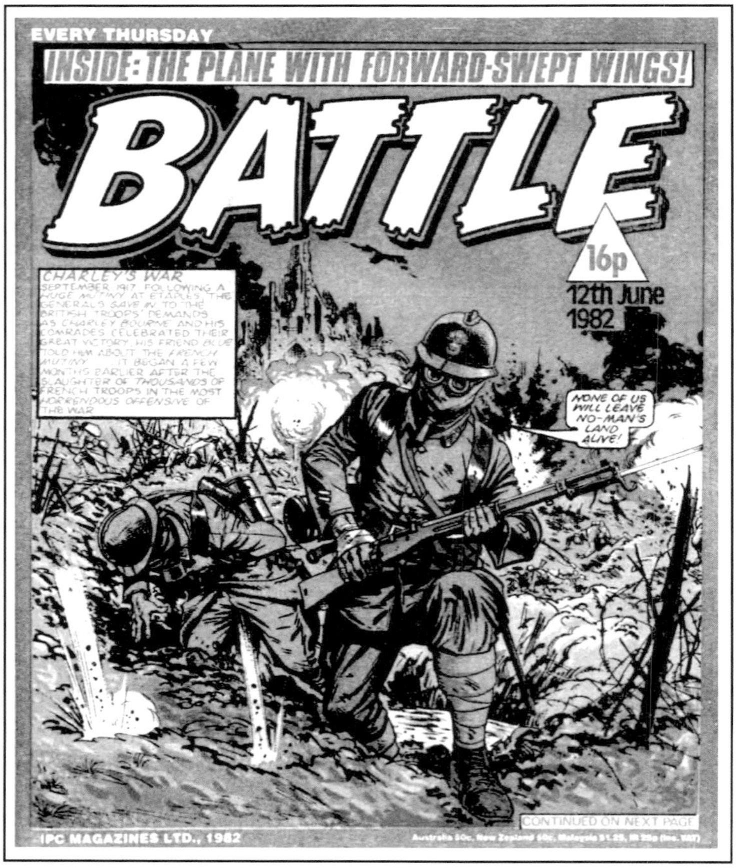
EVERY THURSDAY
INSIDE: THE PLANE WITH FORWARD-SWEPT WINGS!
BATTLE
16p
12th June 1982
CHARLEY'S WAR
SEPTEMBER 1917. FOLLOWING A HUGE MUTINY AT ETAPLES, THE GENERALS GAVE IN TO THE BRITISH TROOPS' DEMANDS. AS CHARLEY BOURNE AND HIS COMRADES CELEBRATED THEIR GREAT VICTORY, HIS FRIEND BLUE TOLD HIM ABOUT THE FRENCH MUTINY . . . IT BEGAN A FEW MONTHS EARLIER AFTER THE SLAUGHTER OF THOUSANDS OF FRENCH TROOPS IN THE MOST HORRENDOUS OFFENSIVE OF THE WAR
NONE OF US WILL LEAVE NO-MAN'S LAND ALIVE!
CONTINUED ON NEXT PAGE
IPC MAGAZINES LTD., 1982

THE FIRST CRACKS

The day after the offensive, seventeen men of the 108th Infantry Regiment abandoned their positions; twelve were subsequently sentenced to death but were later reprieved. Desertions began to mount, but the 2nd Battalion, 18th Infantry Regiment took more decisive action. The unit had been shattered and demoralised when two thirds of the unit – around 400 men – were lost during the opening offensive. Instead of being withdrawn from the frontline to rest and regroup, the casualties were simply replaced and the Battalion sent back to the front on 29 April.

Disgusted, the soldiers, many of them drunk and yelling "Down with the war!" refused. Order was restored early the following morning, but the unit's officers decided to make examples of the mutineers, with around a dozen men picked, apparently at random, to be court-martialled. Many ended in prison; five were sentenced to death, although one escaped as he was being led to the firing squad when German shelling enabled him to make a break for freedom.

A more disturbing incident occurred on 3 May. Soldiers of the 2nd Colonial Division were ordered into formation prior to moving forward to the front. Many were drunk and without weapons; they refused to move into their trenches. Faced with so many rebellious soldiers, their superiors decided on a more sensible approach rather than just randomly court-martialling and executing suspected mutineers. The most respected officers in the unit were sent to try and appeal to the troops' sense of patriotism and honour in an effort to send them forward to replace other, exhausted soldiers at the front.

But, as with many of the mutinies, the problems were not a lack of national pride or sense of duty; the principal concern was the terrible tactics and poor leadership that led to so many needless casualties. However, sobriety and, presumably, hangovers led to a softening of attitudes amongst the soldiers and they finally were marched forward. Some were punished but most of the 2nd Division escaped arrest.

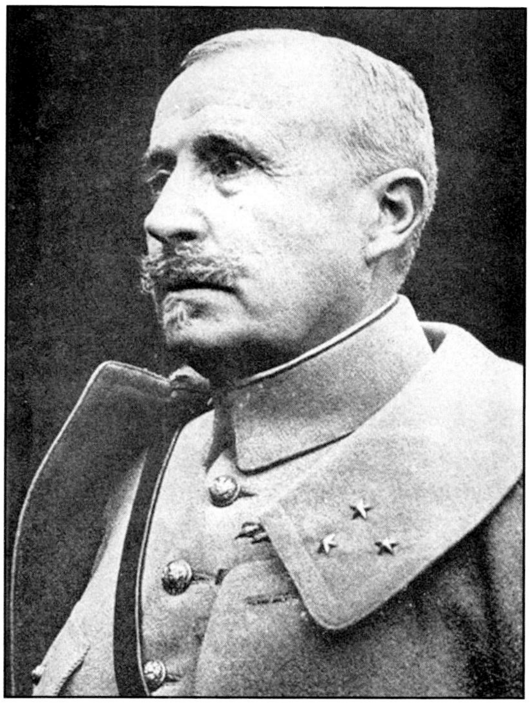

LEFT: French General Nivelle, who was exiled to North Africa for his mistakes.

OFFICERS' MESS

By the end of May, the situation within the French Army was becoming increasingly fraught. The German Army was only sixty miles from Paris when the disgraced Nivelle, who was exiled to North Africa, was replaced by General Henri Philippe Petain. He soon suspended large-scale attacks but on 27 May some 30,000 French soldiers mutinied, left the front line and marched under their own steam back to the rear.

Complaints grew, not just about the poor running of the war and its resulting casualties, but about the abysmal conditions survivors were forced to endure; poor food, disgusting quarters, hardly any leave to see families. Rumours added fuel to the fire; apparent heavy-handed treatment by General Duchene of the 32nd and 66th Infantry Regiments was reported, with every tenth man executed when the units refused to return to the front. More hearsay concerned rioters in Paris attacking women and children, left unprotected because the men were mired in the futile stalemate of the Western Front.

The officers meanwhile feared the spread of a Bolshevik-style revolution that was gripping Russia at the time. Reactionary and anti-war pamphlets were circulating on the front line and soldiers were known to be flying red flags, chanting anti-war slogans and singing revolutionary songs. One, 'La Chanson de Craonne', became particularly loathed by the French High Command and was prohibited from being sung until as late as 1974!

The song was originally called 'La Chanson de Lorette', inspired by Lorette à Ablain-Saint-Nazaire, a battlefield fought over during the early days of the First World War that resulted in over 100,000 casualties. The song subsequently mutated during the course of the war, with versions written about fighting in the Champagne region and about the horrendous French losses at Verdun (see *Charley's War: Blue's Story*).

The 1917 version was centred on Craonne, a village that was the nexus point for some savage fighting during Nivelle's disastrous offensive. The song itself was particularly disparaging of the officer classes, who (in the lyrics) were seen as rich, uncaring shirkers leaving the peasant soldiers to sacrifice themselves defending the wealth of the aristocrats. Little wonder then that it incurred such wrath from the High Command, who sought vainly to discover the authors; they even offered a million francs and an immediate honourable discharge to anyone willing to reveal the writer. The offer was not tempting enough, and the author or authors remain unknown, although it has been credited to Paul Vaillant-Couturier, later the editor-in-chief of the communist newspaper *L'Humanité*.

Despite the ill feeling between the base soldiers and the officers, relations between the two classes remained reasonably cordial, especially with the junior officers who often shared the same atrocious conditions and dangers as the rank and file. Many officers tried to negotiate and reason with angry troops; when men from the 2nd Battalion, 18th Infantry Regiment mutinied after having their leave cancelled and being ordered forward, a regimental Colonel met with the troops. He was told that the revolt was nothing personal – the colonel was even cheered – but enough was enough. Most soldiers were willing to take defensive action but the days of the French Army as an offensive force were by now over.

BELOW: French Attack at German dugout, believed to have been photographed during the Third Battle of Ypres. Photo: German Department of Photos and Film.

'UNFIT TO FIGHT'

On 7 June, Petain went to see British Commander-in-Chief, Field Marshal Sir Douglas Haig in private. He admitted to problems with two divisions moving forward to replace those on the frontline. The reality, whilst not entirely clear even now, is that the situation was somewhat more complicated, Petain admitting that the French Army was now 'unfit to fight'.

Anywhere up to sixty-eight divisions may have been affected, to a lesser or greater degree, by misconduct or mutiny; all were infantry units. It is now believed that at least eleven divisions were left profoundly affected by the mutiny; fifteen were seriously impacted; twenty-five were afflicted by minor outbreaks of mutinous behaviour; and seventeen were troubled by a single outbreak. It's thought around 35,000 men were actively involved in the mutiny – just one per cent of the army. (Haig's own war diaries note that according to his French sources, by the end of May there were 30,000 'rebels' who had to be dealt with.)

However, French forces consisted of 112 infantry divisions – its principal fighting force – resulting in around half of the frontline units being affected.

Not surprisingly, many of the support units who took no active part in the fighting went largely unaffected by the outbreak of dissent. Only twelve artillery regiments, for example, were thought to have been affected by misconduct.

PETAIN'S SOLUTION

By mid-June, the crisis was at its height and the French commander-in-chief had to act fast. Petain's solution to the mutiny was an iron fist in a velvet glove. Whilst many senior commanders were in favour of taking harsh disciplinary measures, Petain was far more subtle, fearing that the sort of arbitrary trials and executions conducted before would merely inflame an already dangerous situation.

There were mass arrests. Officers in the affected units picked men for court-martial, allegedly with the consent of the rank and file. Exact figures are disputed but it is believed 23,385 were convicted. Whilst 929 were sentenced to death, the number actually shot remains in doubt. It is believed around forty to fifty received no reprieve and were killed; some were summarily executed, whist other supposed shootings remain in doubt. Others were not shot for mutiny but for crimes committed during the unrest, including two men executed for murder and rape.

Many more mutineers were imprisoned, including 2,878 sentenced to hard labour (including twenty-three life sentences); 1,492 were given lighter terms, commuted in some cases to suspended sentences.

Petain's velvet glove was the immediate institution of longer and more regular periods of leave for frontline troops; he improved food, housing and bedding; and he had, of course, already suspended one of the root causes of the mutiny: offensive attacks. He believed that he had to "maintain this repression with firmness, but without forgetting that it is being applied to soldiers who for three years now have been with us in the trenches and who are 'our' soldiers."

By the end of 1917, the crisis was over. The British had continued to carry the war to the Germans whilst the French returned to the trenches, and with a new, aggressive government in power in Paris were soon ready to take the offensive once more.

As for the mutiny itself, like events at Etaples involving British troops, it was soon hidden beneath a veil of secrecy and repression. Even at the time, little was known of it; the French High Command keen to keep the growing unrest from the Germans. However, the enemy commanders knew little of the mutiny and, ironically, had similar concerns of their own. At home, Germany was suffering under the iron grip of the Allied economic blockade and there had been strikes and unrest in German factories. The aristocratic High Command must also have been as painfully aware as their French counterparts of the revolts sweeping through Russia. As such, the Germans made no effort to capitalise on the French Army's failures.

Such was the success of the French efforts to hide the mutiny that the event went largely unnoticed and forgotten until a detailed and controversial academic study by Guy Pedroncini first published in 1967, which began resurrecting secret files long hidden in the French Army archives.

However, like the events at Etaples, many records will not be publicly available until 2017, and it's unlikely that many of the facts surrounding this curious episode will ever be truly known. ✛

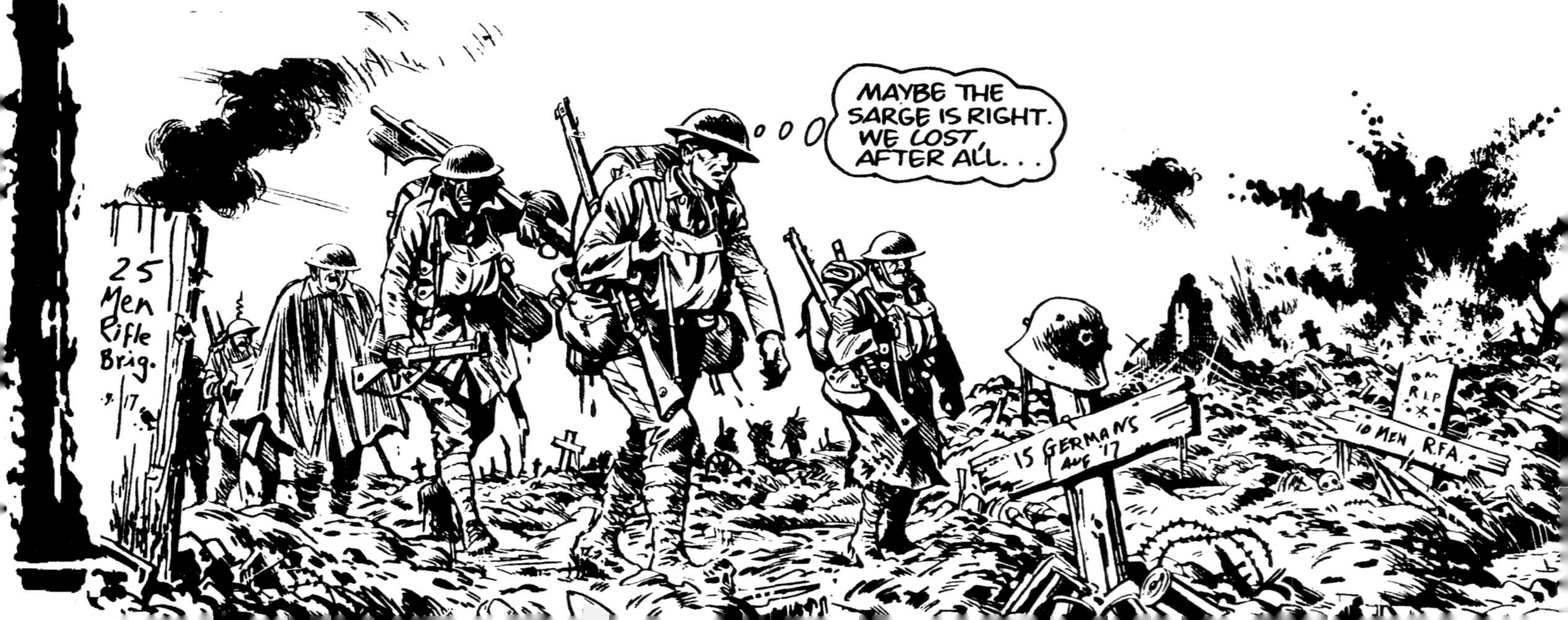
MAYBE THE SARGE IS RIGHT. WE LOST, AFTER ALL. . .
25 Men Rifle Brig.
15 GERMANS Aug '17
10 MEN R.F.A.
R.I.P.

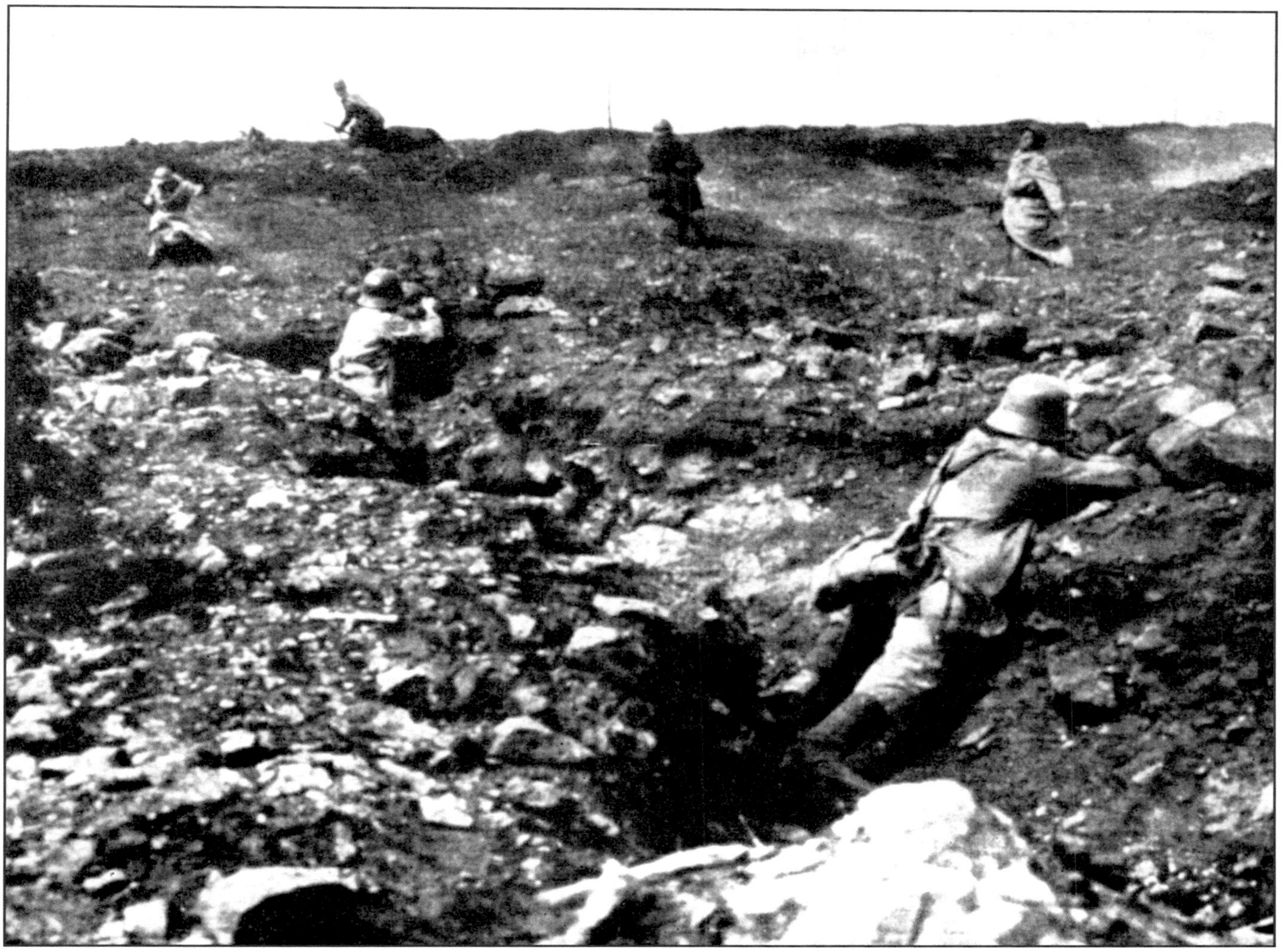

Further Reading:

Les mutineries de 1917 by Guy Pedroncini, Publications de la Sorbonne, Presse Universitaires de France (2nd ed.), Paris, 1983. ISBN: 2130380921.

Web Links:

La Caverne du Dragon, Musée du Chemin des Dames
www.caverne-du-dragon.com/en
Museum dedicated to the Second Battle of Aisne at Chemin des Dames in Oulches-la-Vallée-Foulon. During the First World War, the Chemin des Dames corresponded to a large sector of the front, extending more than thirty kilometres north of the river Aisne between Pinon to the west and Berry-au-Bac to the east. More than seventy villages were involved, some of which were destroyed during the war and never rebuilt, such as Ailles, Beaulne and Troyon.

Chemin des Dames Virtual Memorial

http://www.memorial-chemindesdames.fr
The Virtual Memorial of the Chemin des Dames is run by the Conseil Général de l'Aisne (The Regional Council of Aisne) to pay tribute to the combatants of all nationalities who died at the Chemin des Dames.

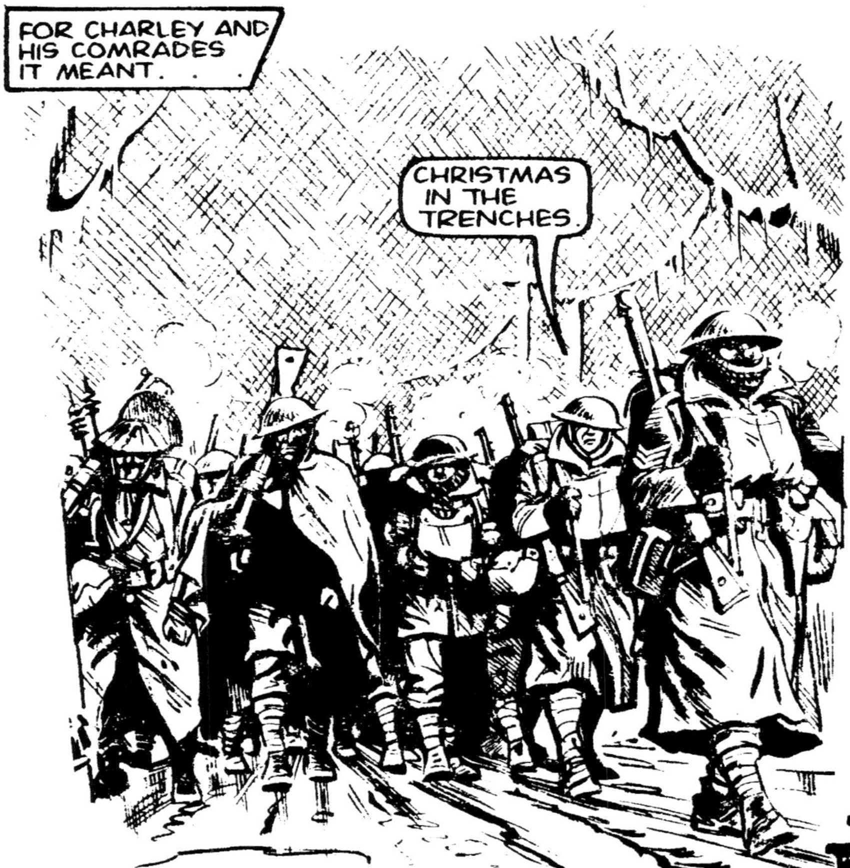
FOR CHARLEY AND HIS COMRADES IT MEANT. . .
CHRISTMAS IN THE TRENCHES.

La Chanson de Lorette

Quand au bout d'huit jours le r'pos terminé,
On va reprendre les tranchées,
Notre place est si utile
Que sans nous on prend la pile.
Mais c'est bien fini, on en a assez,
Personne ne veut plus marcher,
Et le cœur bien gros, comm' dans un sanglot
On dit adieu aux civ'lots.
Même sans tambours, même sans trompette,
On s'en va là-haut en baissant la tête…

Refrain:
Adieu la vie, adieu l'amour,
Adieu toutes les femmes.
C'est bien fini, c'est pour toujours,
De cette guerre infâme.
C'est à Craonne sur le plateau,
Qu'on doit laisser sa peau
Car nous sommes tous condamnés,
C'est nous les sacrifiés!
Huit jours de tranchées, huit jours de souffrance,
Pourtant on a l'espérance
Que ce soir viendra la r'lève
Que nous attendons sans trêve.
Soudain, dans la nuit et le silence,
On voit quelqu'un qui s'avance,
C'est un officier de chasseurs à pied,
Qui vient pour nous remplacer.
Doucement dans l'ombre sous la pluie qui tombe,
Les petits chasseurs vont chercher leurs tombes…

Au Refrain:
C'est malheureux d'voir sur les grands boulevards
Tous ces gros qui font la foire;
Si pour eux la vie est rose,
Pour nous c'est pas la même chose.
Au lieu d'se cacher tous ces embusqués,
Feraient mieux d'monter aux tranchées
Pour défendre leur bien, car nous n'avons rien,
Nous autres les pauv' purotins,
Tous les camarades sont enterrés là,
Pour défendr' les biens de ces messieurs là.

Au Refrain:
Ceux qu'ont le pognon, ceux-là reviendront,
Car c'est pour eux qu'on crève.
Mais c'est fini, car les troufions
Vont tous se mettre en grève.
Ce s'ra votre tour messieurs les gros,
De monter sur l'plateau,
Car si vous voulez faire la guerre,
Payez-la de votre peau!

ABOVE: Paul Vaillant-Couturier, considered the author of the controversial song 'La Chanson de Lorette'. A French author, journalist and politician, he edited the communist newspaper *L'Humanité* in the 1920s.

In English, the song translates as follows:

When At The End of a Week's Leave

We're going to go back to the trenches,
Our place there is so useful that without us we'd take a thrashing.
But it's all over now, we've had it up to here,
Nobody wants to march anymore,
And with hearts downcast, like when you're sobbing,
We're saying good-bye to the civilians.
Even if we don't get drums, even if we don't get trumpets
We're leaving for up there with lowered head.
Good-bye to life, good-bye to love,
Good-bye to all the women,
It's all over now, we've had it for good with this awful war.
It's in Craonne up on the plateau
That we're leaving our skins, 'cause we've all been sentenced to die.
We're the ones that they're sacrificing.
Eight days in the trenches, eight days of suffering,
And yet we still have hope that tonight the relief will come
That we keep waiting for.
Suddenly in the silent night we hear someone approach.
It's an infantry officer who's coming to take over from us.
Quietly, in the shadows under a falling rain,
The poor soldiers are going to look for their graves.

Good-bye to life, good-bye to love,
Good-bye to all the women,
It's all over now, we've had it for good with this awful war.
It's in Craonne up on the plateau that we're leaving our hides, 'cause
we've all been sentenced to die.
We're the ones that they're sacrificing.

On the grand boulevards, it's hard to look
At all the rich and powerful,whooping it up.
For them life is good
But for us it's not the same.
Instead of hiding, all these shirkers
Would do better to go up to the trenches,
To defend what they have, because we have nothing,
All of us poor wretches, all our comrades are being buried there,
To defend the wealth of these gentlemen here.
Those who have the dough, they'll be coming back, 'cause it's for them that we're dying.

But it's all over now, 'cause all of the grunts are going to go on strike.
It'll be your turn, all you rich and powerful gentlemen,
To go up onto the plateau.
And if you want to make war,
Then pay for it with your own skins!

For more information see: *pcfarras.over-blog.com/article-13713984.html*

PREVIOUSLY IN *CHARLEY'S WAR*

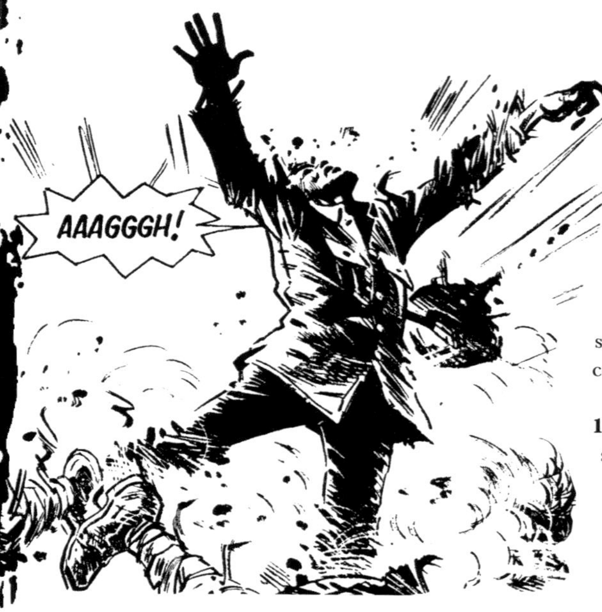

AAAGGGH!

2 June 1916: Charley Bourne, who has joined the army aged sixteen (two years under the official age for conscription), is sent to France, several weeks before the Battle of the Somme.

1 July 1916: The Battle of the Somme begins. Charley and his comrades spare a German soldier they find, but he is shot in cold blood by Lieutenant Snell.

1 August 1916: On Charley's seventeenth birthday, British forces accidentally begin shelling their own side. Charley volunteers to be a communications runner to try to end the bombardment, but is delayed by Snell.

ABOVE: Another casualty of the desperate battle in the trenches.

BELOW: Charley bemoans Captain Snell's bullying style of leadership.

BELOW RIGHT: A German miner battles Charley in the mines below Messines.

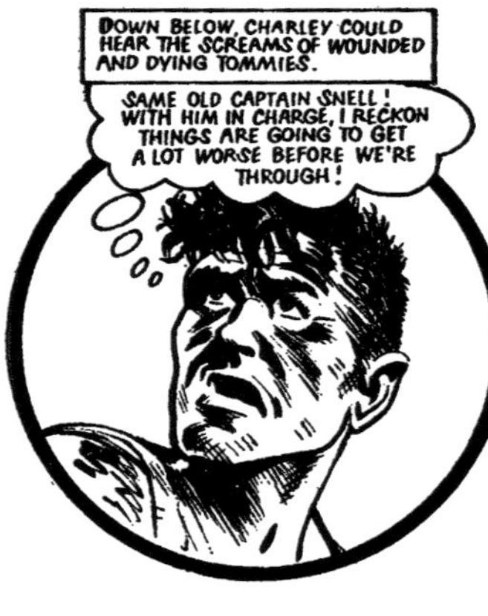

DOWN BELOW, CHARLEY COULD HEAR THE SCREAMS OF WOUNDED AND DYING TOMMIES.
SAME OLD CAPTAIN SNELL! WITH HIM IN CHARGE, I RECKON THINGS ARE GOING TO GET A LOT WORSE BEFORE WE'RE THROUGH!

September 1916: Ginger is killed by a stray shell, and Charley has a temporary breakdown. His unit is reinforced by tanks and, on 15th September, Charley is joined by his cowardly brother-in-law, "Oiley", who deliberately injures himself to be sent home. Charley covers for him.

October 1916: Charley is wounded during the battle against the "Judgement Troopers", but sent back to the lines. Eventually, Colonel Zeiss' plan is halted by the German High Command, but before he can celebrate, Charley is badly injured.

November 1916: Charley, an "unknown soldier" suffering from amnesia, is recuperating in a military hospital when Sergeant Tozer recognises him.

February 18, 1917: Charley survives a U-Boat attack on the York Castle, the hospital ship returning him home.

March 1917: Charley meets a French Foreign Legion deserter, "Blue", and helps him hide as he tells him the grim story of the Battle of Verdun. Eventually, Blue decides to return to his unit. Charley also realises he will soon have to return to the war.

April 1917: Charley rejoins his regiment and is reunited with Weeper and his longtime sergeant, "Old Bill", as it moves up to Flanders to Ypres. The company's duties in the face of snipers and gas attacks are made all the more miserable by Snell's interference and fellow soldiers like the sadistic killer, Grogan. Ypres is hell on Earth...

May 1917: After weeks in reserve trenches, Charley begins a 20-mile march out of the line to billets, Snell leading them on the horse, Warriror. Old Bill loses his sergeant's strips after the march, and even life away from the Front proves harsh. But worse is to come, as Snell is ordered to take charge of a tunnel intended to undermine German guns at Messines. Charley and comrades such as "Budgie" join the Claykickers – the navvies and coalminers digging the huge mines under the German positions. Snell's cruelty continues and the mining proves as dangerous as the Front.

June 1917: Zero hour and all the mines go up – except Snell's. Snell shoots Budgie, believing him a saboteur, and heads into the mine to set it off, even though the delay means blowing up the advancing British troops. Charley goes after Snell but Snell is hit in the head by a ricochet from his own gun and, still alive, is invalided out.

August 1917: Charley is caught up in the Third Battle of Ypres, rescuing his brother, Wilf, then falling in a shellhole whilst avoiding Battle Police. Meanwhile, the harsh training regime at Etaples causes growing unrest in the ranks. Charley meets the sandbaggers – army deserters led by the bowler-hatted Gunboat and a disguised Blue. He's also reunited with Weeper, who's later arrested as a deserter. As Charley goes for a swim, a popular Scottish corporal, Wood, is shot and wounded by a Military Policeman... and the Mutiny begins! ✛

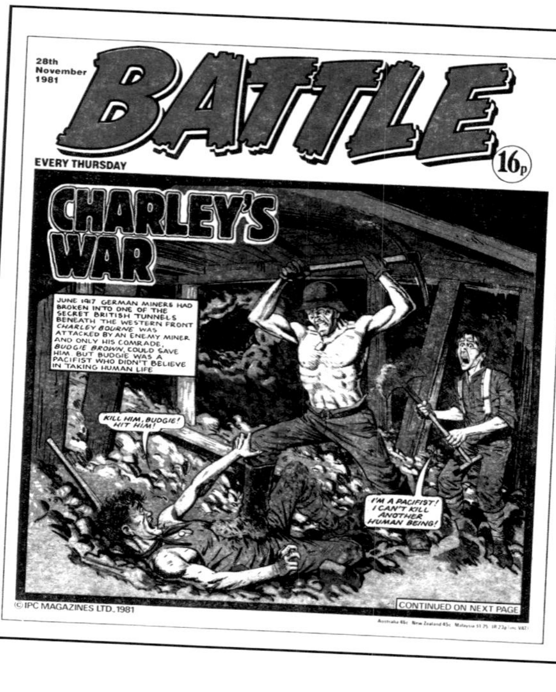

28th November 1981
BATTLE
EVERY THURSDAY
16p
CHARLEY'S WAR
JUNE 1917 GERMAN MINERS HAD BROKEN INTO ONE OF THE SECRET BRITISH TUNNELS BENEATH THE WESTERN FRONT CHARLEY BOURNE WAS ATTACKED BY AN ENEMY MINER AND ONLY HIS COMRADE, BUDGIE BROWN, COULD SAVE HIM. BUT BUDGIE WAS A PACIFIST WHO DIDN'T BELIEVE IN TAKING HUMAN LIFE
KILL HIM, BUDGIE! HIT HIM!
I'M A PACIFIST! I CAN'T KILL ANOTHER HUMAN BEING!
© IPC MAGAZINES LTD. 1981
CONTINUED ON NEXT PAGE

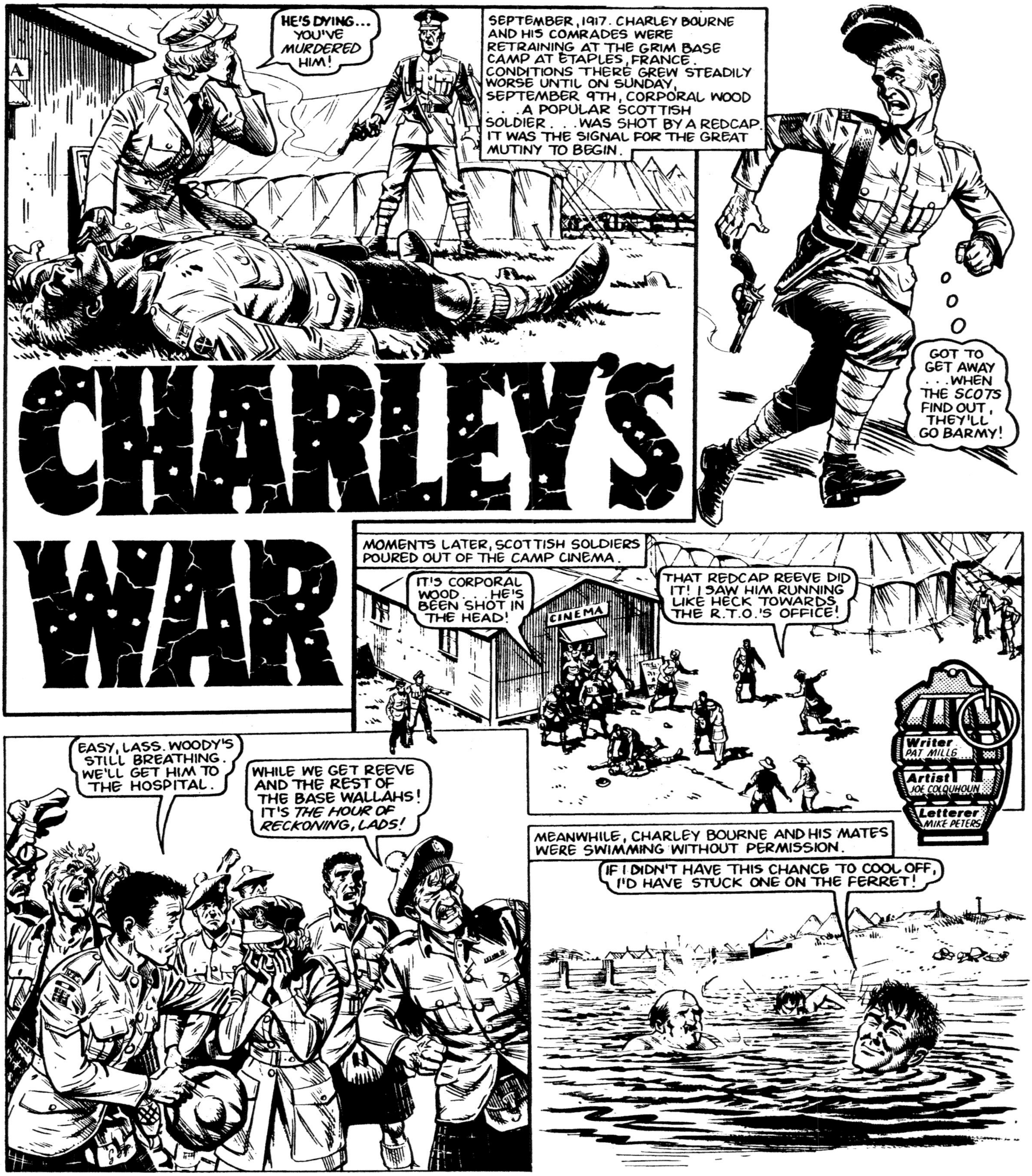
HE'S DYING... YOU'VE MURDERED HIM!
SEPTEMBER, 1917. CHARLEY BOURNE AND HIS COMRADES WERE RETRAINING AT THE GRIM BASE CAMP AT ETAPLES, FRANCE. CONDITIONS THERE GREW STEADILY WORSE UNTIL ON SUNDAY, SEPTEMBER 9TH, CORPORAL WOOD . . . A POPULAR SCOTTISH SOLDIER . . . WAS SHOT BY A REDCAP. IT WAS THE SIGNAL FOR THE GREAT MUTINY TO BEGIN.
CHARLEY'S WAR
GOT TO GET AWAY . . . WHEN THE SCOTS FIND OUT, THEY'LL GO BARMY!
MOMENTS LATER, SCOTTISH SOLDIERS POURED OUT OF THE CAMP CINEMA.
IT'S CORPORAL WOOD . . . HE'S BEEN SHOT IN THE HEAD!
CINEMA
THAT REDCAP REEVE DID IT! I SAW HIM RUNNING LIKE HECK TOWARDS THE R.T.O.'S OFFICE!
Writer PAT MILLS
Artist JOE COLQUHOUN
Letterer MIKE PETERS
EASY, LASS. WOODY'S STILL BREATHING. WE'LL GET HIM TO THE HOSPITAL.
WHILE WE GET REEVE AND THE REST OF THE BASE WALLAHS! IT'S THE HOUR OF RECKONING, LADS!
MEANWHILE, CHARLEY BOURNE AND HIS MATES WERE SWIMMING WITHOUT PERMISSION.
IF I DIDN'T HAVE THIS CHANCE TO COOL OFF, I'D HAVE STUCK ONE ON THE FERRET!

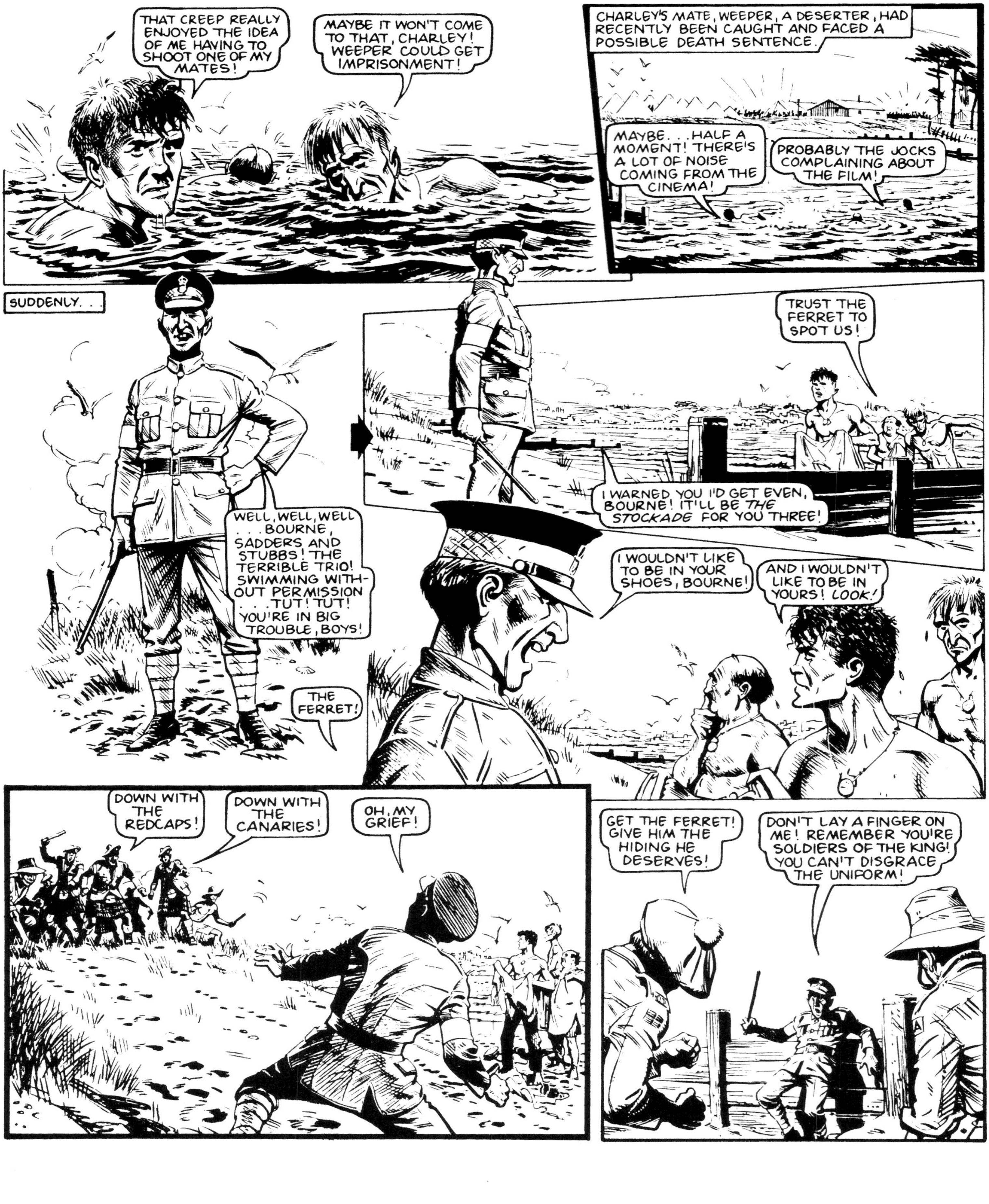
THAT CREEP REALLY ENJOYED THE IDEA OF ME HAVING TO SHOOT ONE OF MY MATES!
MAYBE IT WON'T COME TO THAT, CHARLEY! WEEPER COULD GET IMPRISONMENT!
CHARLEY'S MATE, WEEPER, A DESERTER, HAD RECENTLY BEEN CAUGHT AND FACED A POSSIBLE DEATH SENTENCE.
MAYBE. . . HALF A MOMENT! THERE'S A LOT OF NOISE COMING FROM THE CINEMA!
PROBABLY THE JOCKS COMPLAINING ABOUT THE FILM!
SUDDENLY. . .
WELL, WELL, WELL . . . BOURNE, SADDERS AND STUBBS! THE TERRIBLE TRIO! SWIMMING WITH-OUT PERMISSION . . . TUT! TUT! YOU'RE IN BIG TROUBLE, BOYS!
THE FERRET!
TRUST THE FERRET TO SPOT US!
I WARNED YOU I'D GET EVEN, BOURNE! IT'LL BE *THE STOCKADE* FOR YOU THREE!
I WOULDN'T LIKE TO BE IN YOUR SHOES, BOURNE!
AND I WOULDN'T LIKE TO BE IN YOURS! *LOOK!*
DOWN WITH THE REDCAPS!
DOWN WITH THE CANARIES!
OH, MY GRIEF!
GET THE FERRET! GIVE HIM THE HIDING HE DESERVES!
DON'T LAY A FINGER ON ME! REMEMBER YOU'RE SOLDIERS OF THE KING! YOU CAN'T DISGRACE THE UNIFORM!

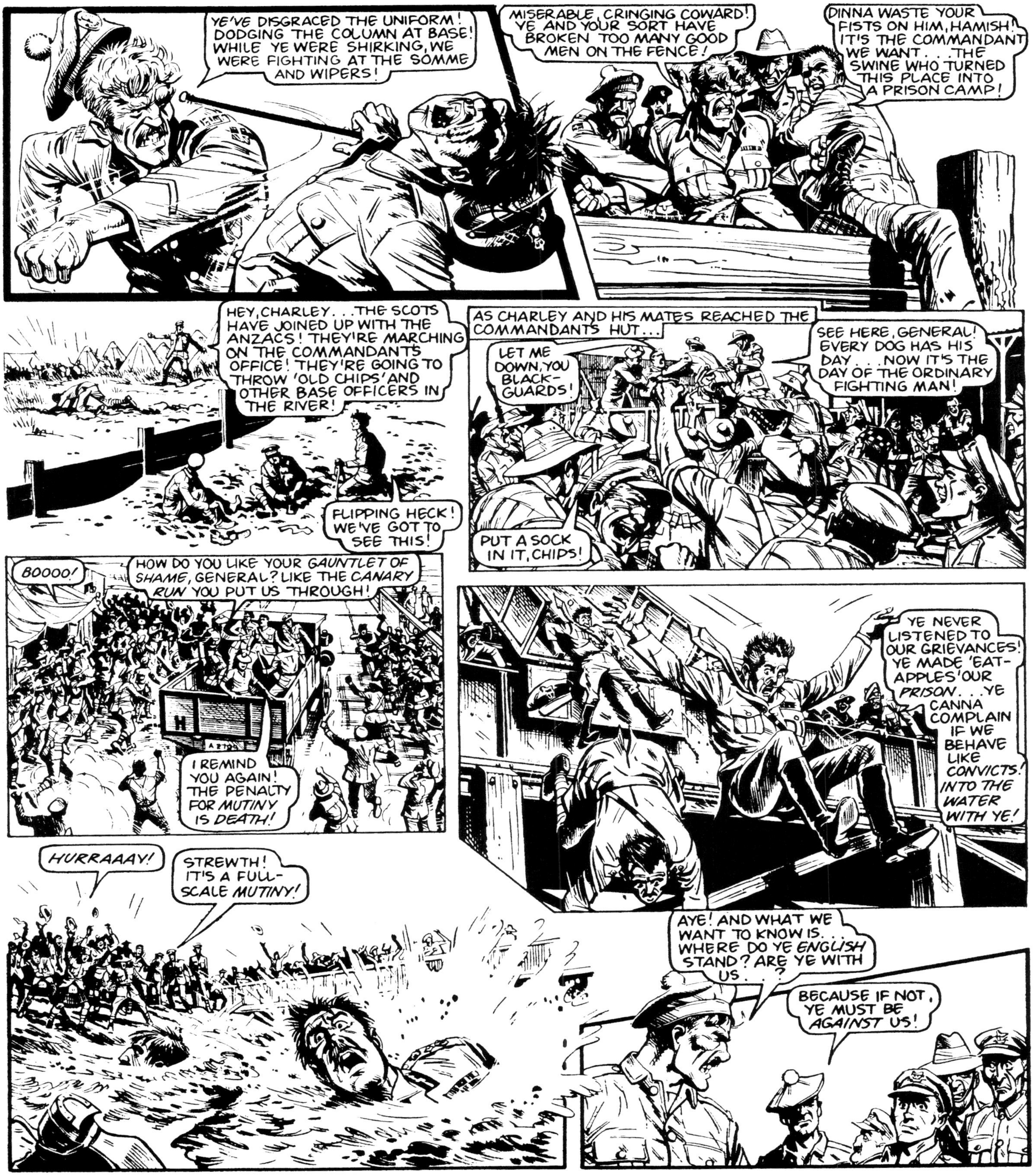
YE'VE DISGRACED THE UNIFORM! DODGING THE COLUMN AT BASE! WHILE YE WERE SHIRKING, WE WERE FIGHTING AT THE SOMME AND WIPERS!
MISERABLE, CRINGING COWARD! YE AND YOUR SORT HAVE BROKEN TOO MANY GOOD MEN ON THE FENCE!
DINNA WASTE YOUR FISTS ON HIM, HAMISH! IT'S THE COMMANDANT WE WANT... THE SWINE WHO TURNED THIS PLACE INTO A PRISON CAMP!
HEY, CHARLEY... THE SCOTS HAVE JOINED UP WITH THE ANZACS! THEY'RE MARCHING ON THE COMMANDANTS OFFICE! THEY'RE GOING TO THROW 'OLD CHIPS' AND OTHER BASE OFFICERS IN THE RIVER!
FLIPPING HECK! WE'VE GOT TO SEE THIS!
AS CHARLEY AND HIS MATES REACHED THE COMMANDANTS HUT...
LET ME DOWN, YOU BLACK-GUARDS!
SEE HERE, GENERAL! EVERY DOG HAS HIS DAY... NOW IT'S THE DAY OF THE ORDINARY FIGHTING MAN!
PUT A SOCK IN IT, CHIPS!
BOOOO!
HOW DO YOU LIKE YOUR GAUNTLET OF SHAME, GENERAL? LIKE THE CANARY RUN YOU PUT US THROUGH!
I REMIND YOU AGAIN! THE PENALTY FOR MUTINY IS DEATH!
YE NEVER LISTENED TO OUR GRIEVANCES! YE MADE 'EAT-APPLES' OUR PRISON... YE CANNA COMPLAIN IF WE BEHAVE LIKE CONVICTS! INTO THE WATER WITH YE!
HURRAAAY!
STREWTH! IT'S A FULL-SCALE MUTINY!
AYE! AND WHAT WE WANT TO KNOW IS... WHERE DO YE ENGLISH STAND? ARE YE WITH US...?
BECAUSE IF NOT, YE MUST BE AGAINST US!

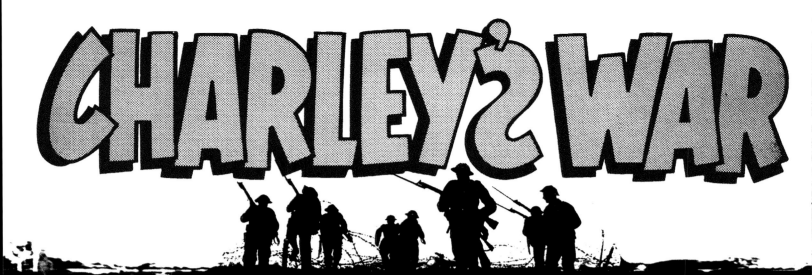

CHARLEY'S WAR

CHARLEY'S WAR. SEPTEMBER 9TH, 1917... ETAPLES BASE CAMP, FRANCE, WHERE 100,000 SOLDIERS WERE SICK OF BEING TREATED LIKE CONVICTS. MATTERS CAME TO A HEAD WHEN A POPULAR SCOTTISH SOLDIER, CORPORAL WOOD, WAS SHOT BY A REDCAP. THE MUTINEERS FORCED THE CAMP COMMANDANT AND HIS OFFICERS INTO LORRIES AND DUMPED THEM IN THE RIVER.

STREWTH! IT'S A FULL-SCALE MUTINY!

CONTINUED ON NEXT PAGE

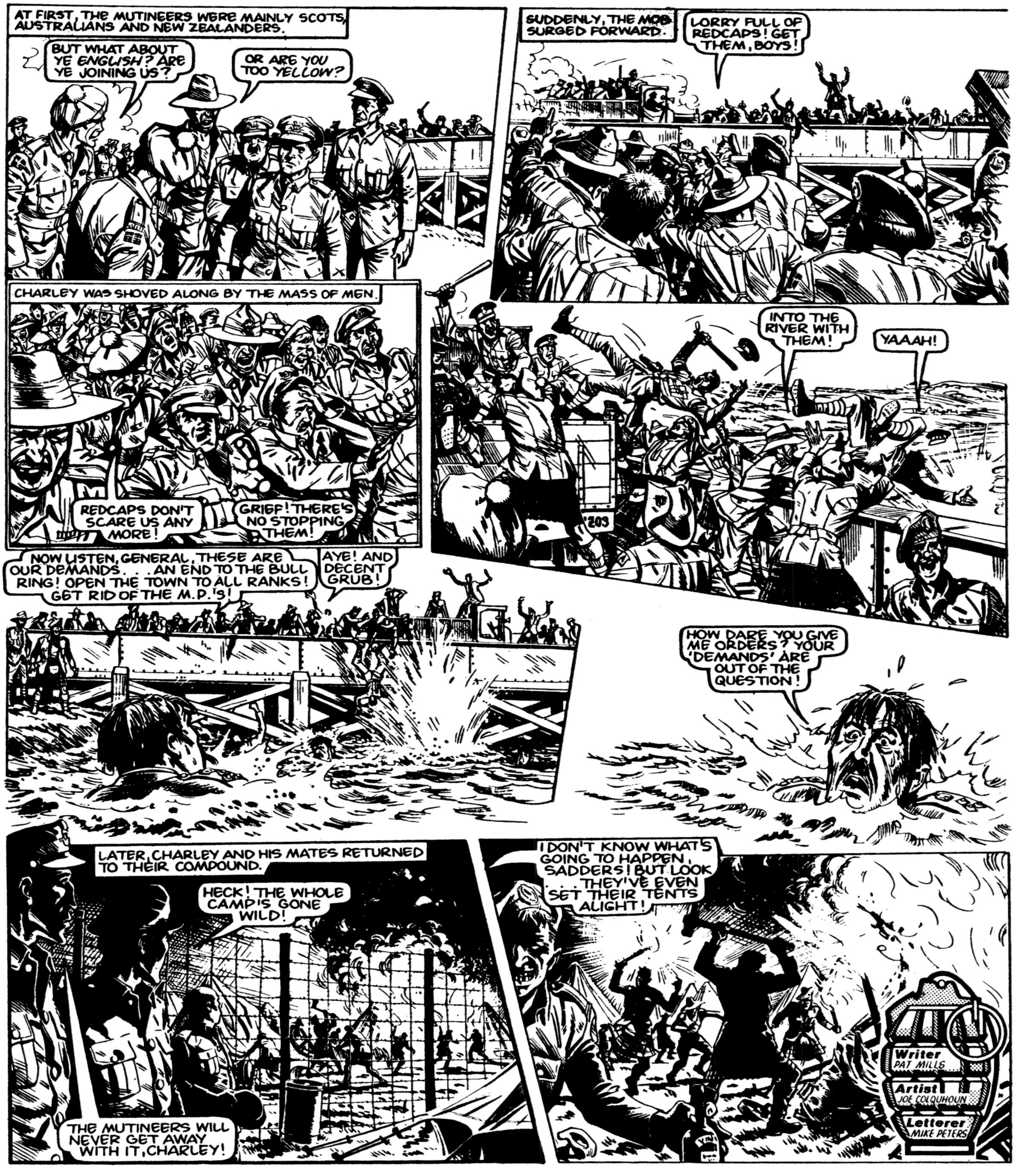

AT FIRST, THE MUTINEERS WERE MAINLY SCOTS, AUSTRALIANS AND NEW ZEALANDERS.
BUT WHAT ABOUT YE ENGLISH? ARE YE JOINING US?
OR ARE YOU TOO YELLOW?
SUDDENLY, THE MOB SURGED FORWARD.
LORRY FULL OF REDCAPS! GET THEM, BOYS!
CHARLEY WAS SHOVED ALONG BY THE MASS OF MEN.
REDCAPS DON'T SCARE US ANY MORE!
GRIEF! THERE'S NO STOPPING THEM!
INTO THE RIVER WITH THEM!
YAAAH!
NOW LISTEN, GENERAL, THESE ARE OUR DEMANDS. . . AN END TO THE BULL RING! OPEN THE TOWN TO ALL RANKS! GET RID OF THE M.P.'S!
AYE! AND DECENT GRUB!
HOW DARE YOU GIVE ME ORDERS? YOUR 'DEMANDS' ARE OUT OF THE QUESTION!
LATER, CHARLEY AND HIS MATES RETURNED TO THEIR COMPOUND.
HECK! THE WHOLE CAMP'S GONE WILD!
THE MUTINEERS WILL NEVER GET AWAY WITH IT, CHARLEY!
I DON'T KNOW WHAT'S GOING TO HAPPEN, SADDERS! BUT LOOK . . . THEY'VE EVEN SET THEIR TENTS ALIGHT!
Writer PAT MILLS
Artist JOE COLQUHOUN
Letterer MIKE PETERS

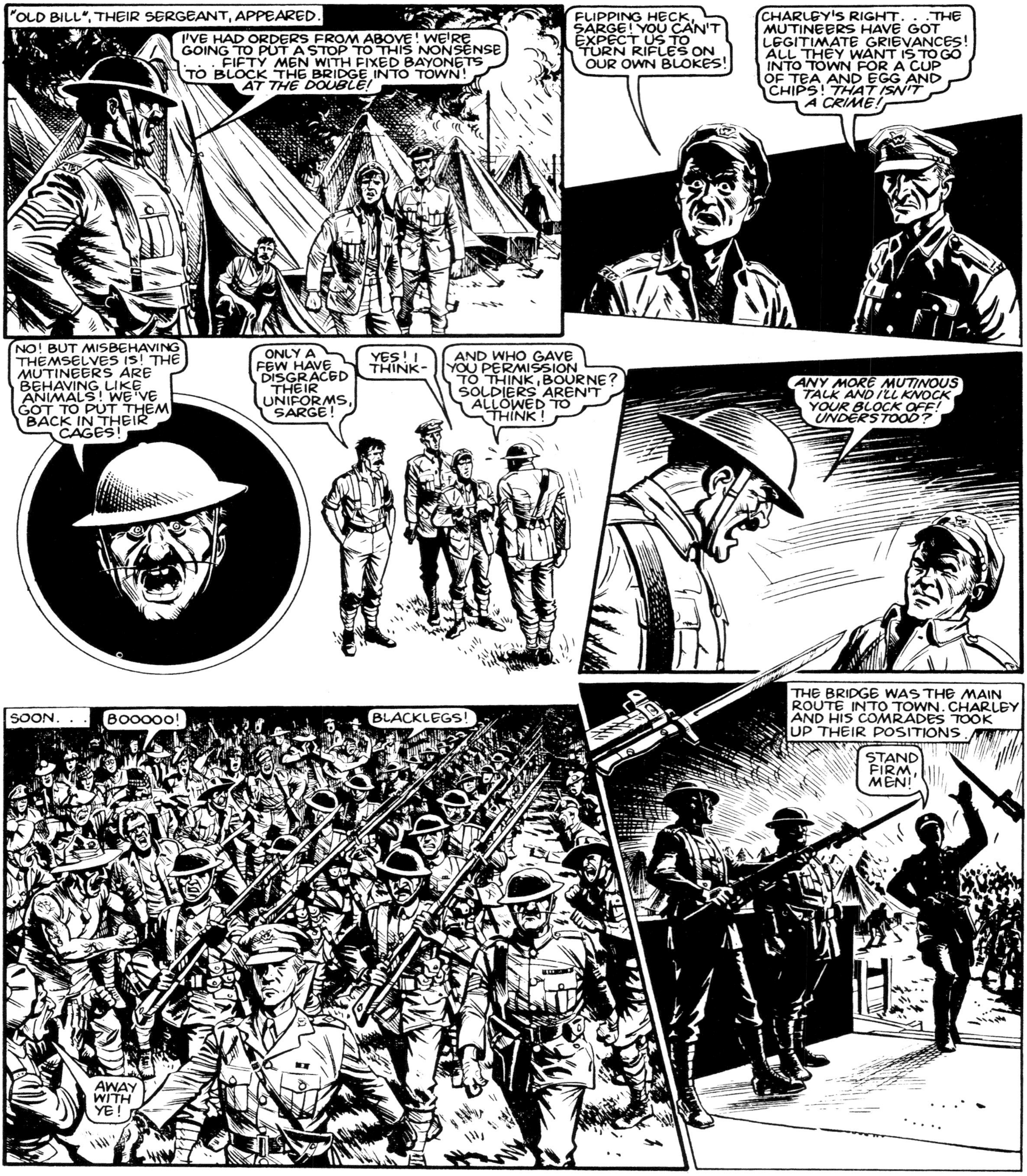
"OLD BILL", THEIR SERGEANT, APPEARED.
I'VE HAD ORDERS FROM ABOVE! WE'RE GOING TO PUT A STOP TO THIS NONSENSE . . . FIFTY MEN WITH FIXED BAYONETS TO BLOCK THE BRIDGE INTO TOWN! AT THE DOUBLE!
FLIPPING HECK, SARGE! YOU CAN'T EXPECT US TO TURN RIFLES ON OUR OWN BLOKES!
CHARLEY'S RIGHT. . . THE MUTINEERS HAVE GOT LEGITIMATE GRIEVANCES! ALL THEY WANT IS TO GO INTO TOWN FOR A CUP OF TEA AND EGG AND CHIPS! THAT ISN'T A CRIME!
NO! BUT MISBEHAVING THEMSELVES IS! THE MUTINEERS ARE BEHAVING LIKE ANIMALS! WE'VE GOT TO PUT THEM BACK IN THEIR CAGES!
ONLY A FEW HAVE DISGRACED THEIR UNIFORMS, SARGE!
YES! I THINK-
AND WHO GAVE YOU PERMISSION TO THINK, BOURNE? SOLDIERS AREN'T ALLOWED TO THINK!
ANY MORE MUTINOUS TALK AND I'LL KNOCK YOUR BLOCK OFF! UNDERSTOOD?
SOON. . .
BOOOOO!
BLACKLEGS!
AWAY WITH YE!
THE BRIDGE WAS THE MAIN ROUTE INTO TOWN. CHARLEY AND HIS COMRADES TOOK UP THEIR POSITIONS.
STAND FIRM, MEN!

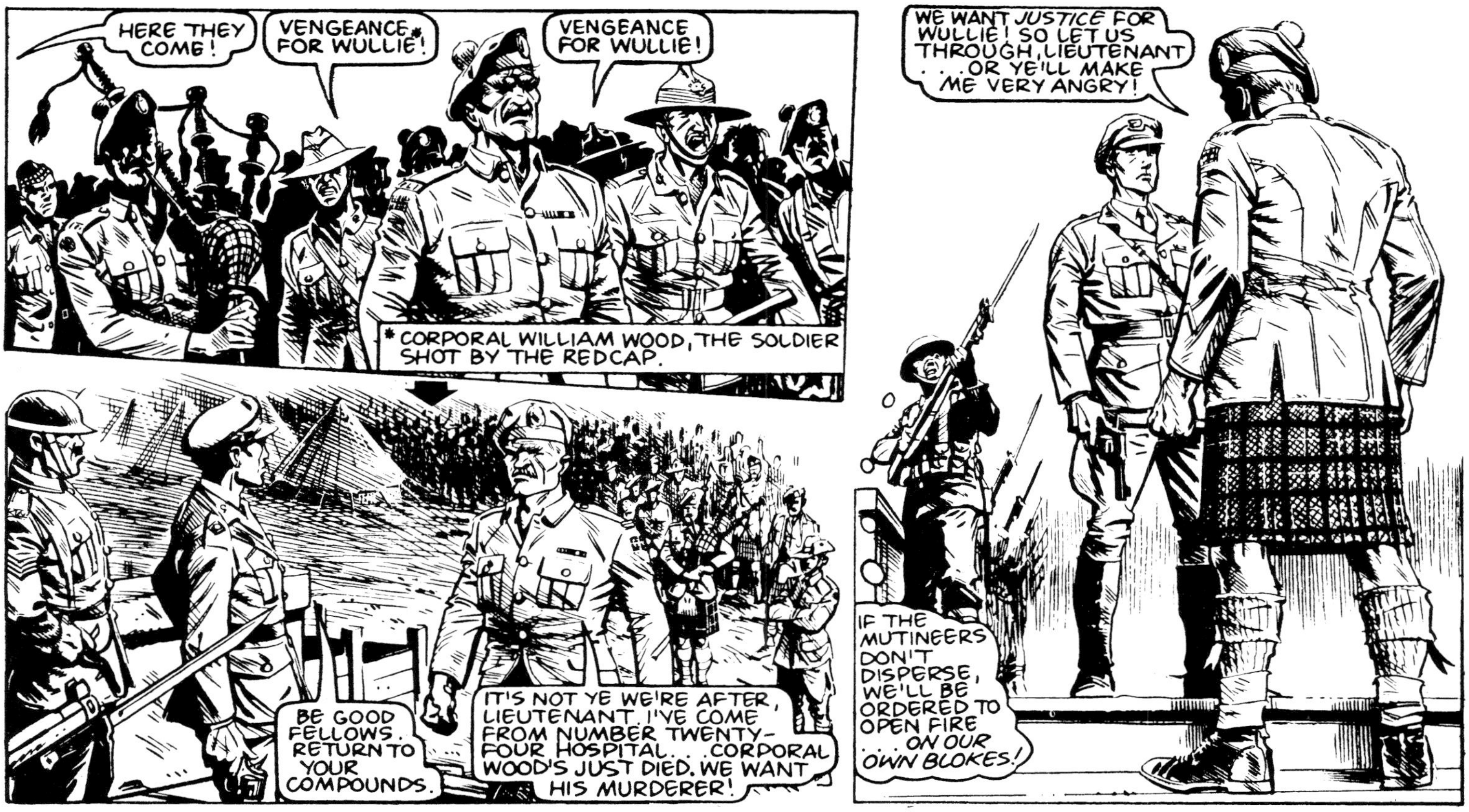

HERE THEY COME!
VENGEANCE* FOR WULLIE!
VENGEANCE FOR WULLIE!
*CORPORAL WILLIAM WOOD, THE SOLDIER SHOT BY THE REDCAP.
BE GOOD FELLOWS. RETURN TO YOUR COMPOUNDS.
IT'S NOT YE WE'RE AFTER, LIEUTENANT. I'VE COME FROM NUMBER TWENTY-FOUR HOSPITAL. . .CORPORAL WOOD'S JUST DIED. WE WANT HIS MURDERER!
WE WANT *JUSTICE* FOR WULLIE! SO LET US THROUGH, LIEUTENANT . . .OR YE'LL MAKE ME VERY ANGRY!
IF THE MUTINEERS DON'T DISPERSE, WE'LL BE ORDERED TO OPEN FIRE . . .ON OUR OWN BLOKES!

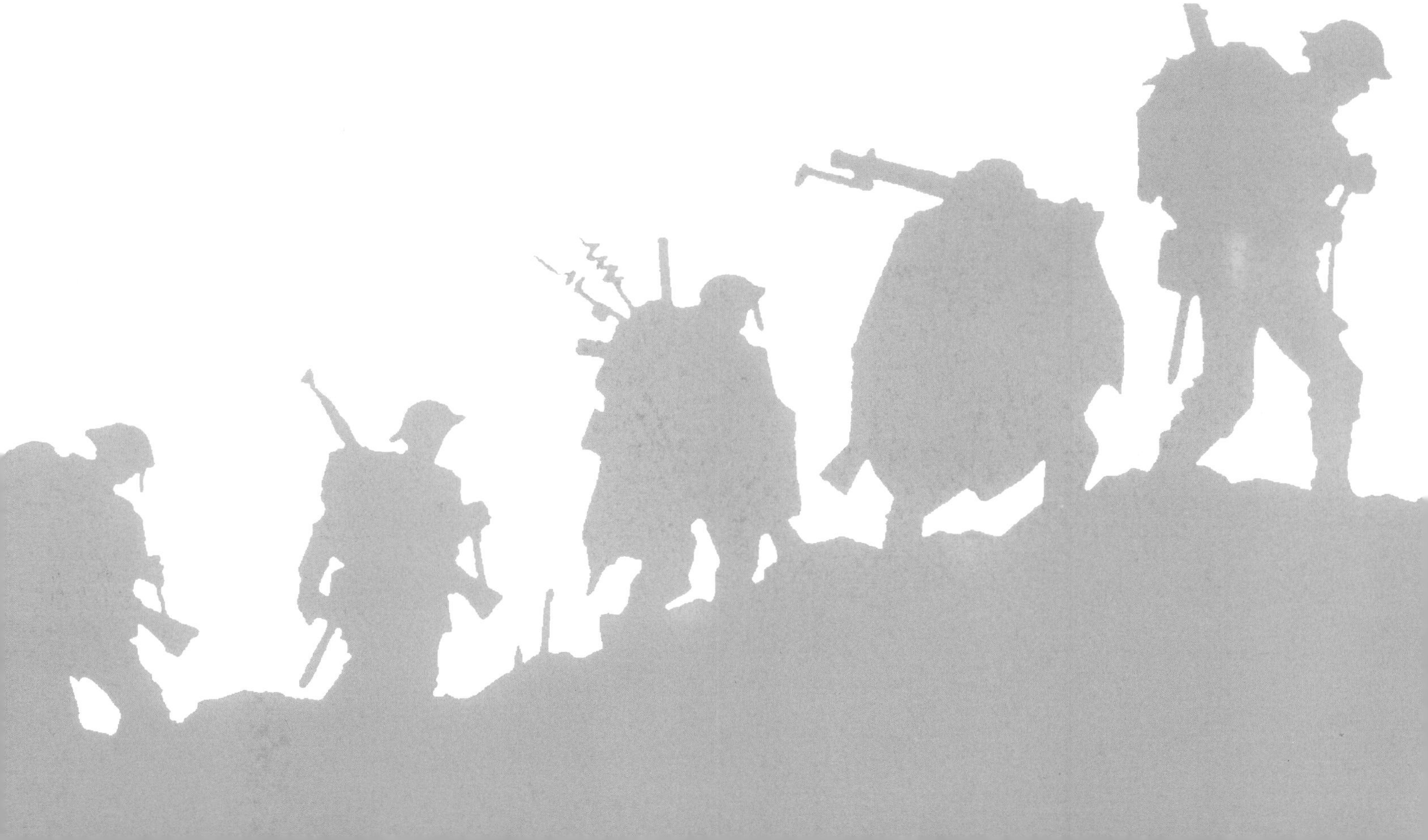

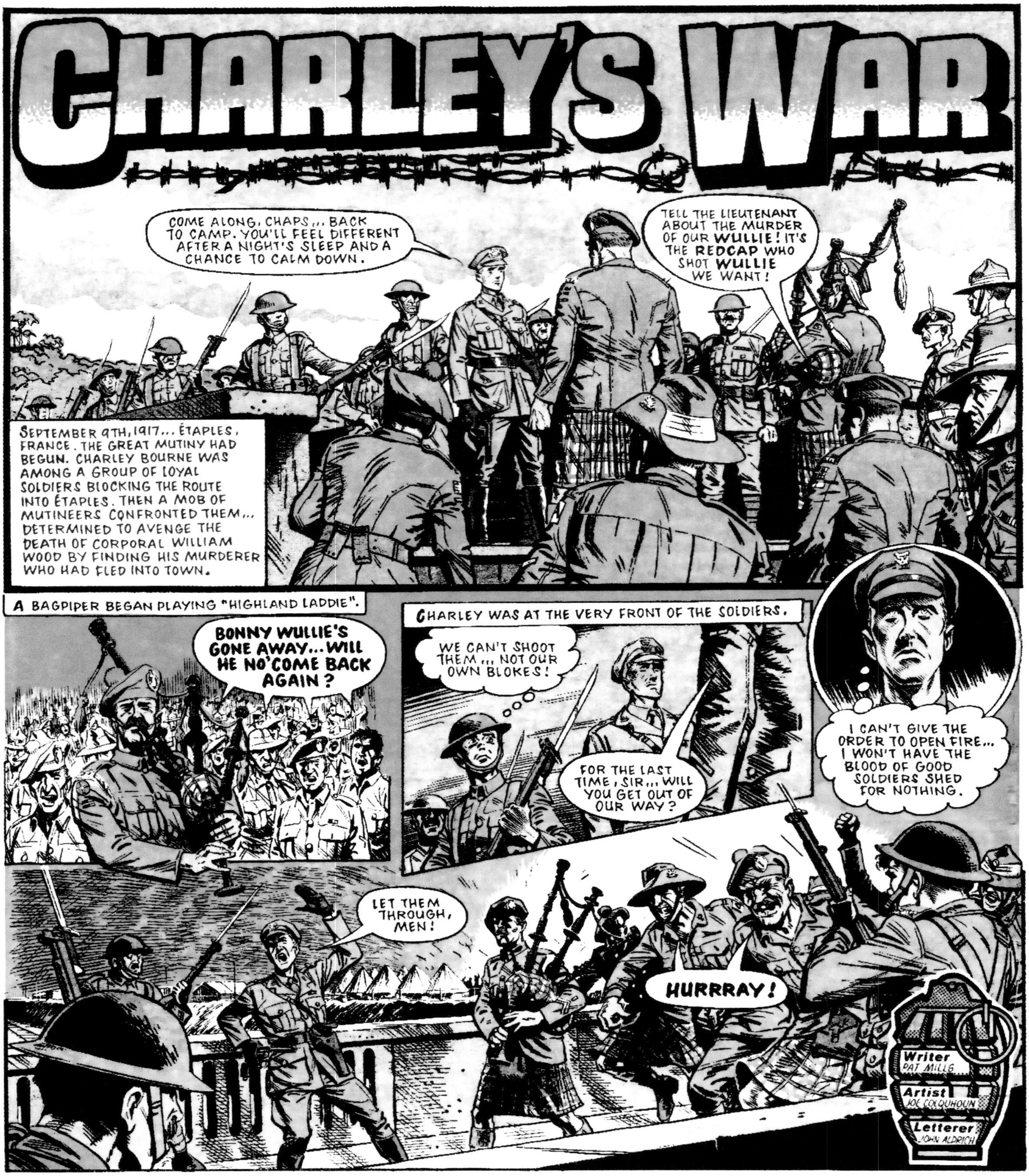

CHARLEY'S WAR
COME ALONG, CHAPS... BACK TO CAMP. YOU'LL FEEL DIFFERENT AFTER A NIGHT'S SLEEP AND A CHANCE TO CALM DOWN.
TELL THE LIEUTENANT ABOUT THE MURDER OF OUR WULLIE! IT'S THE REDCAP WHO SHOT WULLIE WE WANT!
SEPTEMBER 9TH, 1917... ÉTAPLES, FRANCE. THE GREAT MUTINY HAD BEGUN. CHARLEY BOURNE WAS AMONG A GROUP OF LOYAL SOLDIERS BLOCKING THE ROUTE INTO ÉTAPLES. THEN A MOB OF MUTINEERS CONFRONTED THEM... DETERMINED TO AVENGE THE DEATH OF CORPORAL WILLIAM WOOD BY FINDING HIS MURDERER WHO HAD FLED INTO TOWN.
A BAGPIPER BEGAN PLAYING "HIGHLAND LADDIE".
BONNY WULLIE'S GONE AWAY... WILL HE NO' COME BACK AGAIN?
CHARLEY WAS AT THE VERY FRONT OF THE SOLDIERS.
WE CAN'T SHOOT THEM... NOT OUR OWN BLOKES!
FOR THE LAST TIME, SIR... WILL YOU GET OUT OF OUR WAY?
I CAN'T GIVE THE ORDER TO OPEN FIRE... I WON'T HAVE THE BLOOD OF GOOD SOLDIERS SHED FOR NOTHING.
LET THEM THROUGH, MEN!
HURRRAY!
Writer PAT MILLS
Artist JOE COLQUHOUN
Letterer JOHN ALDRICH

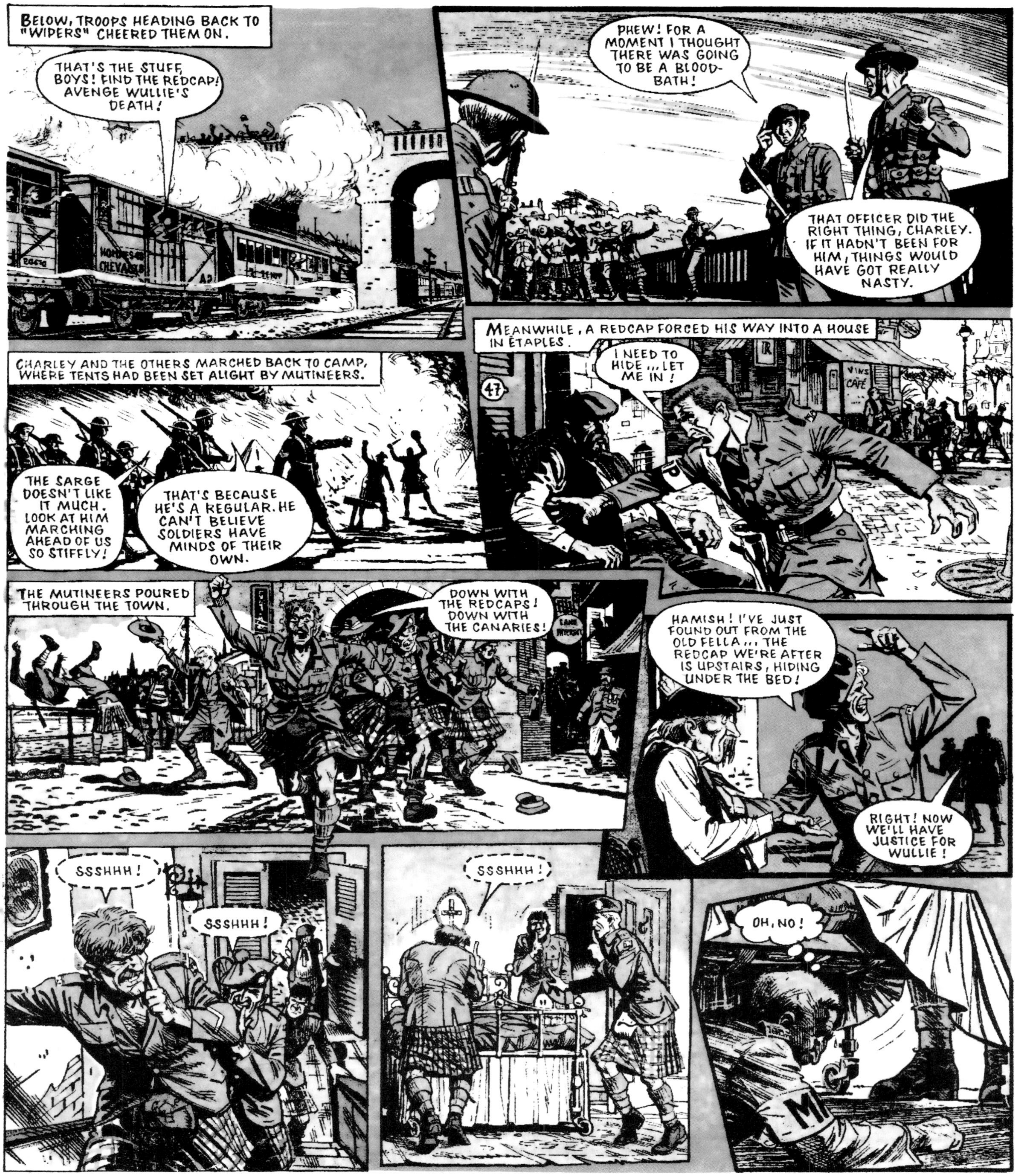
BELOW, TROOPS HEADING BACK TO "WIPERS" CHEERED THEM ON.
THAT'S THE STUFF, BOYS! FIND THE REDCAP! AVENGE WULLIE'S DEATH!
PHEW! FOR A MOMENT I THOUGHT THERE WAS GOING TO BE A BLOOD-BATH!
THAT OFFICER DID THE RIGHT THING, CHARLEY. IF IT HADN'T BEEN FOR HIM, THINGS WOULD HAVE GOT REALLY NASTY.
CHARLEY AND THE OTHERS MARCHED BACK TO CAMP, WHERE TENTS HAD BEEN SET ALIGHT BY MUTINEERS.
!
THE SARGE DOESN'T LIKE IT MUCH. LOOK AT HIM MARCHING AHEAD OF US SO STIFFLY!
THAT'S BECAUSE HE'S A REGULAR. HE CAN'T BELIEVE SOLDIERS HAVE MINDS OF THEIR OWN.
MEANWHILE, A REDCAP FORCED HIS WAY INTO A HOUSE IN ÉTAPLES.
I NEED TO HIDE ... LET ME IN!
47
VINS
CAFÉ
THE MUTINEERS POURED THROUGH THE TOWN.
DOWN WITH THE REDCAPS! DOWN WITH THE CANARIES!
HAMISH! I'VE JUST FOUND OUT FROM THE OLD FELLA ... THE REDCAP WE'RE AFTER IS UPSTAIRS, HIDING UNDER THE BED!
RIGHT! NOW WE'LL HAVE JUSTICE FOR WULLIE!
SSSHHH!
SSSHHH!
SSSHHH!
OH, NO!

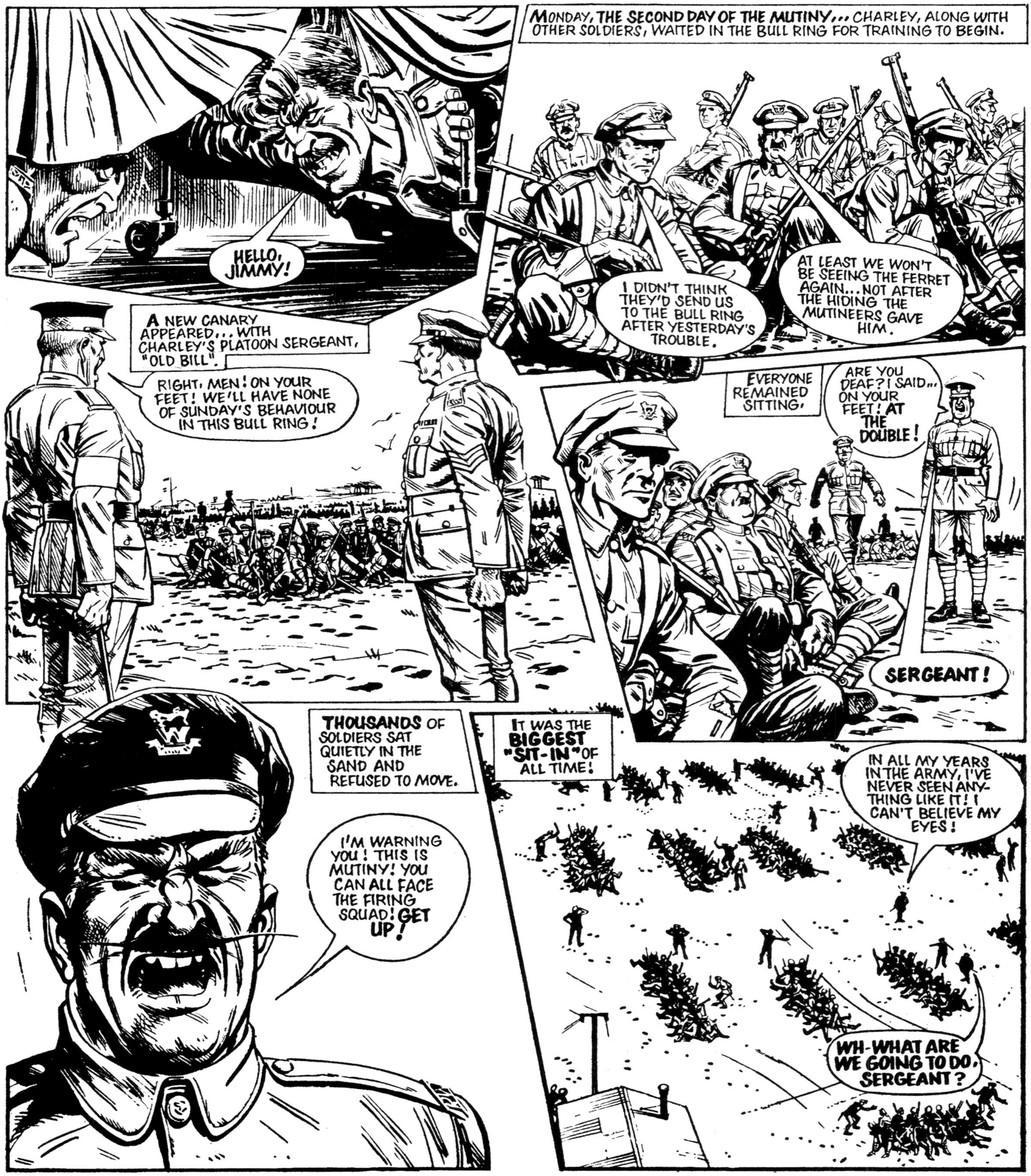
HELLO, JIMMY!
MONDAY, THE SECOND DAY OF THE MUTINY... CHARLEY, ALONG WITH OTHER SOLDIERS, WAITED IN THE BULL RING FOR TRAINING TO BEGIN.
I DIDN'T THINK THEY'D SEND US TO THE BULL RING AFTER YESTERDAY'S TROUBLE.
AT LEAST WE WON'T BE SEEING THE FERRET AGAIN... NOT AFTER THE HIDING THE MUTINEERS GAVE HIM.
A NEW CANARY APPEARED... WITH CHARLEY'S PLATOON SERGEANT, "OLD BILL".
RIGHT, MEN! ON YOUR FEET! WE'LL HAVE NONE OF SUNDAY'S BEHAVIOUR IN THIS BULL RING!
EVERYONE REMAINED SITTING.
ARE YOU DEAF?! I SAID... ON YOUR FEET! AT THE DOUBLE!
SERGEANT!
THOUSANDS OF SOLDIERS SAT QUIETLY IN THE SAND AND REFUSED TO MOVE.
I'M WARNING YOU! THIS IS MUTINY! YOU CAN ALL FACE THE FIRING SQUAD! GET UP!
IT WAS THE BIGGEST "SIT-IN" OF ALL TIME!
IN ALL MY YEARS IN THE ARMY, I'VE NEVER SEEN ANYTHING LIKE IT! I CAN'T BELIEVE MY EYES!
WH-WHAT ARE WE GOING TO DO, SERGEANT?

CHARLEY'S WAR

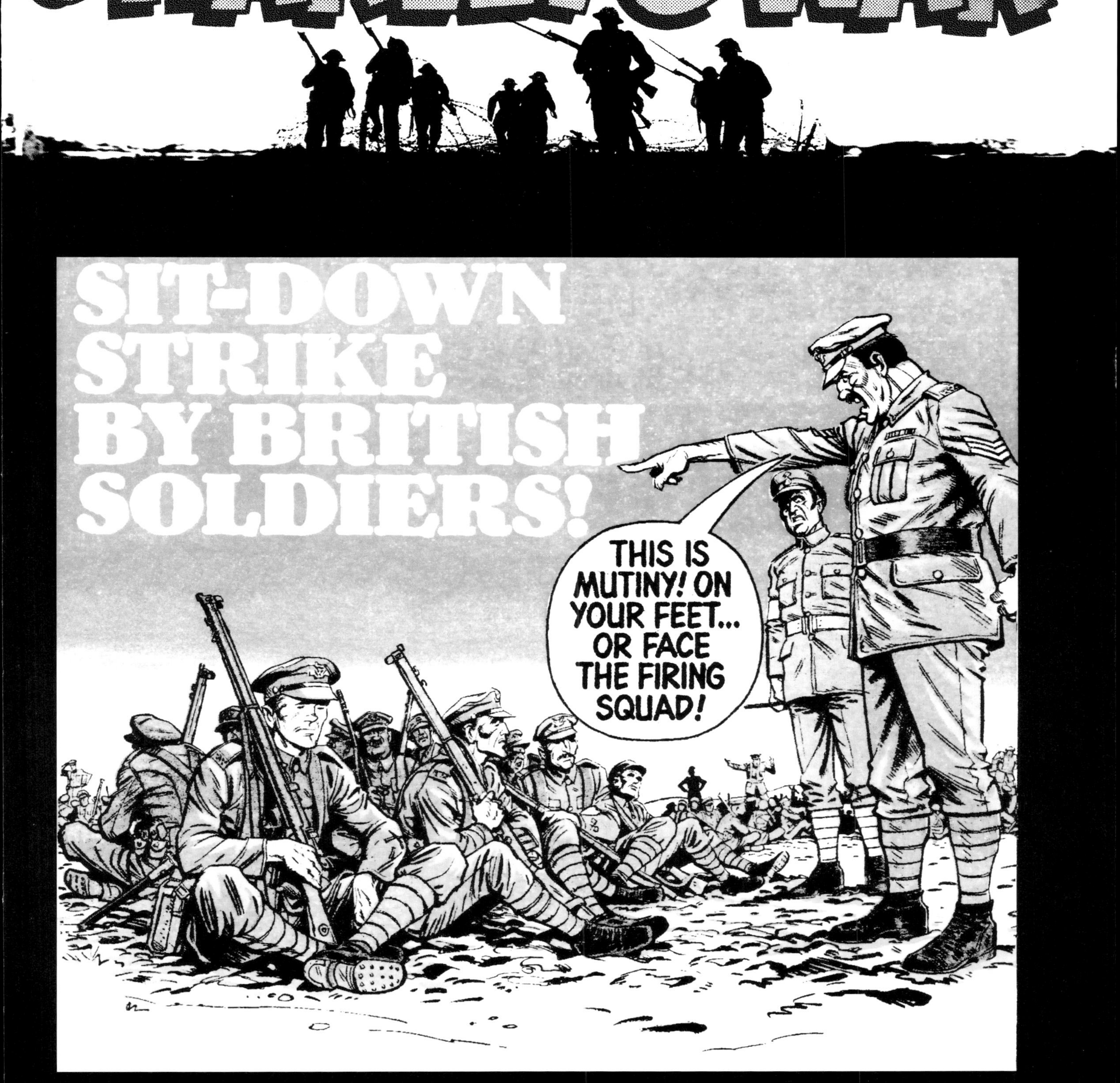
SIT-DOWN STRIKE BY BRITISH SOLDIERS!
THIS IS MUTINY! ON YOUR FEET... OR FACE THE FIRING SQUAD!

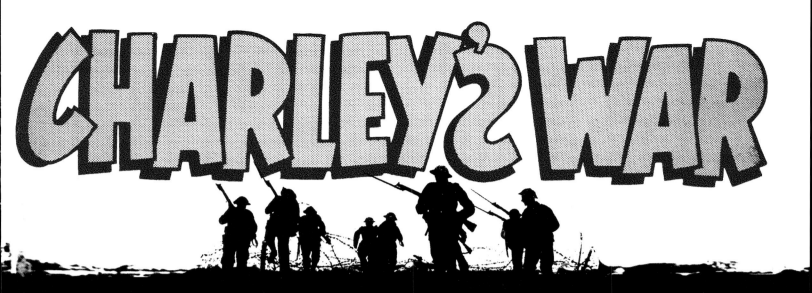

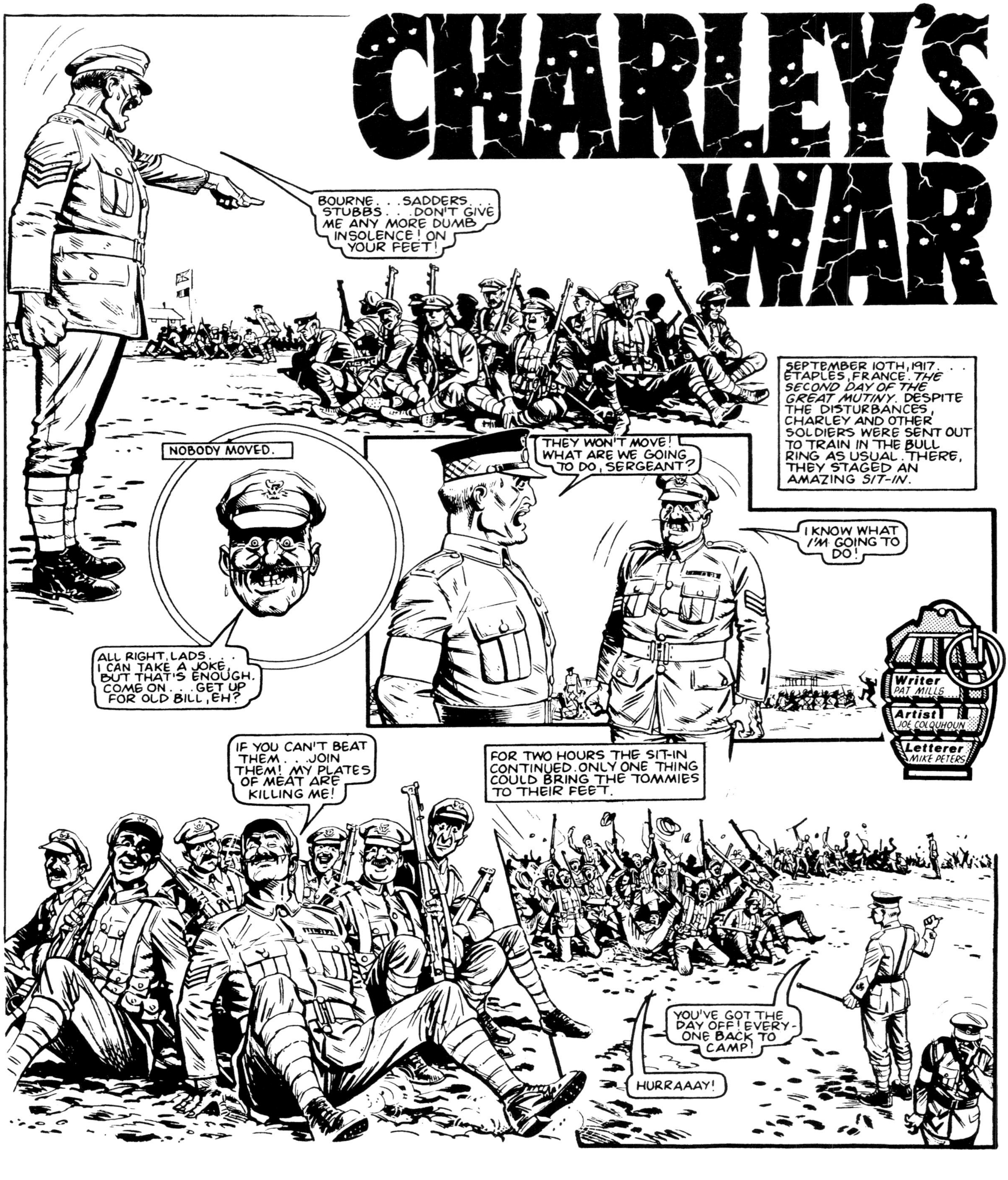
CHARLEY'S WAR
BOURNE. . . SADDERS. . . STUBBS. . . DON'T GIVE ME ANY MORE DUMB INSOLENCE! ON YOUR FEET!
SEPTEMBER 10TH, 1917. . . ETAPLES, FRANCE. THE SECOND DAY OF THE GREAT MUTINY. DESPITE THE DISTURBANCES, CHARLEY AND OTHER SOLDIERS WERE SENT OUT TO TRAIN IN THE BULL RING AS USUAL. THERE, THEY STAGED AN AMAZING SIT-IN.
NOBODY MOVED.
ALL RIGHT, LADS. . . I CAN TAKE A JOKE, BUT THAT'S ENOUGH. COME ON. . . GET UP FOR OLD BILL, EH?
THEY WON'T MOVE! WHAT ARE WE GOING TO DO, SERGEANT?
I KNOW WHAT I'M GOING TO DO!
Writer PAT MILLS
Artist JOE COLQUHOUN
Letterer MIKE PETERS
IF YOU CAN'T BEAT THEM. . . JOIN THEM! MY PLATES OF MEAT ARE KILLING ME!
FOR TWO HOURS THE SIT-IN CONTINUED. ONLY ONE THING COULD BRING THE TOMMIES TO THEIR FEET.
YOU'VE GOT THE DAY OFF! EVERY-ONE BACK TO CAMP!
HURRAAAY!

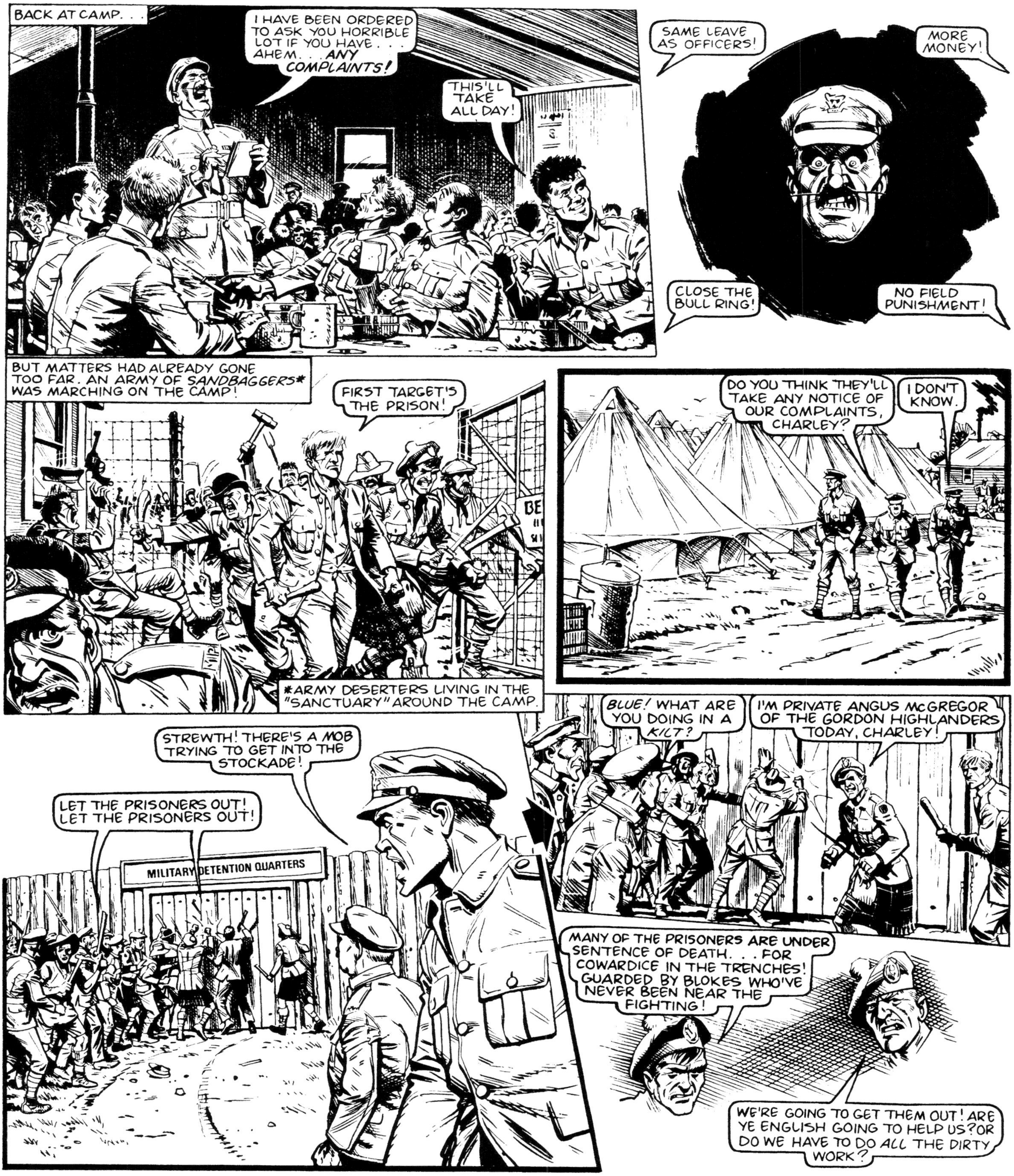
BACK AT CAMP. . .
I HAVE BEEN ORDERED TO ASK YOU HORRIBLE LOT IF YOU HAVE. . . AHEM. . . ANY COMPLAINTS!
THIS'LL TAKE ALL DAY!
SAME LEAVE AS OFFICERS!
MORE MONEY!
CLOSE THE BULL RING!
NO FIELD PUNISHMENT!
BUT MATTERS HAD ALREADY GONE TOO FAR. AN ARMY OF SANDBAGGERS* WAS MARCHING ON THE CAMP!
FIRST TARGET'S THE PRISON!
*ARMY DESERTERS LIVING IN THE "SANCTUARY" AROUND THE CAMP.
DO YOU THINK THEY'LL TAKE ANY NOTICE OF OUR COMPLAINTS, CHARLEY?
I DON'T KNOW.
STREWTH! THERE'S A MOB TRYING TO GET INTO THE STOCKADE!
LET THE PRISONERS OUT! LET THE PRISONERS OUT!
MILITARY DETENTION QUARTERS
BLUE! WHAT ARE YOU DOING IN A KILT?
I'M PRIVATE ANGUS McGREGOR OF THE GORDON HIGHLANDERS TODAY, CHARLEY!
MANY OF THE PRISONERS ARE UNDER SENTENCE OF DEATH. . . FOR COWARDICE IN THE TRENCHES! GUARDED BY BLOKES WHO'VE NEVER BEEN NEAR THE FIGHTING!
WE'RE GOING TO GET THEM OUT! ARE YE ENGLISH GOING TO HELP US? OR DO WE HAVE TO DO ALL THE DIRTY WORK?

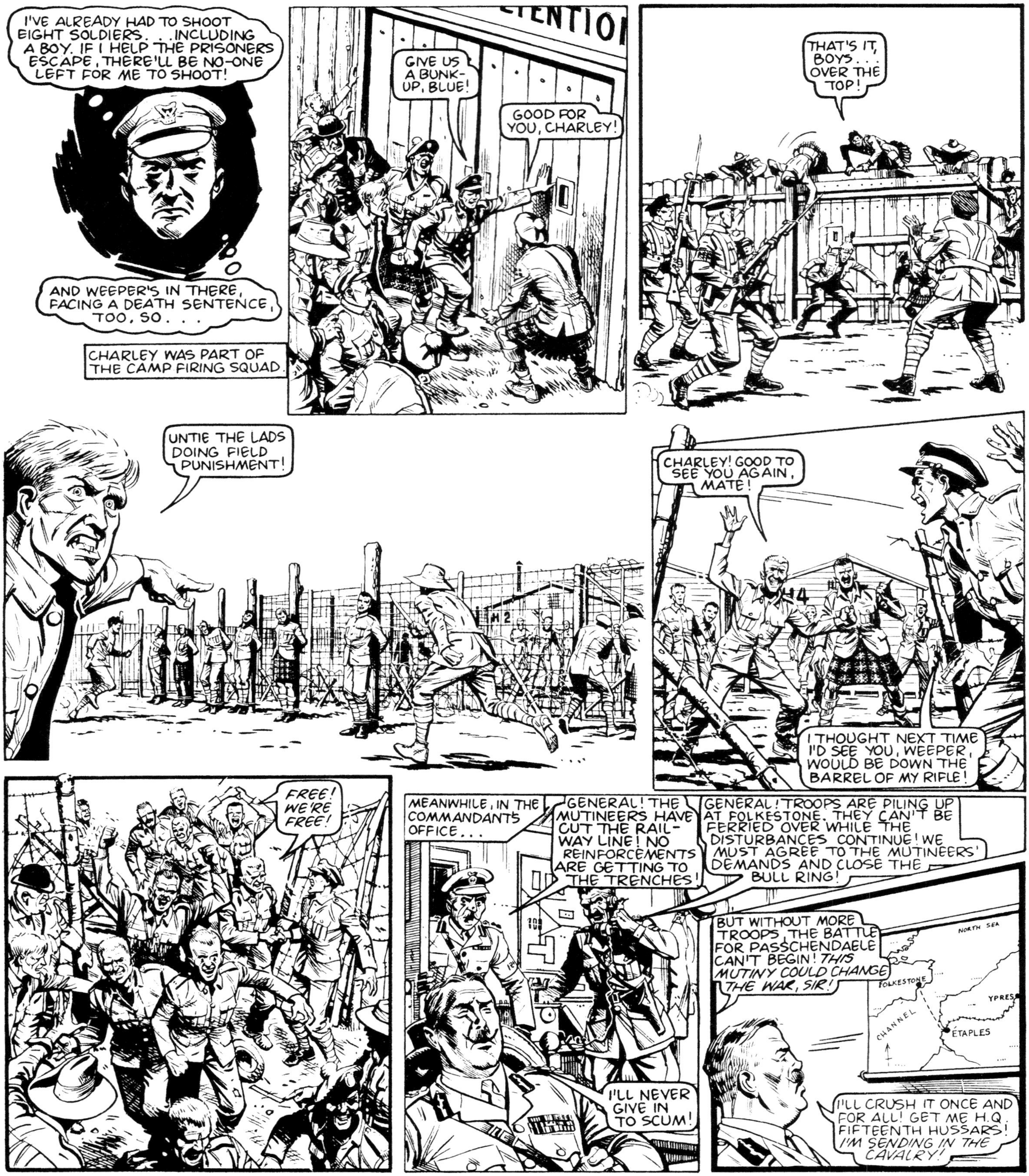
I'VE ALREADY HAD TO SHOOT EIGHT SOLDIERS. . . INCLUDING A BOY. IF I HELP THE PRISONERS ESCAPE, THERE'LL BE NO-ONE LEFT FOR ME TO SHOOT!
AND WEEPER'S IN THERE, FACING A DEATH SENTENCE, TOO, SO . . .
CHARLEY WAS PART OF THE CAMP FIRING SQUAD.
GIVE US A BUNK-UP, BLUE!
GOOD FOR YOU, CHARLEY!
THAT'S IT, BOYS. . . OVER THE TOP!
UNTIE THE LADS DOING FIELD PUNISHMENT!
CHARLEY! GOOD TO SEE YOU AGAIN, MATE!
I THOUGHT NEXT TIME I'D SEE YOU, WEEPER, WOULD BE DOWN THE BARREL OF MY RIFLE!
FREE! WE'RE FREE!
MEANWHILE, IN THE COMMANDANTS OFFICE. . .
GENERAL! THE MUTINEERS HAVE CUT THE RAIL-WAY LINE! NO REINFORCEMENTS ARE GETTING TO THE TRENCHES!
GENERAL! TROOPS ARE PILING UP AT FOLKESTONE. THEY CAN'T BE FERRIED OVER WHILE THE DISTURBANCES CONTINUE! WE MUST AGREE TO THE MUTINEERS' DEMANDS AND CLOSE THE BULL RING!
I'LL NEVER GIVE IN TO SCUM!
BUT WITHOUT MORE TROOPS, THE BATTLE FOR PASSCHENDAELE CAN'T BEGIN! THIS MUTINY COULD CHANGE THE WAR, SIR!
NORTH SEA
FOLKESTONE
YPRES
CHANNEL
ETAPLES
I'LL CRUSH IT ONCE AND FOR ALL! GET ME H.Q. FIFTEENTH HUSSARS! I'M SENDING IN THE CAVALRY!

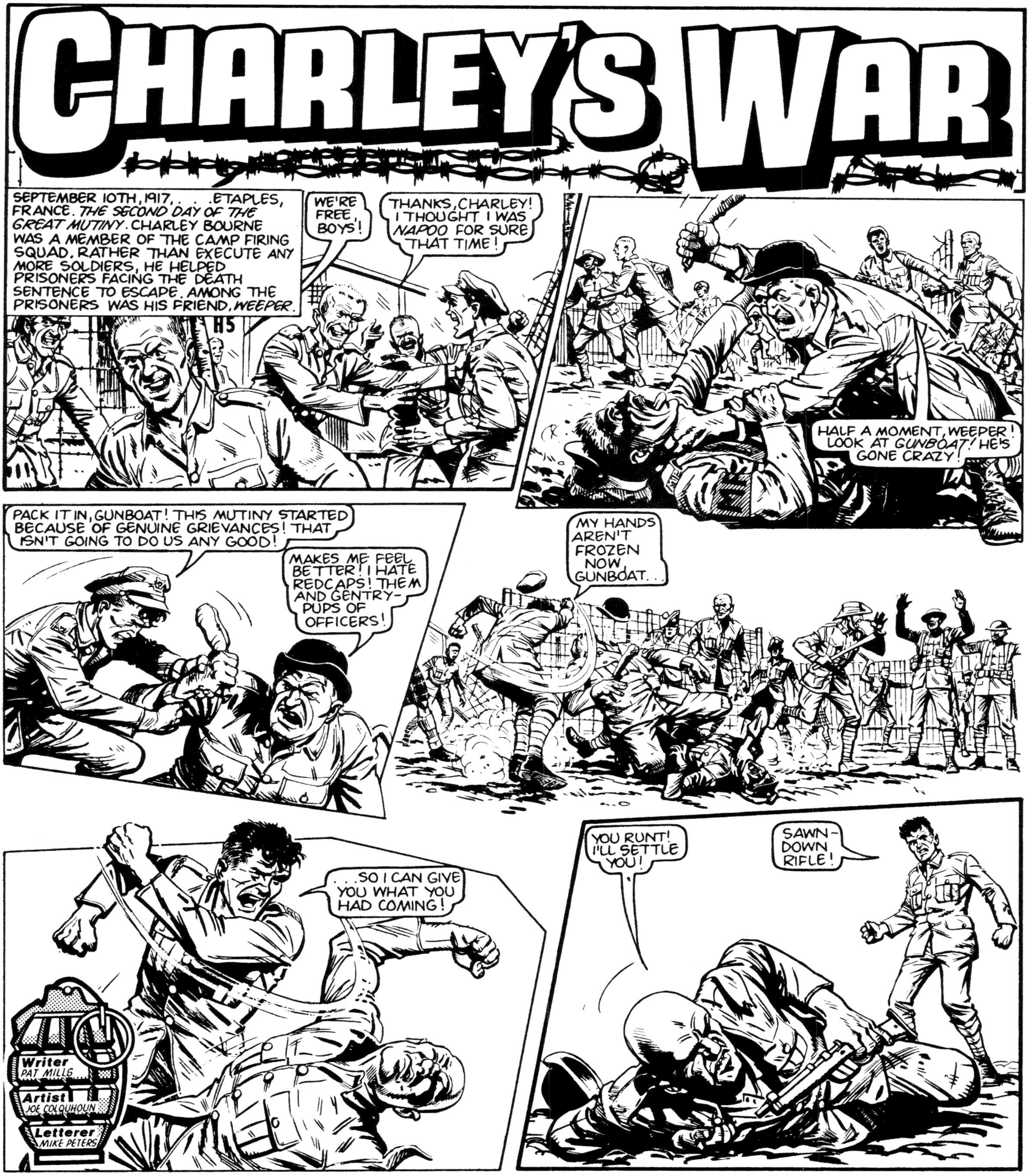
CHARLEY'S WAR
SEPTEMBER 10TH, 1917, . . . ETAPLES, FRANCE. THE SECOND DAY OF THE GREAT MUTINY. CHARLEY BOURNE WAS A MEMBER OF THE CAMP FIRING SQUAD. RATHER THAN EXECUTE ANY MORE SOLDIERS, HE HELPED PRISONERS FACING THE DEATH SENTENCE TO ESCAPE. AMONG THE PRISONERS WAS HIS FRIEND, WEEPER.
WE'RE FREE, BOYS!
THANKS, CHARLEY! I THOUGHT I WAS NAPOO FOR SURE THAT TIME!
H5
HALF A MOMENT, WEEPER! LOOK AT GUNBOAT! HE'S GONE CRAZY!
PACK IT IN, GUNBOAT! THIS MUTINY STARTED BECAUSE OF GENUINE GRIEVANCES! THAT ISN'T GOING TO DO US ANY GOOD!
MAKES ME FEEL BETTER! I HATE REDCAPS! THEM AND GENTRY-PUPS OF OFFICERS!
MY HANDS AREN'T FROZEN NOW, GUNBOAT. . .
. . . SO I CAN GIVE YOU WHAT YOU HAD COMING!
Writer PAT MILLS
Artist JOE COLQUHOUN
Letterer MIKE PETERS
YOU RUNT! I'LL SETTLE YOU!
SAWN-DOWN RIFLE!

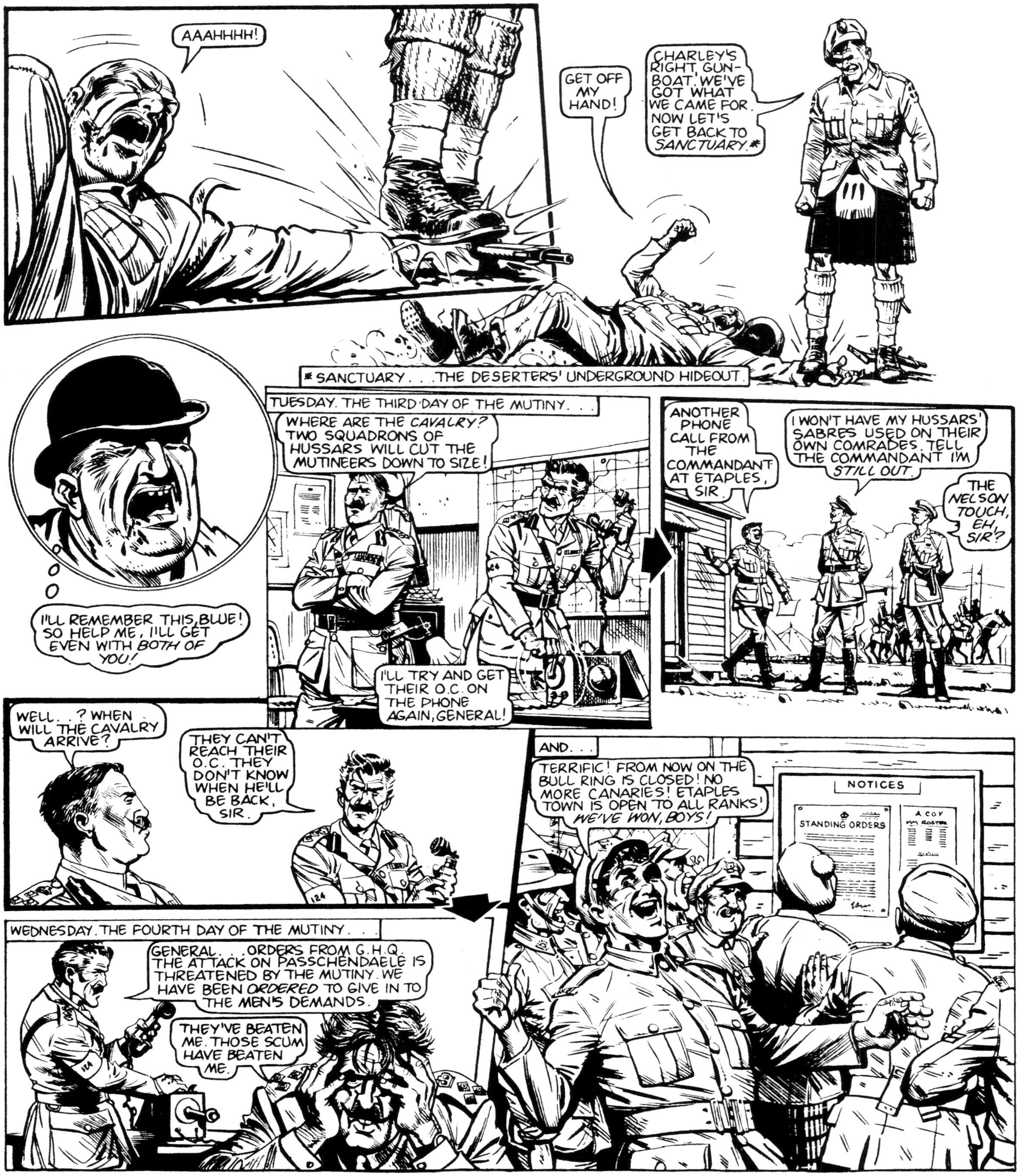

AAAHHHH!
GET OFF MY HAND!
CHARLEY'S RIGHT, GUN-BOAT. WE'VE GOT WHAT WE CAME FOR. NOW LET'S GET BACK TO SANCTUARY.*
* SANCTUARY . . . THE DESERTERS' UNDERGROUND HIDEOUT.
I'LL REMEMBER THIS, BLUE! SO HELP ME, I'LL GET EVEN WITH BOTH OF YOU!
TUESDAY. THE THIRD DAY OF THE MUTINY . . .
WHERE ARE THE CAVALRY? TWO SQUADRONS OF HUSSARS WILL CUT THE MUTINEERS DOWN TO SIZE!
I'LL TRY AND GET THEIR O.C. ON THE PHONE AGAIN, GENERAL!
ANOTHER PHONE CALL FROM THE COMMANDANT AT ETAPLES, SIR.
I WON'T HAVE MY HUSSARS' SABRES USED ON THEIR OWN COMRADES. TELL THE COMMANDANT I'M STILL OUT.
THE NELSON TOUCH, EH, SIR?
WELL . . ? WHEN WILL THE CAVALRY ARRIVE?
THEY CAN'T REACH THEIR O.C. THEY DON'T KNOW WHEN HE'LL BE BACK, SIR.
WEDNESDAY. THE FOURTH DAY OF THE MUTINY . . .
GENERAL . . . ORDERS FROM G.H.Q. THE ATTACK ON PASSCHENDAELE IS THREATENED BY THE MUTINY. WE HAVE BEEN ORDERED TO GIVE IN TO THE MEN'S DEMANDS.
THEY'VE BEATEN ME. THOSE SCUM HAVE BEATEN ME.
AND . . .
TERRIFIC! FROM NOW ON THE BULL RING IS CLOSED! NO MORE CANARIES! ETAPLES TOWN IS OPEN TO ALL RANKS! WE'VE WON, BOYS!
NOTICES
STANDING ORDERS
A COY

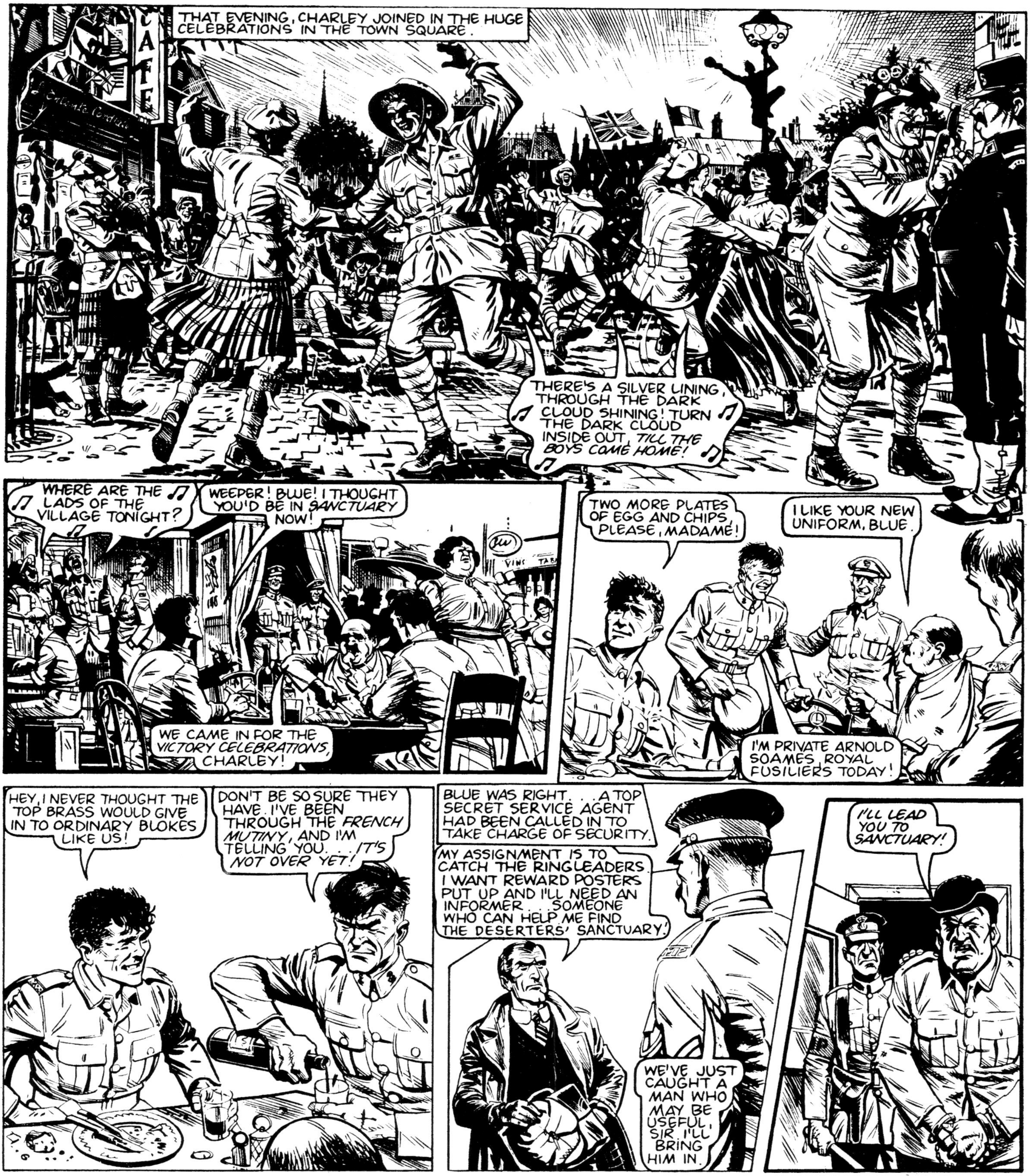

THAT EVENING, CHARLEY JOINED IN THE HUGE CELEBRATIONS IN THE TOWN SQUARE.
CAFE
THERE'S A SILVER LINING, THROUGH THE DARK CLOUD SHINING! TURN THE DARK CLOUD INSIDE OUT, TILL THE BOYS COME HOME!
WHERE ARE THE LADS OF THE VILLAGE TONIGHT?
WEEPER! BLUE! I THOUGHT YOU'D BE IN SANCTUARY NOW!
WE CAME IN FOR THE VICTORY CELEBRATIONS, CHARLEY!
TWO MORE PLATES OF EGG AND CHIPS, PLEASE, MADAME!
I LIKE YOUR NEW UNIFORM, BLUE.
I'M PRIVATE ARNOLD SOAMES, ROYAL FUSILIERS TODAY!
HEY, I NEVER THOUGHT THE TOP BRASS WOULD GIVE IN TO ORDINARY BLOKES LIKE US!
DON'T BE SO SURE THEY HAVE. I'VE BEEN THROUGH THE FRENCH MUTINY, AND I'M TELLING YOU. . . IT'S NOT OVER YET!
BLUE WAS RIGHT. . . A TOP SECRET SERVICE AGENT HAD BEEN CALLED IN TO TAKE CHARGE OF SECURITY.
MY ASSIGNMENT IS TO CATCH THE RINGLEADERS. I WANT REWARD POSTERS PUT UP AND I'LL NEED AN INFORMER . . . SOMEONE WHO CAN HELP ME FIND THE DESERTERS' SANCTUARY!
WE'VE JUST CAUGHT A MAN WHO MAY BE USEFUL, SIR. I'LL BRING HIM IN.
I'LL LEAD YOU TO SANCTUARY!

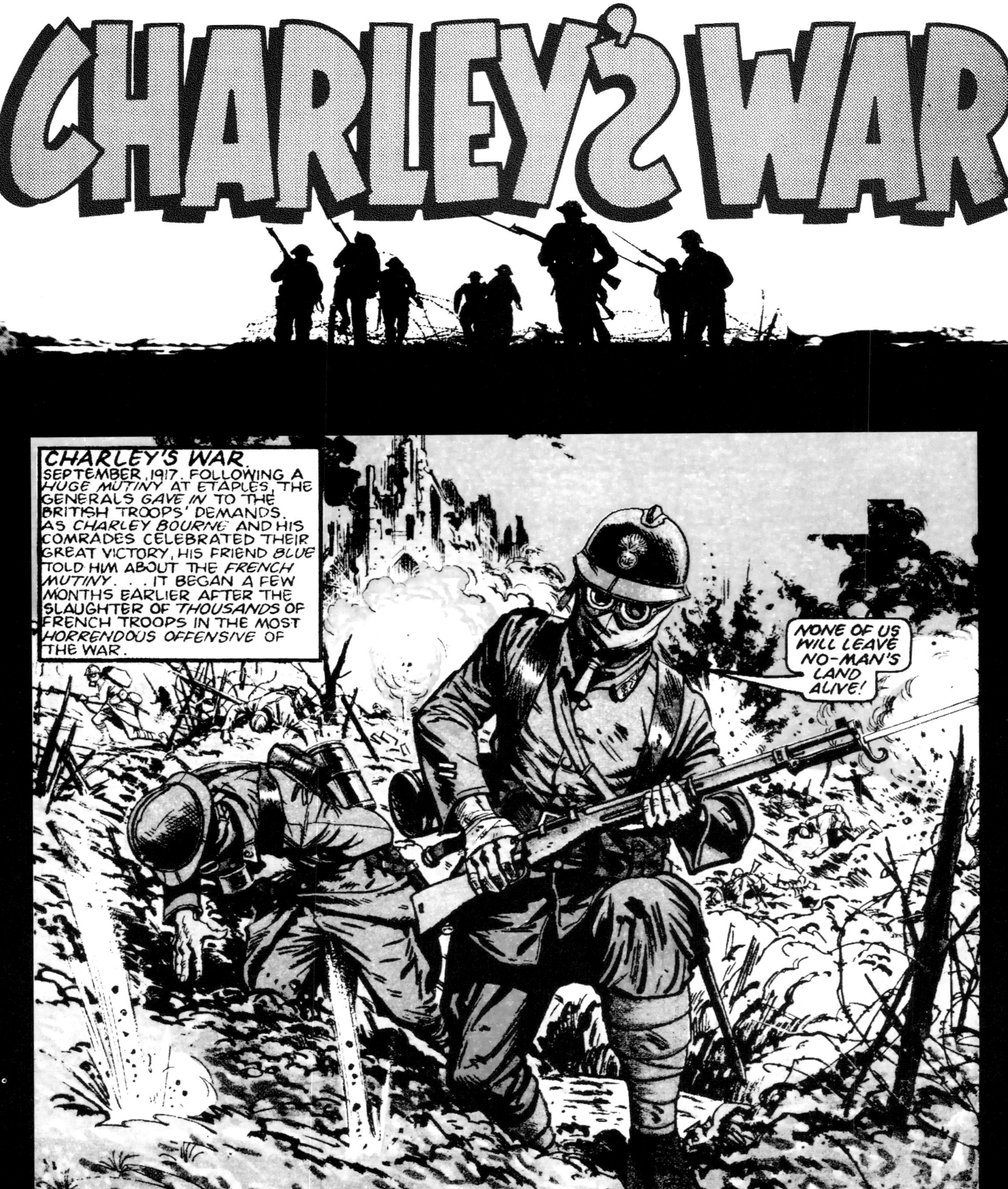
CHARLEY'S WAR
CHARLEY'S WAR. SEPTEMBER, 1917. FOLLOWING A HUGE MUTINY AT ETAPLES, THE GENERALS GAVE IN TO THE BRITISH TROOPS' DEMANDS. AS CHARLEY BOURNE AND HIS COMRADES CELEBRATED THEIR GREAT VICTORY, HIS FRIEND BLUE TOLD HIM ABOUT THE FRENCH MUTINY. . . IT BEGAN A FEW MONTHS EARLIER AFTER THE SLAUGHTER OF THOUSANDS OF FRENCH TROOPS IN THE MOST HORRENDOUS OFFENSIVE OF THE WAR.
NONE OF US WILL LEAVE NO-MAN'S LAND ALIVE!
CONTINUED ON NEXT PAGE

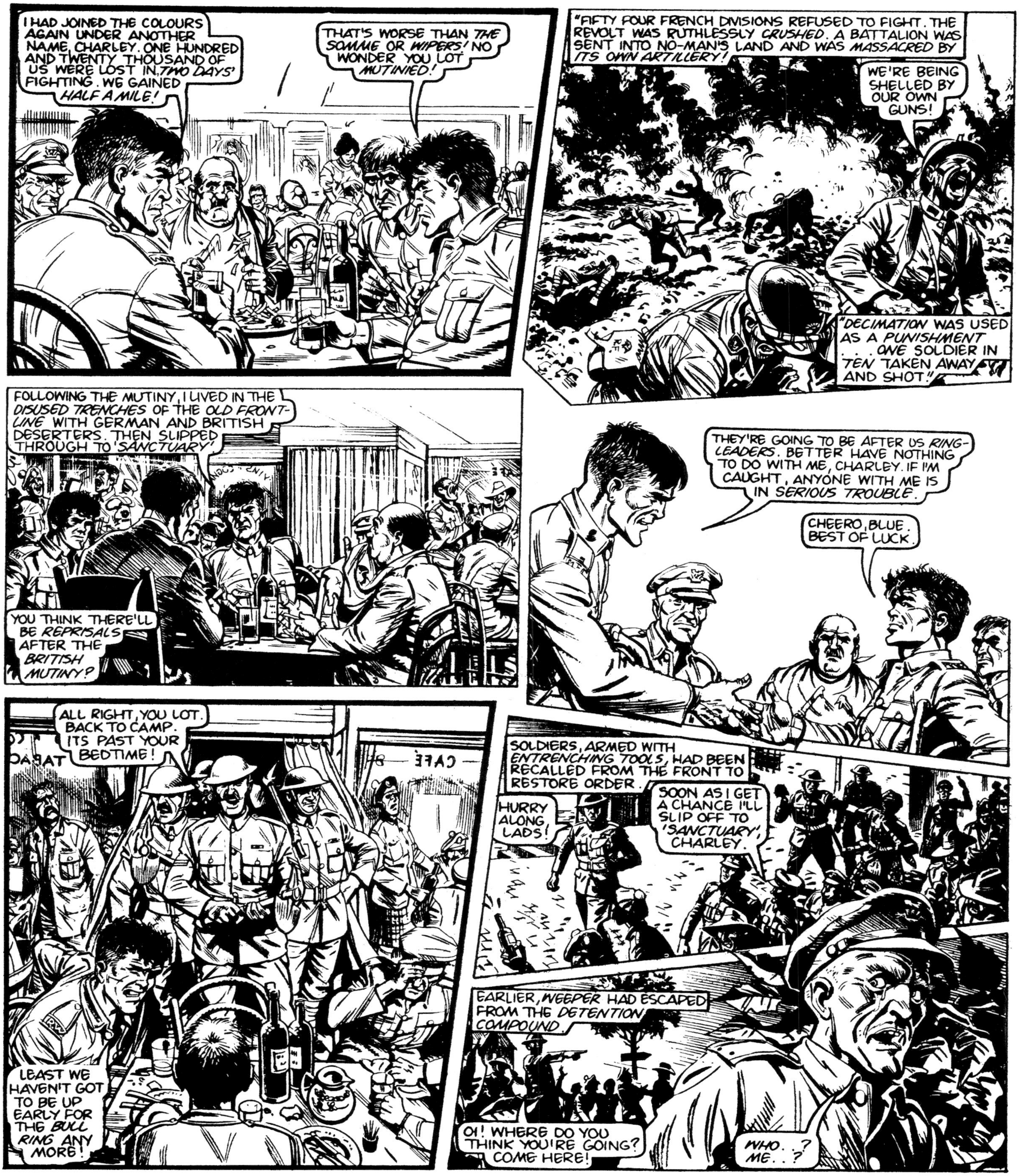

I HAD JOINED THE COLOURS AGAIN UNDER ANOTHER NAME, CHARLEY. ONE HUNDRED AND TWENTY THOUSAND OF US WERE LOST IN TWO DAYS' FIGHTING. WE GAINED HALF A MILE!
THAT'S WORSE THAN THE SOMME OR WIPERS! NO WONDER YOU LOT MUTINIED!
"FIFTY FOUR FRENCH DIVISIONS REFUSED TO FIGHT. THE REVOLT WAS RUTHLESSLY CRUSHED. A BATTALION WAS SENT INTO NO-MAN'S LAND AND WAS MASSACRED BY ITS OWN ARTILLERY!
WE'RE BEING SHELLED BY OUR OWN GUNS!
"DECIMATION WAS USED AS A PUNISHMENT . . . ONE SOLDIER IN TEN TAKEN AWAY AND SHOT!"
FOLLOWING THE MUTINY, I LIVED IN THE DISUSED TRENCHES OF THE OLD FRONT-LINE WITH GERMAN AND BRITISH DESERTERS. THEN SLIPPED THROUGH TO 'SANCTUARY'.
YOU THINK THERE'LL BE REPRISALS AFTER THE BRITISH MUTINY?
THEY'RE GOING TO BE AFTER US RING-LEADERS. BETTER HAVE NOTHING TO DO WITH ME, CHARLEY. IF I'M CAUGHT, ANYONE WITH ME IS IN SERIOUS TROUBLE.
CHEERO, BLUE. BEST OF LUCK.
ALL RIGHT, YOU LOT. BACK TO CAMP. ITS PAST YOUR BEDTIME!
CAFE
LEAST WE HAVEN'T GOT TO BE UP EARLY FOR THE BULL RING ANY MORE!
SOLDIERS, ARMED WITH ENTRENCHING TOOLS, HAD BEEN RECALLED FROM THE FRONT TO RESTORE ORDER.
HURRY ALONG, LADS!
SOON AS I GET A CHANCE I'LL SLIP OFF TO 'SANCTUARY', CHARLEY.
EARLIER, WEEPER HAD ESCAPED FROM THE DETENTION COMPOUND.
OI! WHERE DO YOU THINK YOU'RE GOING? COME HERE!
WHO. .? ME. . ?

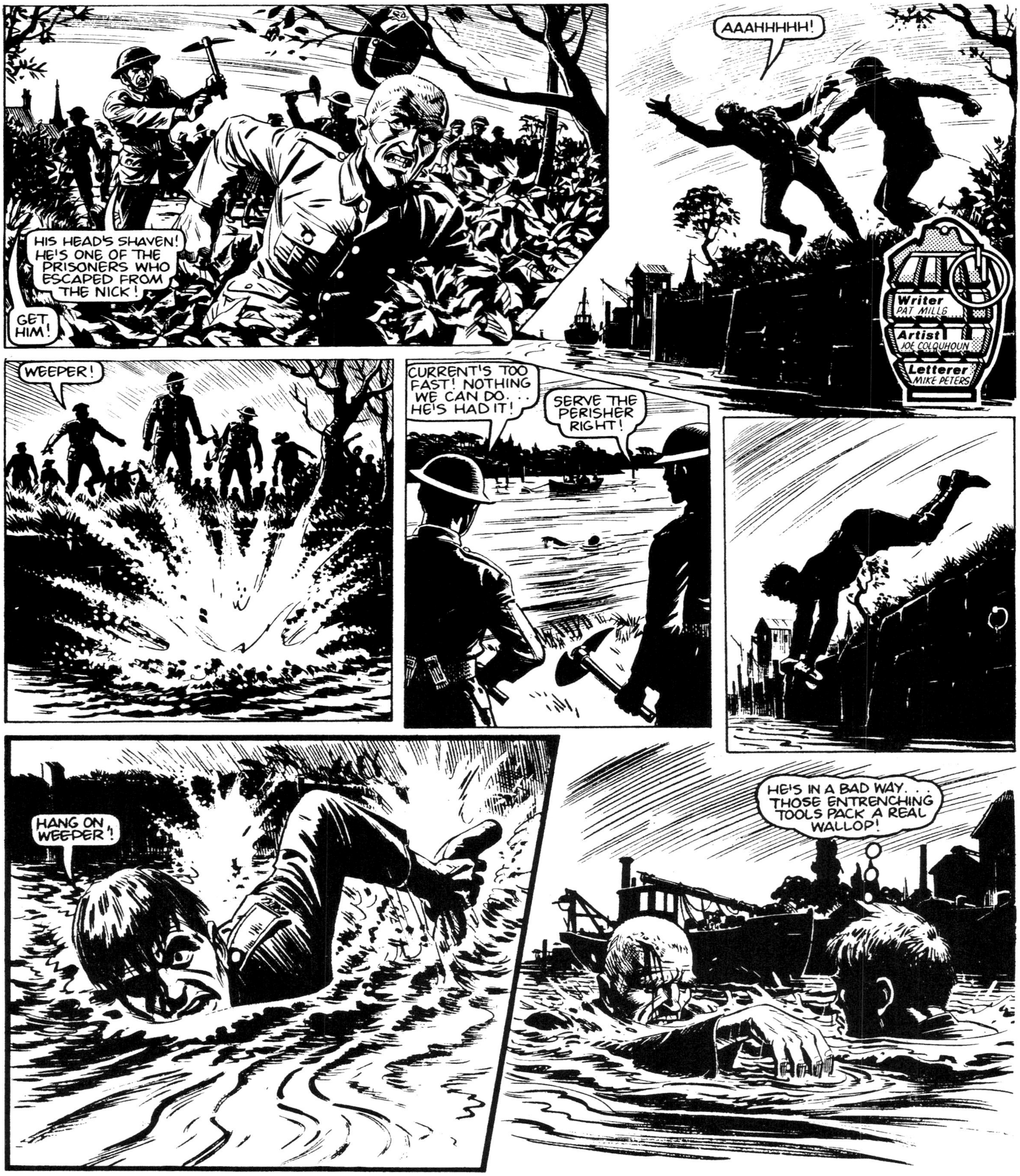

HIS HEAD'S SHAVEN! HE'S ONE OF THE PRISONERS WHO ESCAPED FROM THE NICK!
GET HIM!
AAAHHHHH!
Writer PAT MILLS
Artist JOE COLQUHOUN
Letterer MIKE PETERS
WEEPER!
CURRENT'S TOO FAST! NOTHING WE CAN DO... HE'S HAD IT!
SERVE THE PERISHER RIGHT!
HANG ON WEEPER!
HE'S IN A BAD WAY... THOSE ENTRENCHING TOOLS PACK A REAL WALLOP!

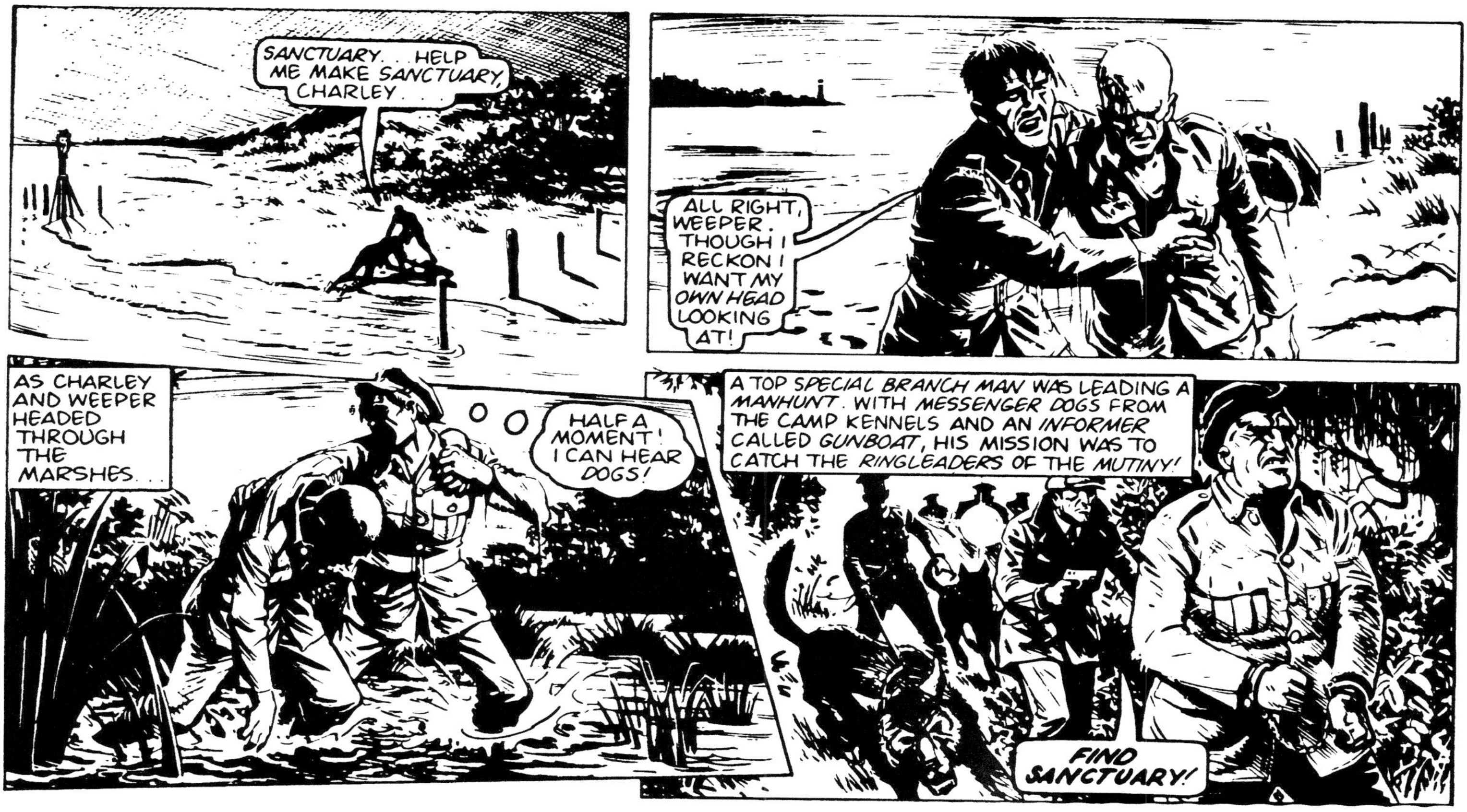
SANCTUARY... HELP ME MAKE SANCTUARY, CHARLEY.
ALL RIGHT, WEEPER. THOUGH I RECKON I WANT MY OWN HEAD LOOKING AT!
AS CHARLEY AND WEEPER HEADED THROUGH THE MARSHES...
HALF A MOMENT! I CAN HEAR DOGS!
A TOP SPECIAL BRANCH MAN WAS LEADING A MANHUNT. WITH MESSENGER DOGS FROM THE CAMP KENNELS AND AN INFORMER CALLED GUNBOAT, HIS MISSION WAS TO CATCH THE RINGLEADERS OF THE MUTINY!
FIND SANCTUARY!

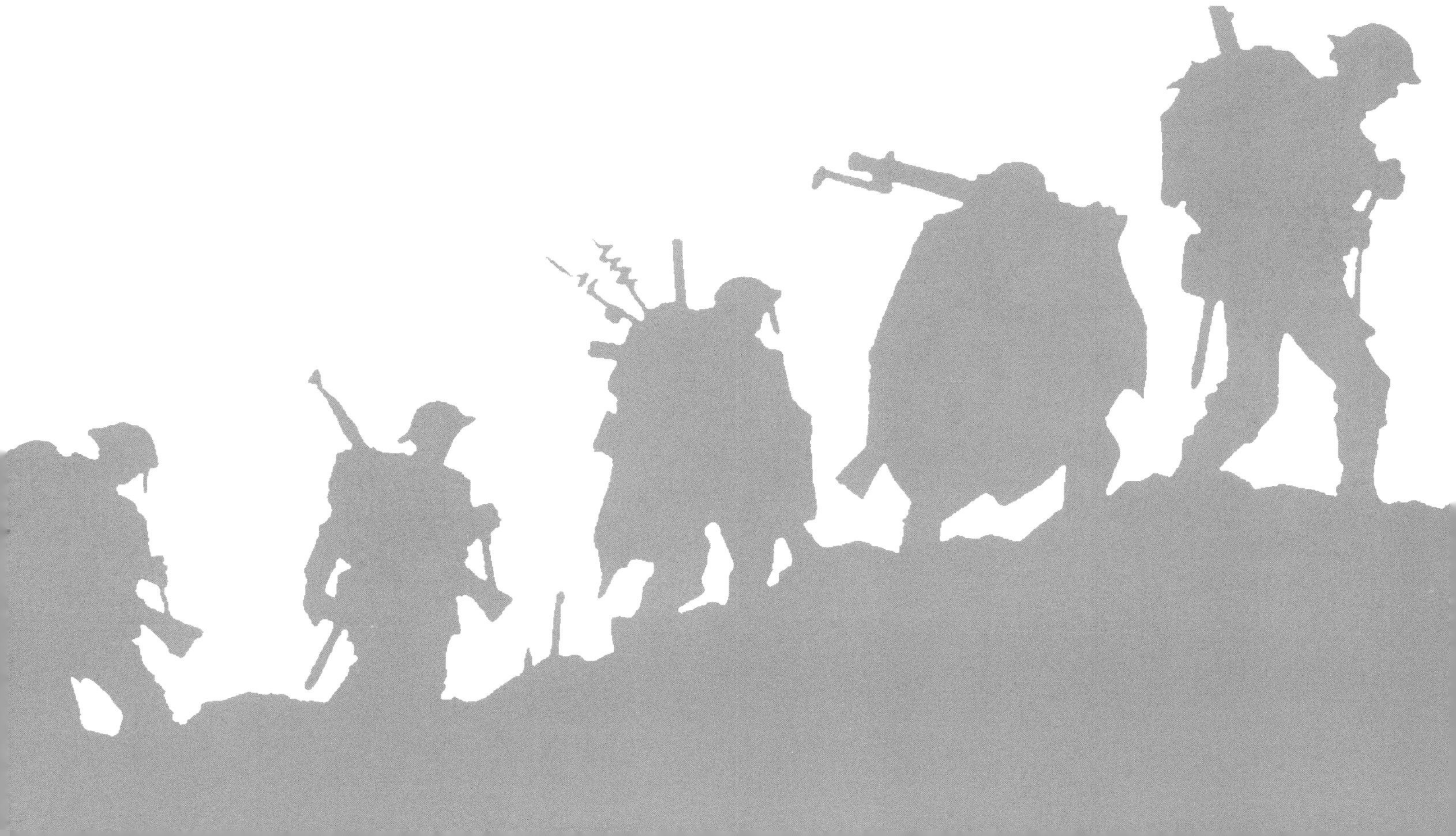

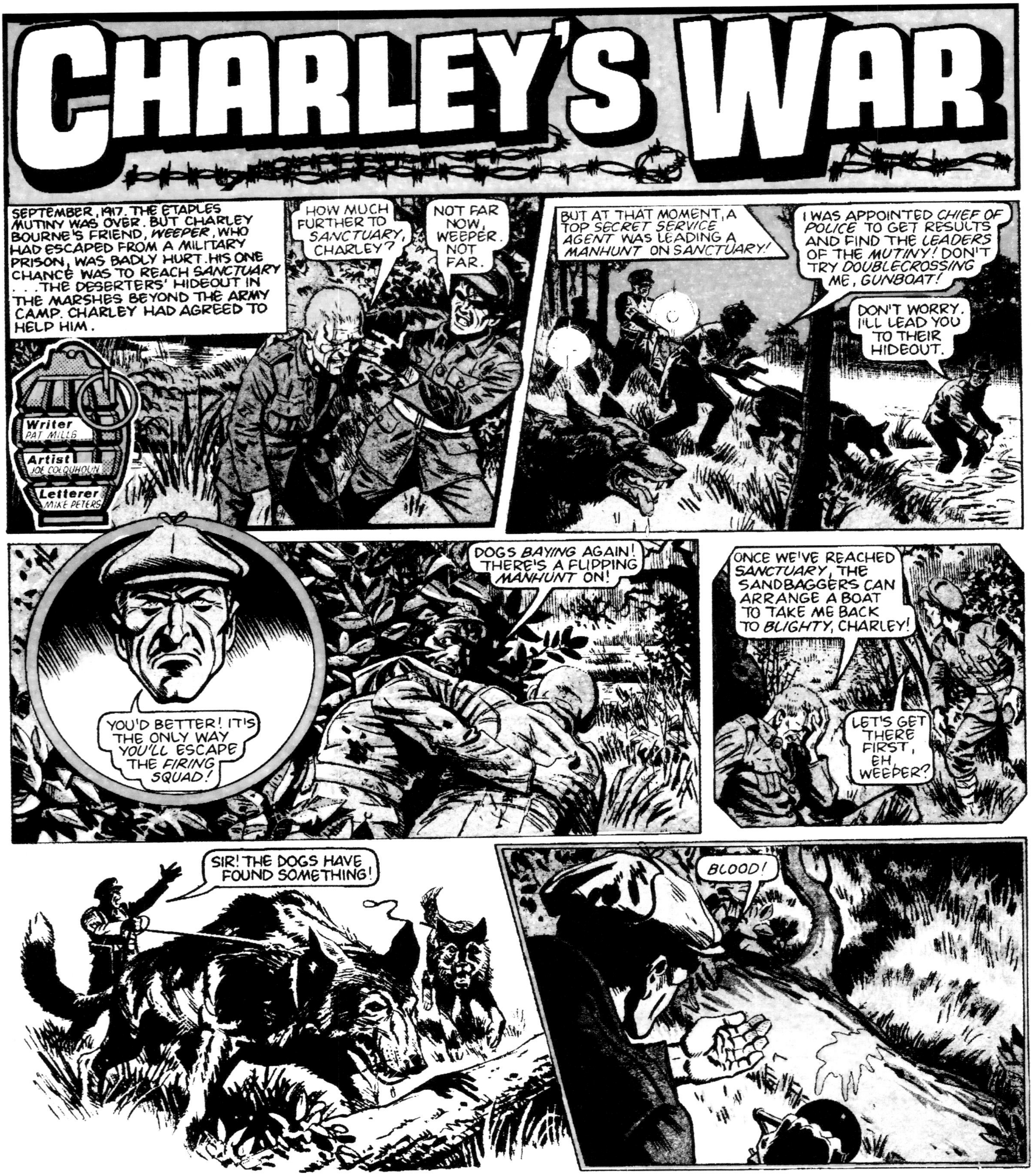
CHARLEY'S WAR
SEPTEMBER, 1917. THE ETAPLES MUTINY WAS OVER. BUT CHARLEY BOURNE'S FRIEND, WEEPER, WHO HAD ESCAPED FROM A MILITARY PRISON, WAS BADLY HURT. HIS ONE CHANCE WAS TO REACH SANCTUARY . . . THE DESERTERS' HIDEOUT IN THE MARSHES BEYOND THE ARMY CAMP. CHARLEY HAD AGREED TO HELP HIM.
Writer PAT MILLS
Artist JOE COLQUHOUN
Letterer MIKE PETERS
HOW MUCH FURTHER TO SANCTUARY, CHARLEY?
NOT FAR NOW, WEEPER. NOT FAR.
BUT AT THAT MOMENT, A TOP SECRET SERVICE AGENT WAS LEADING A MANHUNT ON SANCTUARY!
I WAS APPOINTED CHIEF OF POLICE TO GET RESULTS AND FIND THE LEADERS OF THE MUTINY! DON'T TRY DOUBLECROSSING ME, GUNBOAT!
DON'T WORRY. I'LL LEAD YOU TO THEIR HIDEOUT.
YOU'D BETTER! IT'S THE ONLY WAY YOU'LL ESCAPE THE FIRING SQUAD!
DOGS BAYING AGAIN! THERE'S A FLIPPING MANHUNT ON!
ONCE WE'VE REACHED SANCTUARY, THE SANDBAGGERS CAN ARRANGE A BOAT TO TAKE ME BACK TO BLIGHTY, CHARLEY!
LET'S GET THERE FIRST, EH, WEEPER?
SIR! THE DOGS HAVE FOUND SOMETHING!
BLOOD!

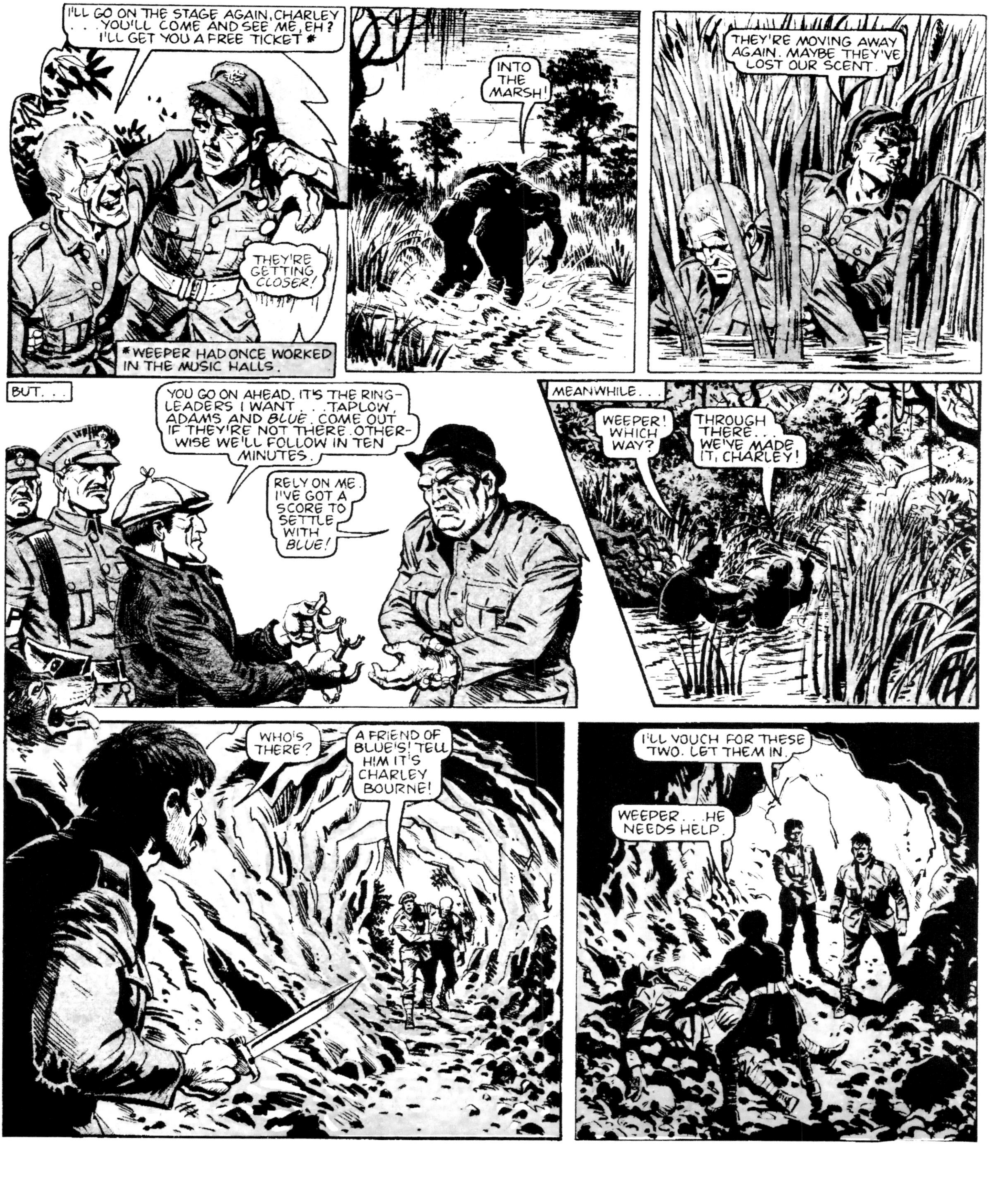

I'LL GO ON THE STAGE AGAIN, CHARLEY . . . YOU'LL COME AND SEE ME, EH? I'LL GET YOU A FREE TICKET *
THEY'RE GETTING CLOSER!
* WEEPER HAD ONCE WORKED IN THE MUSIC HALLS.
INTO THE MARSH!
THEY'RE MOVING AWAY AGAIN. MAYBE THEY'VE LOST OUR SCENT.
BUT. . .
YOU GO ON AHEAD. IT'S THE RING-LEADERS I WANT . . . TAPLOW, ADAMS AND BLUE. COME OUT IF THEY'RE NOT THERE. OTHERWISE WE'LL FOLLOW IN TEN MINUTES.
RELY ON ME. I'VE GOT A SCORE TO SETTLE WITH BLUE!
MEANWHILE. . .
WEEPER! WHICH WAY?
THROUGH THERE. . . WE'VE MADE IT, CHARLEY!
WHO'S THERE?
A FRIEND OF BLUE'S! TELL HIM IT'S CHARLEY BOURNE!
I'LL VOUCH FOR THESE TWO. LET THEM IN.
WEEPER. . . HE NEEDS HELP.

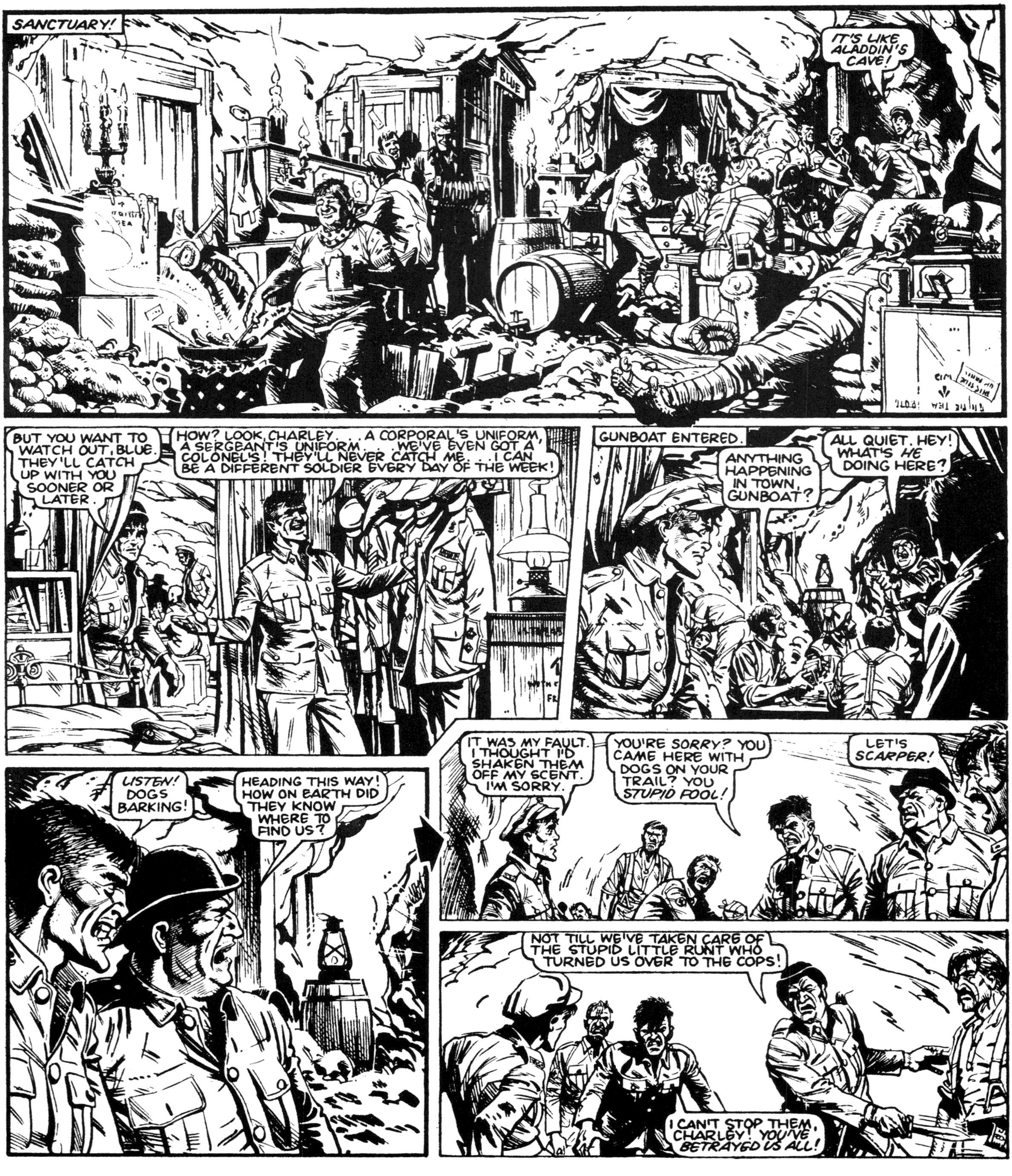

SANCTUARY!
IT'S LIKE ALADDIN'S CAVE!
BUT YOU WANT TO WATCH OUT, BLUE. THEY'LL CATCH UP WITH YOU SOONER OR LATER.
HOW? LOOK, CHARLEY . . . A CORPORAL'S UNIFORM, A SERGEANT'S UNIFORM . . . WE'VE EVEN GOT A COLONEL'S! THEY'LL NEVER CATCH ME . . . I CAN BE A DIFFERENT SOLDIER EVERY DAY OF THE WEEK!
GUNBOAT ENTERED.
ANYTHING HAPPENING IN TOWN, GUNBOAT?
ALL QUIET. HEY! WHAT'S HE DOING HERE?
LISTEN! DOGS BARKING!
HEADING THIS WAY! HOW ON EARTH DID THEY KNOW WHERE TO FIND US?
IT WAS MY FAULT. I THOUGHT I'D SHAKEN THEM OFF MY SCENT. I'M SORRY.
YOU'RE SORRY? YOU CAME HERE WITH DOGS ON YOUR TRAIL? YOU STUPID FOOL!
LET'S SCARPER!
NOT TILL WE'VE TAKEN CARE OF THE STUPID LITTLE RUNT WHO TURNED US OVER TO THE COPS!
I CAN'T STOP THEM, CHARLEY! YOU'VE BETRAYED US ALL!

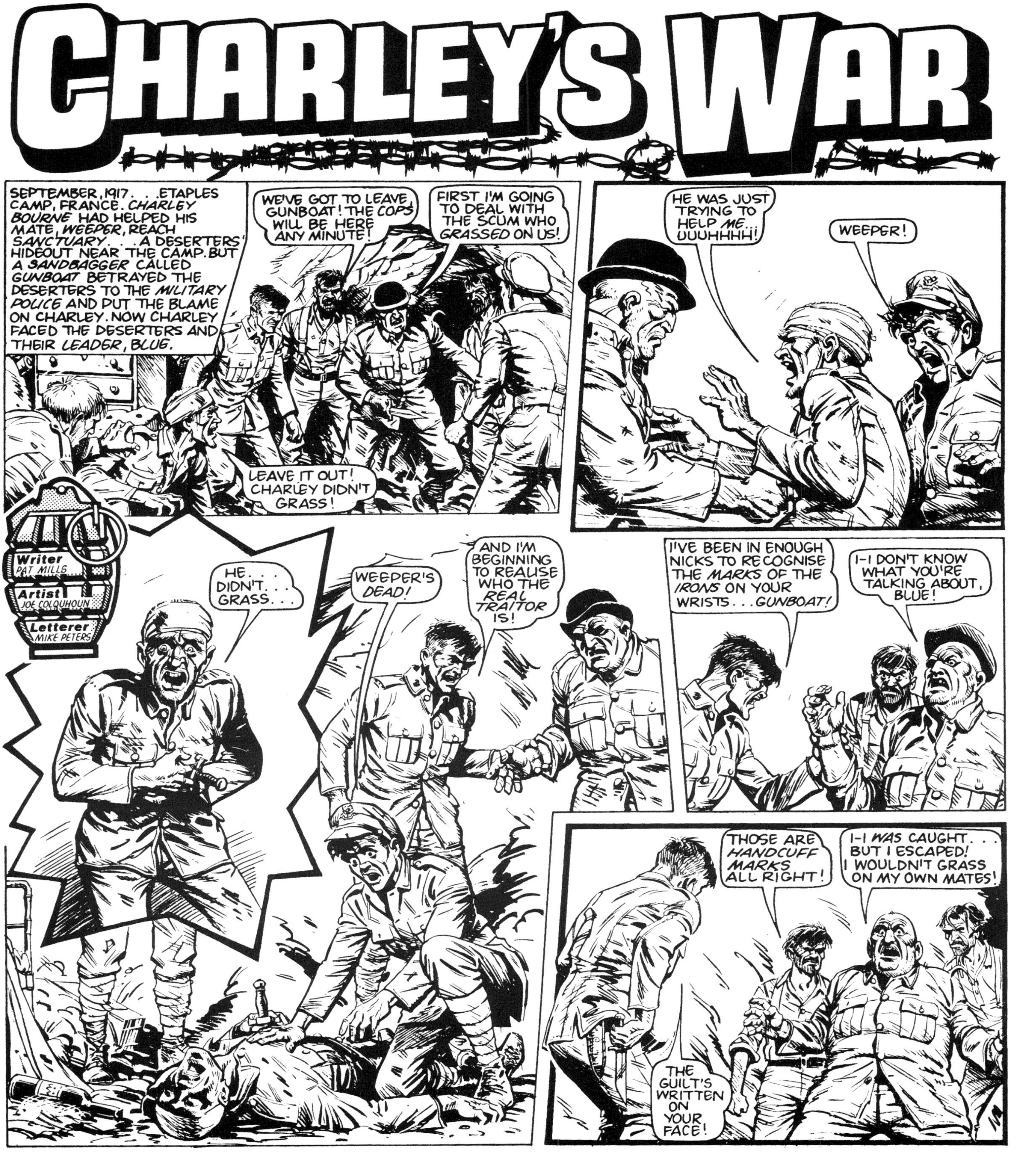

CHARLEY'S WAR
SEPTEMBER, 1917. . . ETAPLES CAMP, FRANCE. CHARLEY BOURNE HAD HELPED HIS MATE, WEEPER, REACH SANCTUARY. . . A DESERTERS' HIDEOUT NEAR THE CAMP. BUT A SANDBAGGER CALLED GUNBOAT BETRAYED THE DESERTERS TO THE MILITARY POLICE AND PUT THE BLAME ON CHARLEY. NOW CHARLEY FACED THE DESERTERS AND THEIR LEADER, BLUE.
WE'VE GOT TO LEAVE GUNBOAT! THE COPS WILL BE HERE ANY MINUTE!
FIRST I'M GOING TO DEAL WITH THE SCUM WHO GRASSED ON US!
LEAVE IT OUT! CHARLEY DIDN'T GRASS!
HE WAS JUST TRYING TO HELP ME... UUUHHHH!
WEEPER!
Writer PAT MILLS
Artist JOE COLQUHOUN
Letterer MIKE PETERS
HE. . . DIDN'T. . . GRASS. . .
WEEPER'S DEAD!
AND I'M BEGINNING TO REALISE WHO THE REAL TRAITOR IS!
I'VE BEEN IN ENOUGH NICKS TO RECOGNISE THE MARKS OF THE IRONS ON YOUR WRISTS. . . GUNBOAT!
I-I DON'T KNOW WHAT YOU'RE TALKING ABOUT, BLUE!
THOSE ARE HANDCUFF MARKS ALL RIGHT!
I-I WAS CAUGHT. . . BUT I ESCAPED! I WOULDN'T GRASS ON MY OWN MATES!
THE GUILT'S WRITTEN ON YOUR FACE!

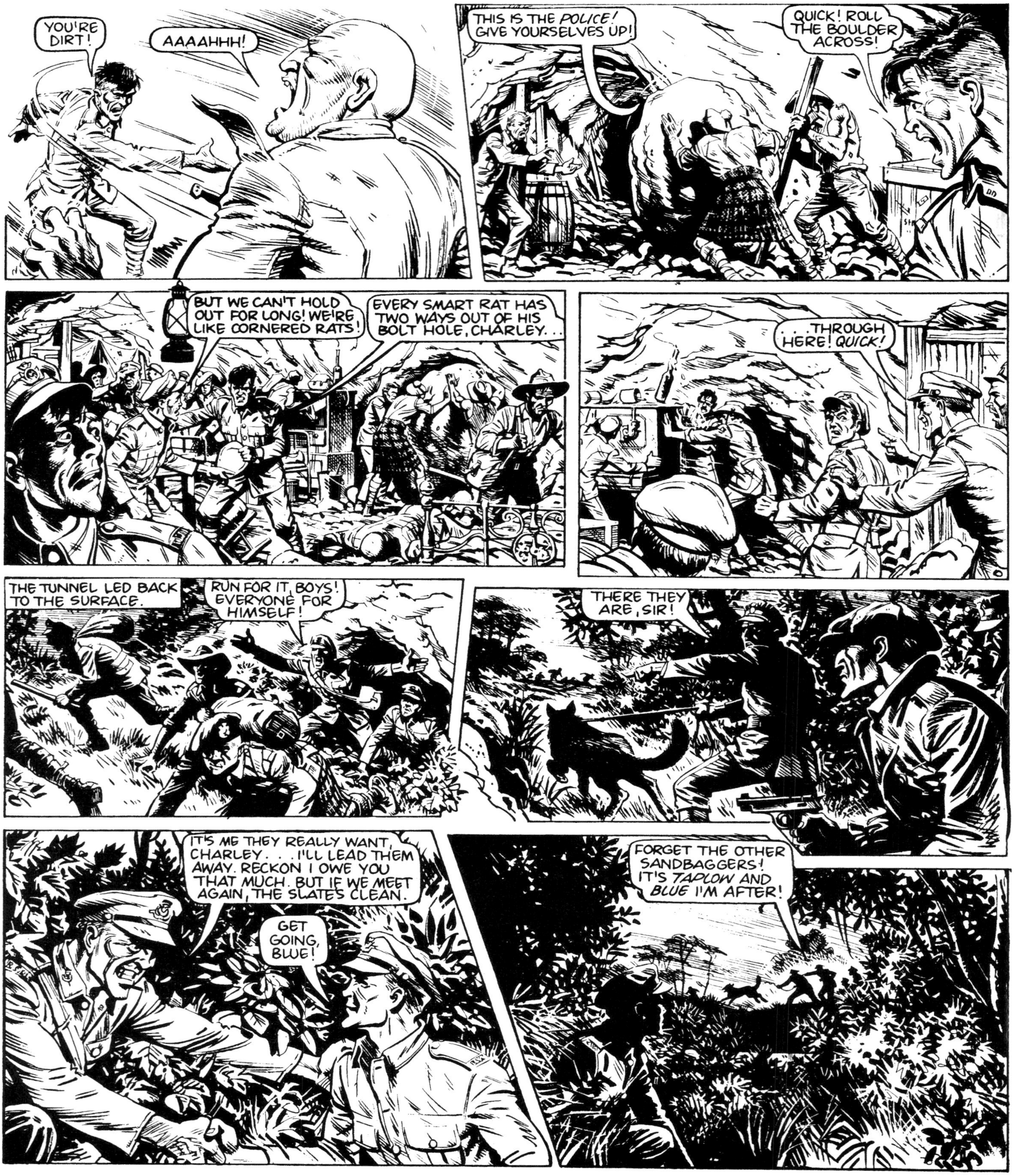
YOU'RE DIRT!
AAAAHHH!
THIS IS THE POLICE! GIVE YOURSELVES UP!
QUICK! ROLL THE BOULDER ACROSS!
BUT WE CAN'T HOLD OUT FOR LONG! WE'RE LIKE CORNERED RATS!
EVERY SMART RAT HAS TWO WAYS OUT OF HIS BOLT HOLE, CHARLEY...
...THROUGH HERE! QUICK!
THE TUNNEL LED BACK TO THE SURFACE.
RUN FOR IT, BOYS! EVERYONE FOR HIMSELF!
THERE THEY ARE, SIR!
IT'S ME THEY REALLY WANT, CHARLEY... I'LL LEAD THEM AWAY. RECKON I OWE YOU THAT MUCH. BUT IF WE MEET AGAIN, THE SLATE'S CLEAN.
GET GOING, BLUE!
FORGET THE OTHER SANDBAGGERS! IT'S TAPLOW AND BLUE I'M AFTER!

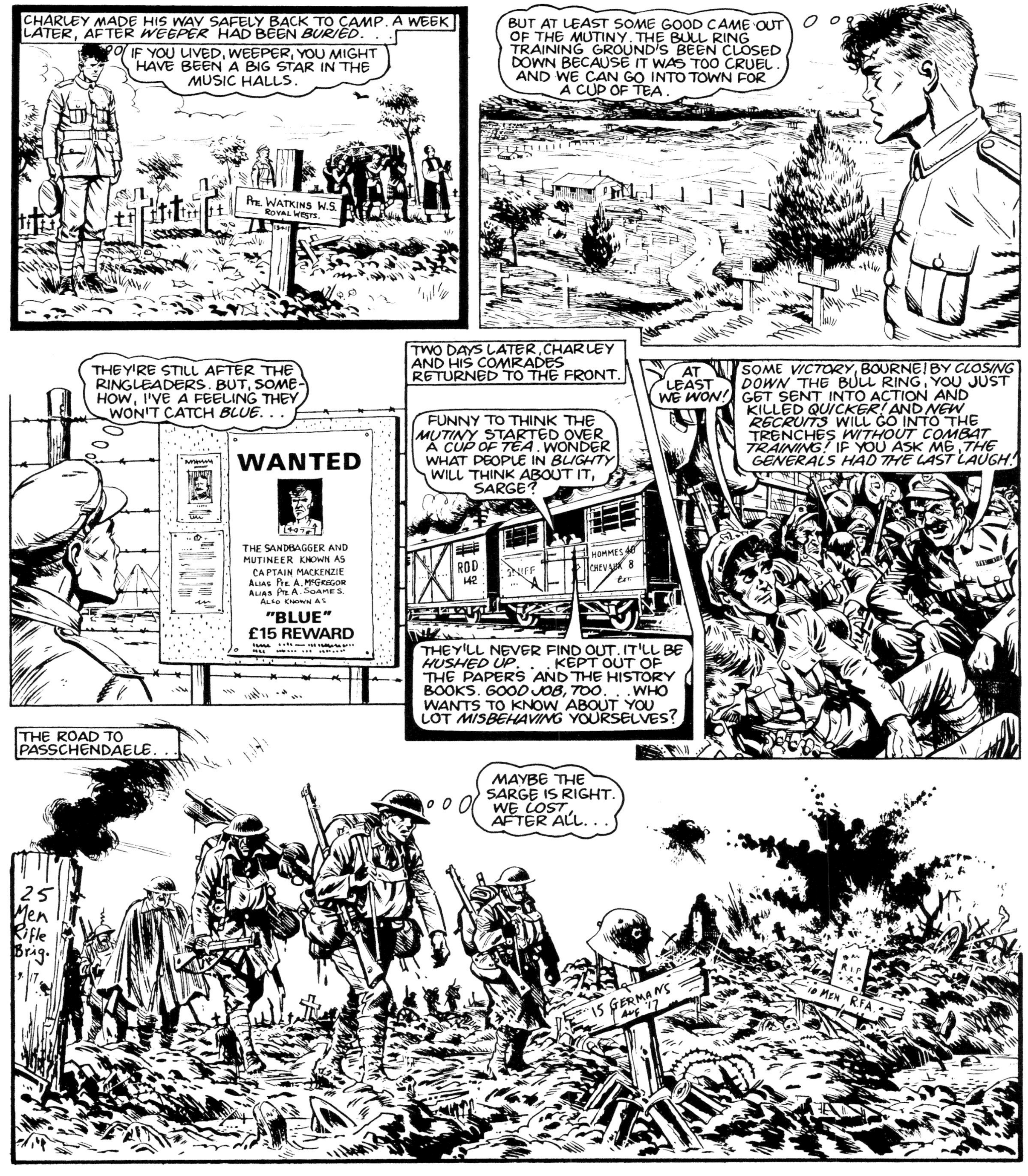
CHARLEY MADE HIS WAY SAFELY BACK TO CAMP. A WEEK LATER, AFTER WEEPER HAD BEEN BURIED. . .
IF YOU LIVED, WEEPER, YOU MIGHT HAVE BEEN A BIG STAR IN THE MUSIC HALLS.
PTE. WATKINS W.S.
ROYAL WESTS.
BUT AT LEAST SOME GOOD CAME OUT OF THE MUTINY. THE BULL RING TRAINING GROUND'S BEEN CLOSED DOWN BECAUSE IT WAS TOO CRUEL. AND WE CAN GO INTO TOWN FOR A CUP OF TEA.
THEY'RE STILL AFTER THE RINGLEADERS. BUT, SOMEHOW, I'VE A FEELING THEY WON'T CATCH BLUE. . .
WANTED
THE SANDBAGGER AND MUTINEER KNOWN AS CAPTAIN MACKENZIE ALIAS PTE A. McGREGOR ALIAS PTE A. SOAMES. ALSO KNOWN AS
"BLUE"
£15 REWARD
TWO DAYS LATER, CHARLEY AND HIS COMRADES RETURNED TO THE FRONT.
FUNNY TO THINK THE MUTINY STARTED OVER A CUP OF TEA. WONDER WHAT PEOPLE IN BLIGHTY WILL THINK ABOUT IT, SARGE?
ROD 142
HOMMES 40
CHEVAUX 8
THEY'LL NEVER FIND OUT. IT'LL BE HUSHED UP. . . KEPT OUT OF THE PAPERS AND THE HISTORY BOOKS. GOOD JOB, TOO. . . WHO WANTS TO KNOW ABOUT YOU LOT MISBEHAVING YOURSELVES?
AT LEAST WE WON!
SOME VICTORY, BOURNE! BY CLOSING DOWN THE BULL RING, YOU JUST GET SENT INTO ACTION AND KILLED QUICKER! AND NEW RECRUITS WILL GO INTO THE TRENCHES WITHOUT COMBAT TRAINING! IF YOU ASK ME, THE GENERALS HAD THE LAST LAUGH!
THE ROAD TO PASSCHENDAELE. . .
MAYBE THE SARGE IS RIGHT. WE LOST, AFTER ALL. . .
25 Men Rifle Brig.
15 GERMANS AUG '17
10 MEN R.F.A.

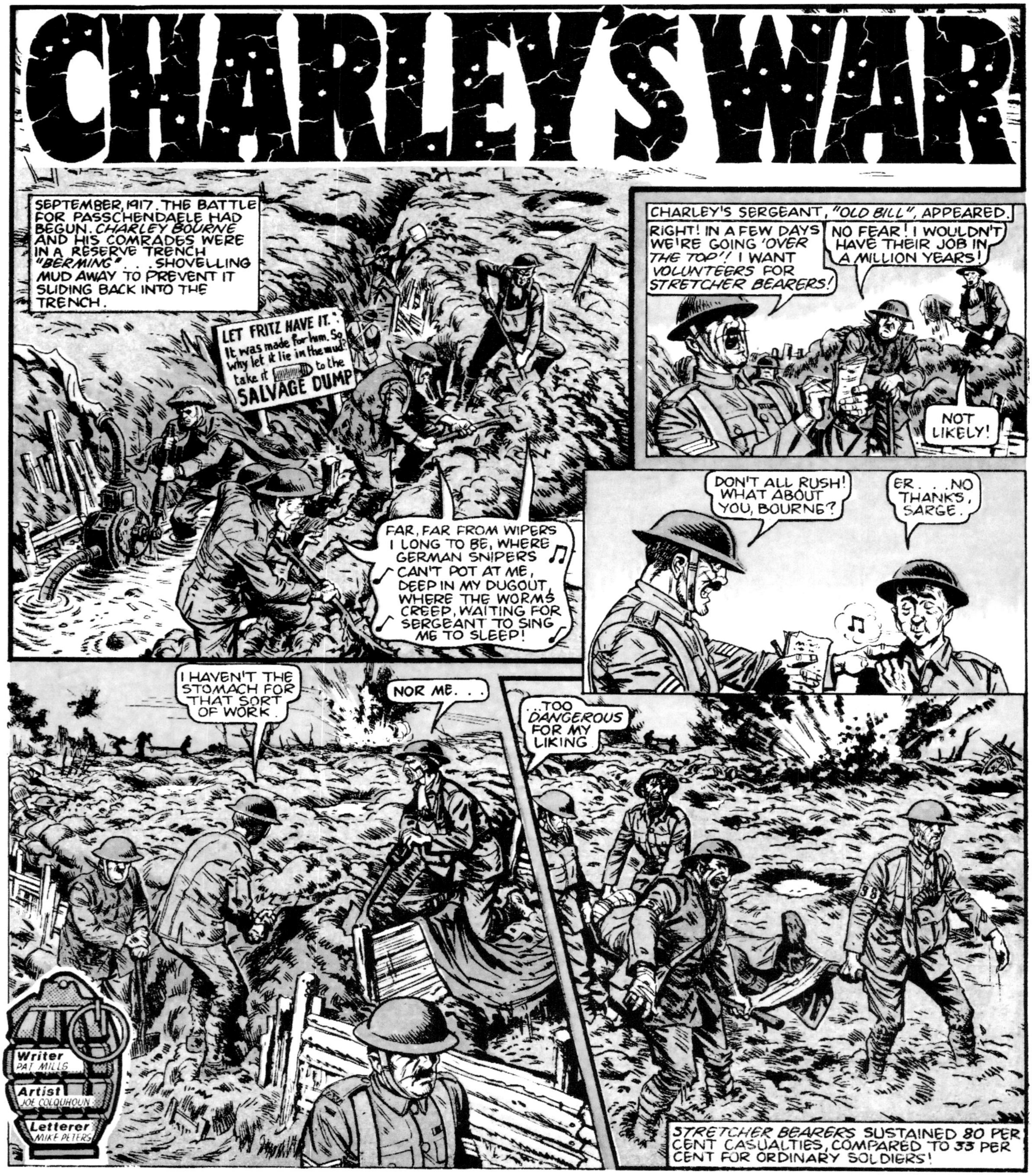
CHARLEY'S WAR
SEPTEMBER, 1917. THE BATTLE FOR PASSCHENDAELE HAD BEGUN. CHARLEY BOURNE AND HIS COMRADES WERE IN A RESERVE TRENCH "BERMING" . . . SHOVELLING MUD AWAY TO PREVENT IT SLIDING BACK INTO THE TRENCH.
LET FRITZ HAVE IT. It was made for him. So why let it lie in the mud? take it to the SALVAGE DUMP
FAR, FAR FROM WIPERS I LONG TO BE, WHERE GERMAN SNIPERS CAN'T POT AT ME, DEEP IN MY DUGOUT, WHERE THE WORMS CREEP, WAITING FOR SERGEANT TO SING ME TO SLEEP!
CHARLEY'S SERGEANT, "OLD BILL", APPEARED.
RIGHT! IN A FEW DAYS WE'RE GOING 'OVER THE TOP'! I WANT VOLUNTEERS FOR STRETCHER BEARERS!
NO FEAR! I WOULDN'T HAVE THEIR JOB IN A MILLION YEARS!
NOT LIKELY!
DON'T ALL RUSH! WHAT ABOUT YOU, BOURNE?
ER. . . NO THANKS, SARGE.
I HAVEN'T THE STOMACH FOR THAT SORT OF WORK.
NOR ME. . .
. . .TOO DANGEROUS FOR MY LIKING.
STRETCHER BEARERS SUSTAINED 80 PER CENT CASUALTIES, COMPARED TO 33 PER CENT FOR ORDINARY SOLDIERS!
Writer PAT MILLS
Artist JOE COLQUHOUN
Letterer MIKE PETERS

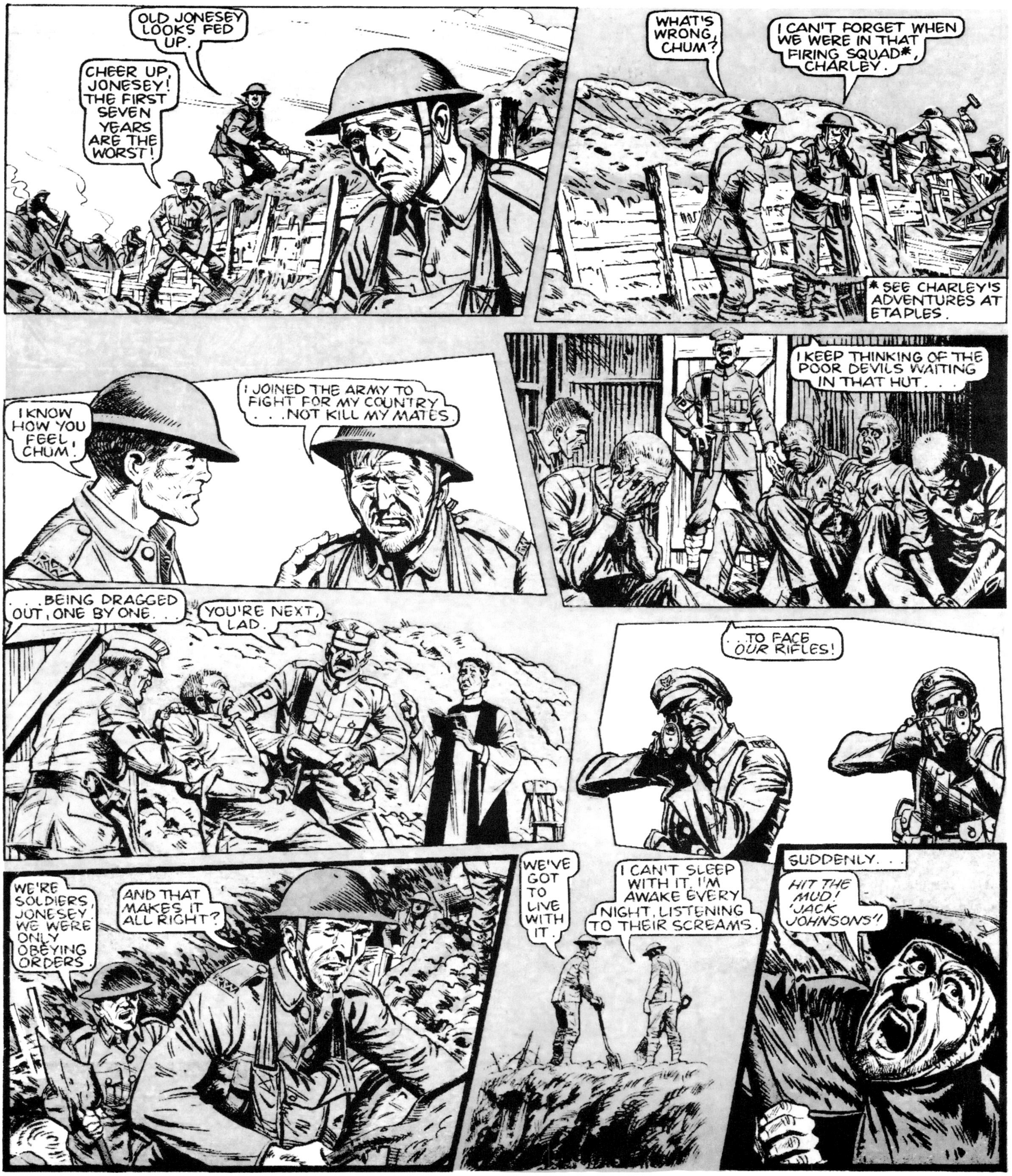

OLD JONESEY LOOKS FED UP.
CHEER UP, JONESEY! THE FIRST SEVEN YEARS ARE THE WORST!
WHAT'S WRONG, CHUM?
I CAN'T FORGET WHEN WE WERE IN THAT FIRING SQUAD*, CHARLEY.
* SEE CHARLEY'S ADVENTURES AT ETAPLES.
I KNOW HOW YOU FEEL, CHUM.
I JOINED THE ARMY TO FIGHT FOR MY COUNTRY . . . NOT KILL MY MATES.
I KEEP THINKING OF THE POOR DEVILS WAITING IN THAT HUT . . .
. . . BEING DRAGGED OUT, ONE BY ONE . . .
YOU'RE NEXT, LAD.
. . . TO FACE OUR RIFLES!
WE'RE SOLDIERS, JONESEY. WE WERE ONLY OBEYING ORDERS.
AND THAT MAKES IT ALL RIGHT?
WE'VE GOT TO LIVE WITH IT.
I CAN'T SLEEP WITH IT. I'M AWAKE EVERY NIGHT, LISTENING TO THEIR SCREAMS.
SUDDENLY . . .
HIT THE MUD! 'JACK JOHNSONS'!

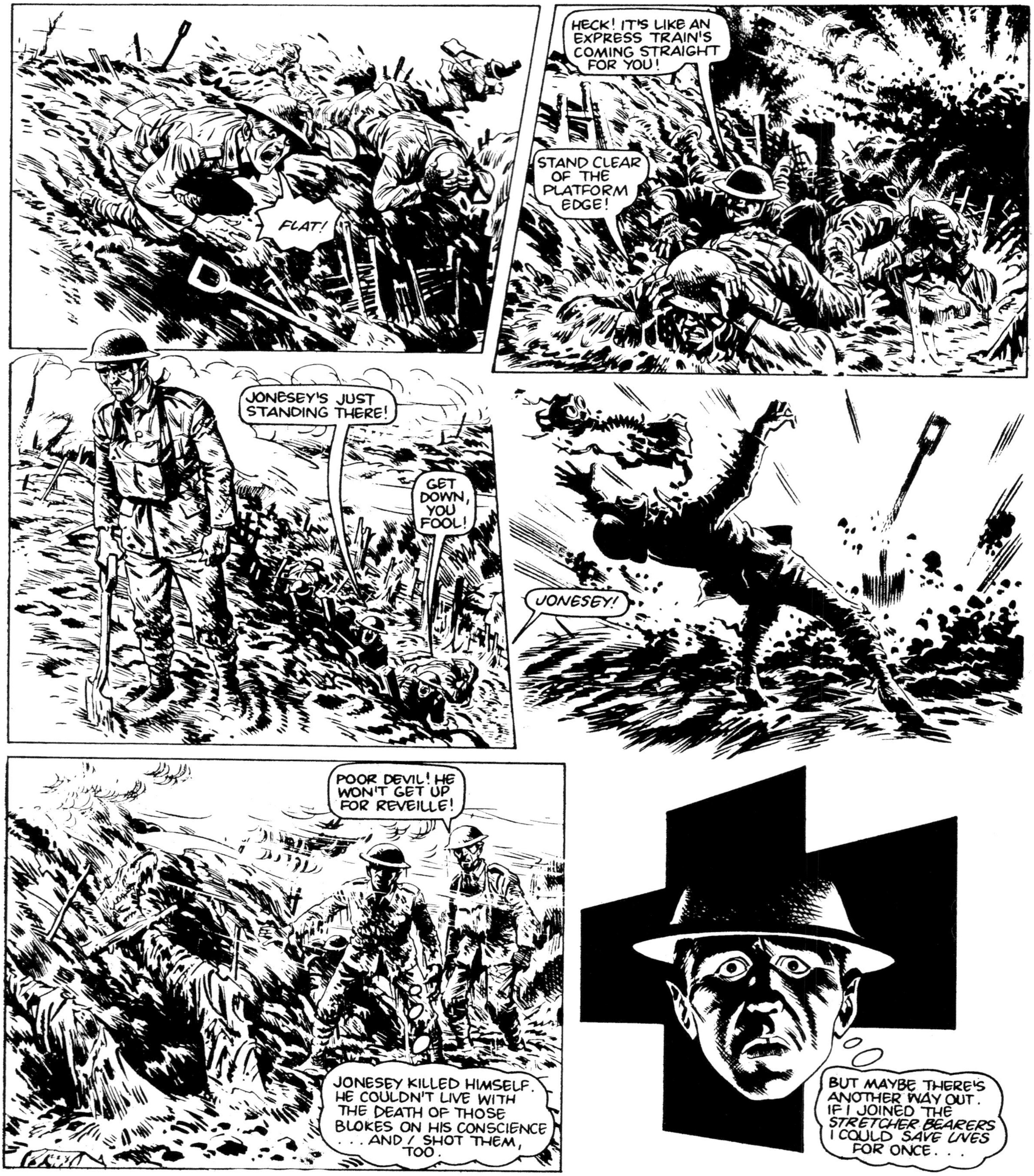
FLAT!
HECK! IT'S LIKE AN EXPRESS TRAIN'S COMING STRAIGHT FOR YOU!
STAND CLEAR OF THE PLATFORM EDGE!
JONESEY'S JUST STANDING THERE!
GET DOWN, YOU FOOL!
JONESEY!
POOR DEVIL! HE WON'T GET UP FOR REVEILLE!
JONESEY KILLED HIMSELF. HE COULDN'T LIVE WITH THE DEATH OF THOSE BLOKES ON HIS CONSCIENCE . . . AND I SHOT THEM, TOO.
BUT MAYBE THERE'S ANOTHER WAY OUT. IF I JOINED THE STRETCHER BEARERS I COULD SAVE LIVES FOR ONCE . . .

CHARLEY'S WAR

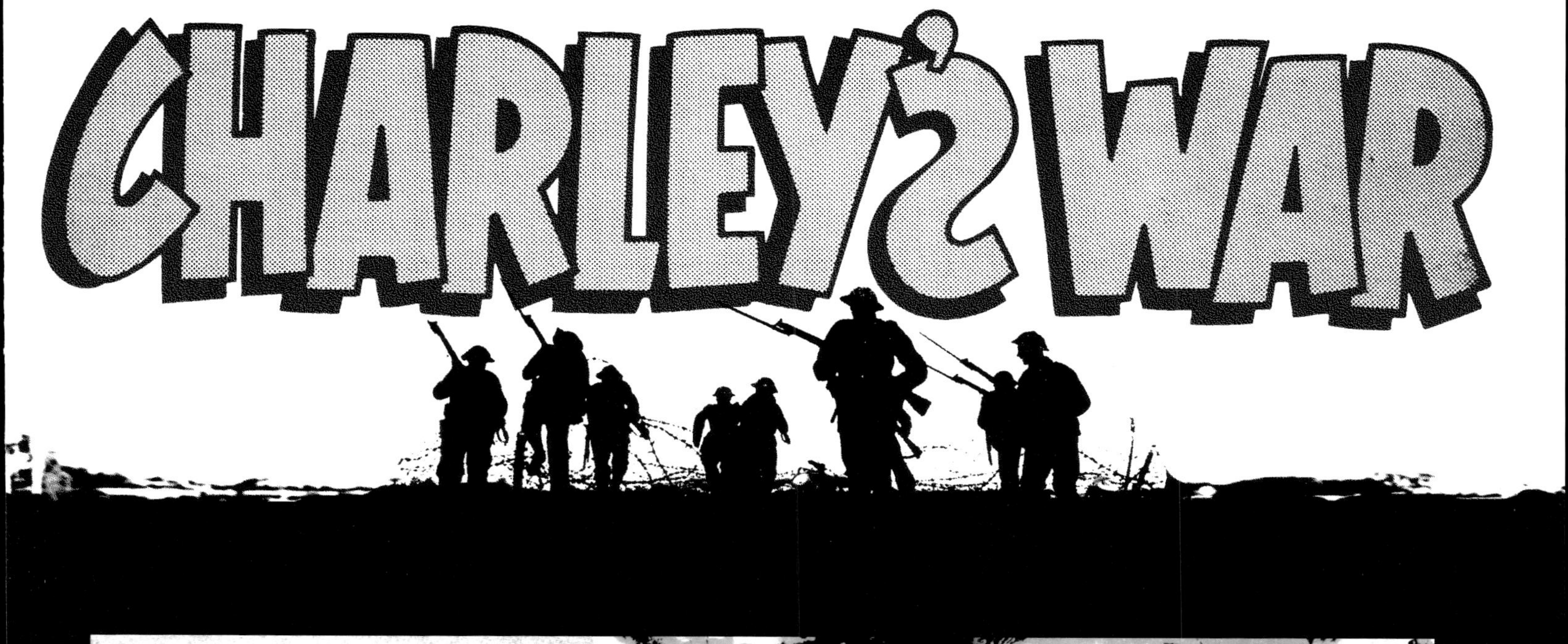

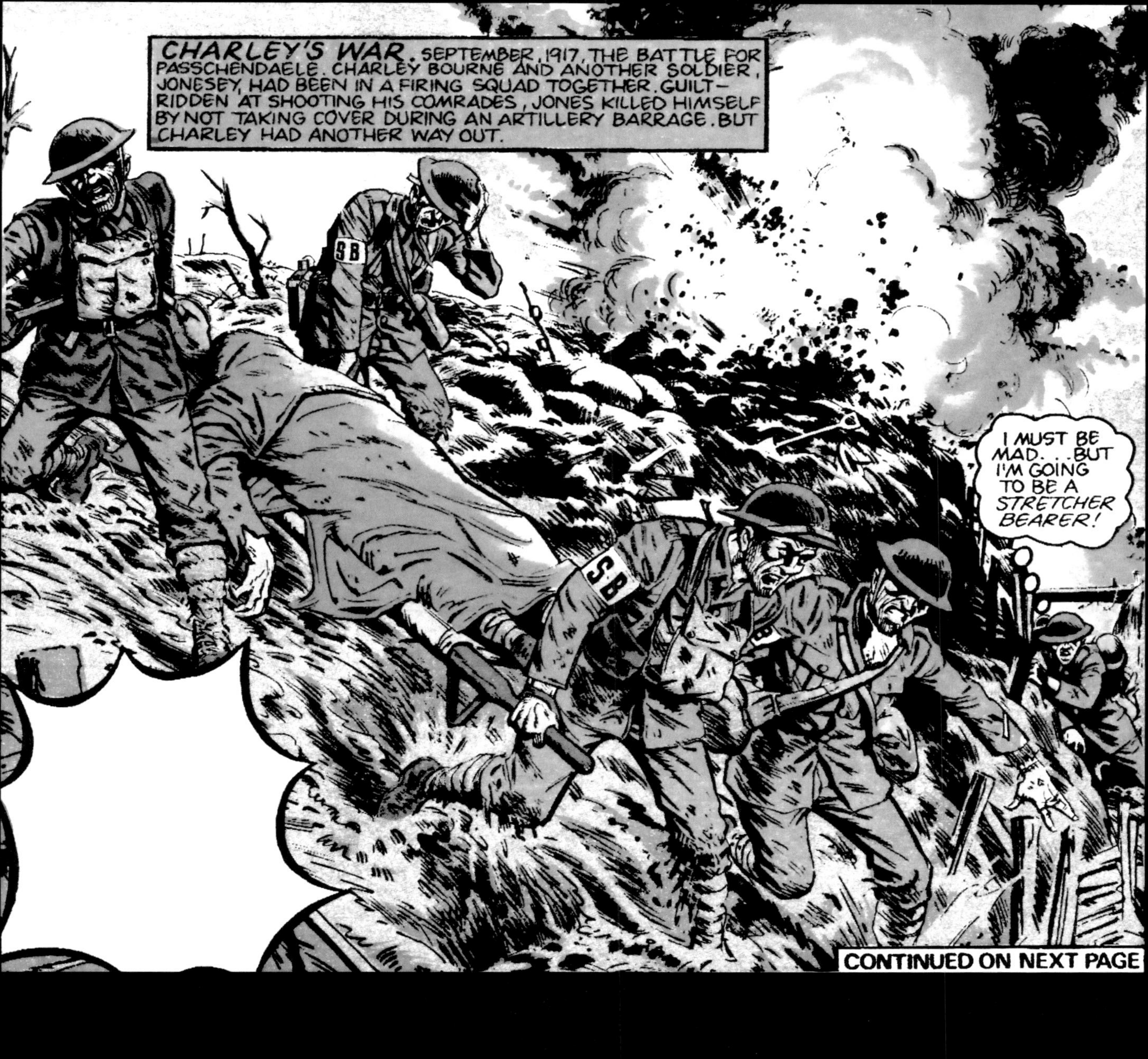

CHARLEY'S WAR. SEPTEMBER, 1917, THE BATTLE FOR PASSCHENDAELE. CHARLEY BOURNE AND ANOTHER SOLDIER, JONESEY, HAD BEEN IN A FIRING SQUAD TOGETHER. GUILT-RIDDEN AT SHOOTING HIS COMRADES, JONES KILLED HIMSELF BY NOT TAKING COVER DURING AN ARTILLERY BARRAGE. BUT CHARLEY HAD ANOTHER WAY OUT.
I MUST BE MAD. . .BUT I'M GOING TO BE A STRETCHER BEARER!
SB

CONTINUED ON NEXT PAGE

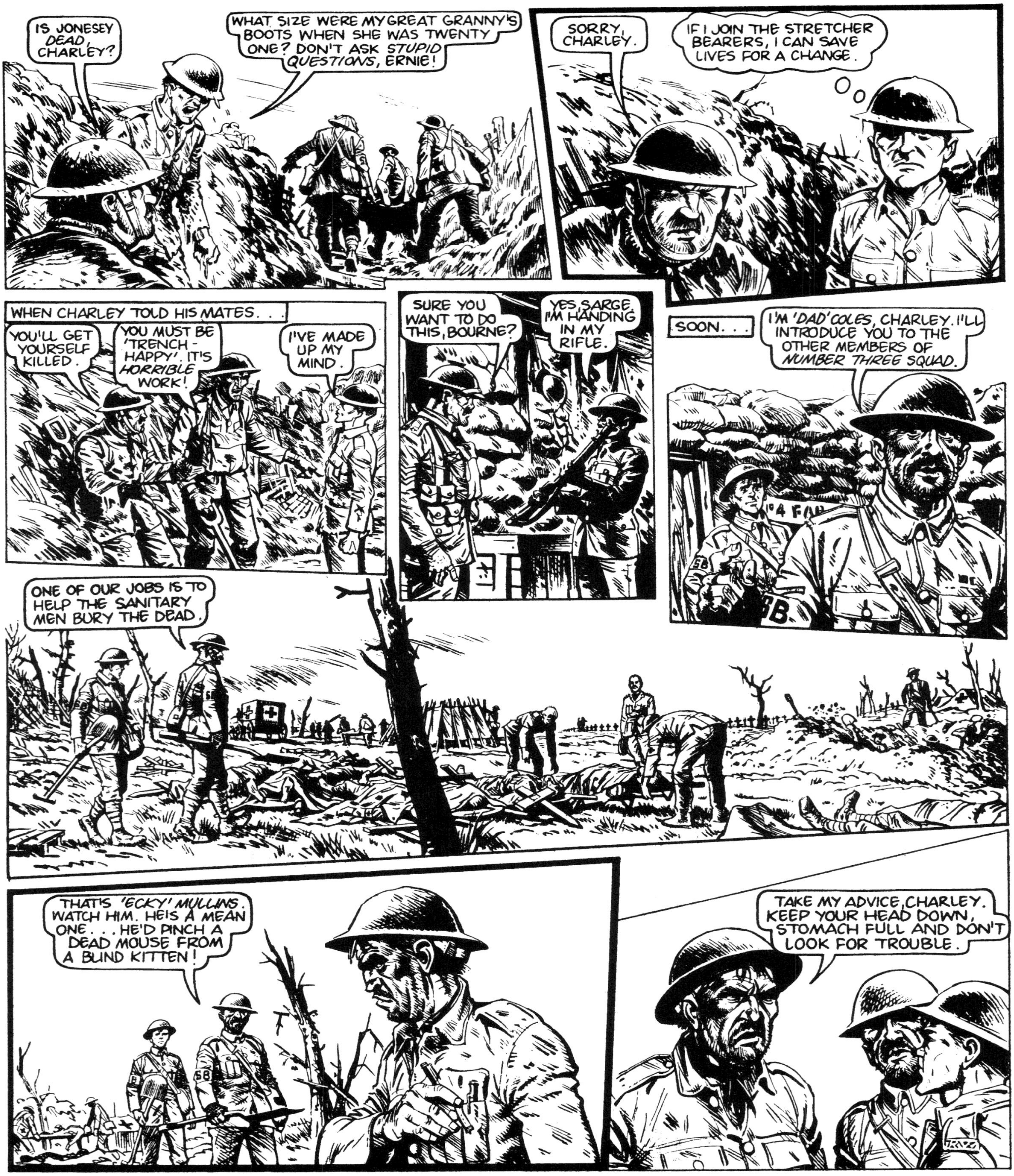
IS JONESEY DEAD, CHARLEY?
WHAT SIZE WERE MY GREAT GRANNY'S BOOTS WHEN SHE WAS TWENTY ONE? DON'T ASK STUPID QUESTIONS, ERNIE!
SORRY, CHARLEY.
IF I JOIN THE STRETCHER BEARERS, I CAN SAVE LIVES FOR A CHANGE.
WHEN CHARLEY TOLD HIS MATES...
YOU'LL GET YOURSELF KILLED.
YOU MUST BE 'TRENCH-HAPPY'. IT'S HORRIBLE WORK!
I'VE MADE UP MY MIND.
SURE YOU WANT TO DO THIS, BOURNE?
YES, SARGE. I'M HANDING IN MY RIFLE.
SOON...
I'M 'DAD' COLES, CHARLEY. I'LL INTRODUCE YOU TO THE OTHER MEMBERS OF NUMBER THREE SQUAD.
ONE OF OUR JOBS IS TO HELP THE SANITARY MEN BURY THE DEAD.
THAT'S 'ECKY' MULLINS. WATCH HIM. HE'S A MEAN ONE... HE'D PINCH A DEAD MOUSE FROM A BLIND KITTEN!
TAKE MY ADVICE, CHARLEY. KEEP YOUR HEAD DOWN, STOMACH FULL AND DON'T LOOK FOR TROUBLE.

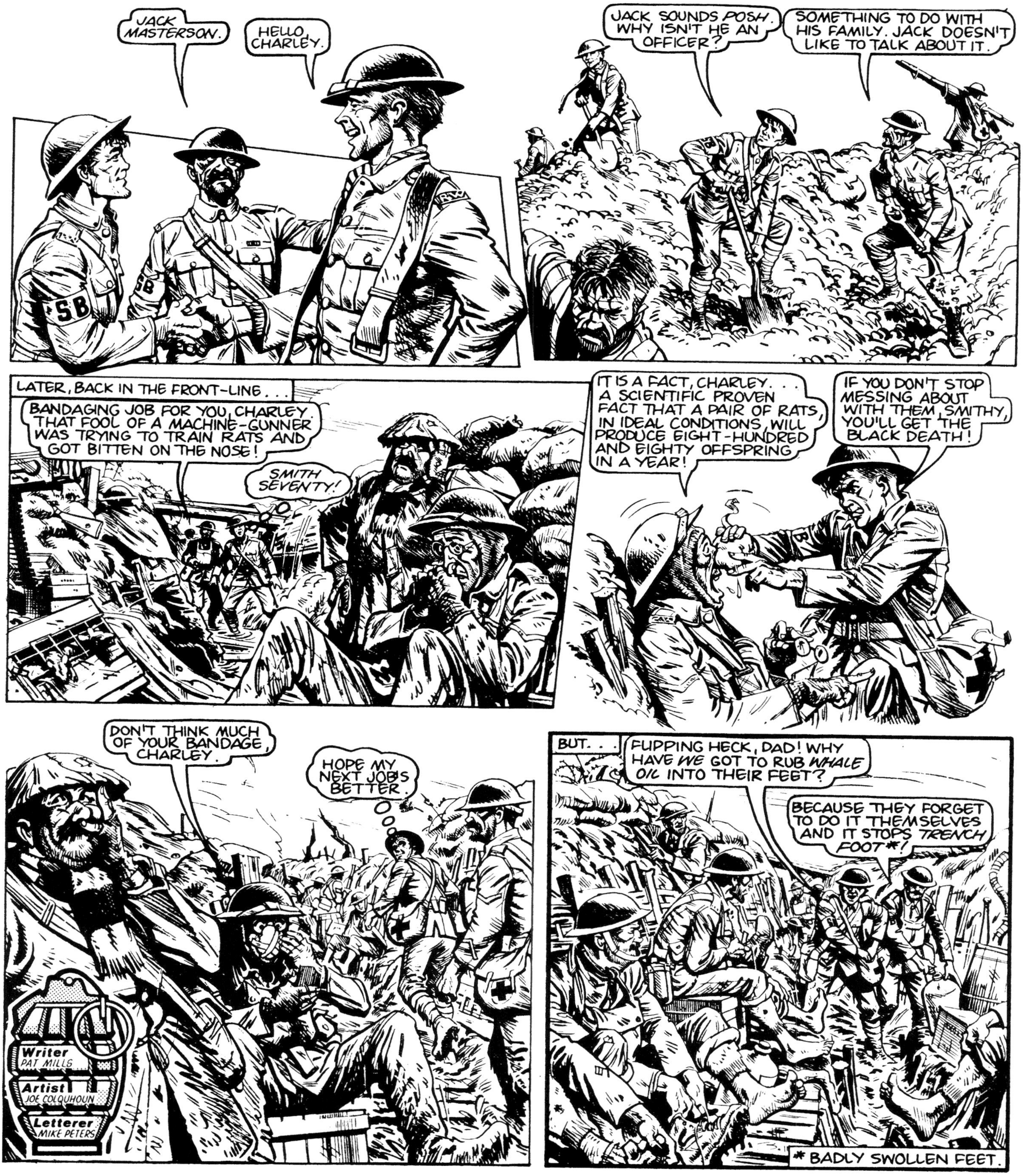
JACK MASTERSON.
HELLO, CHARLEY.
JACK SOUNDS POSH. WHY ISN'T HE AN OFFICER?
SOMETHING TO DO WITH HIS FAMILY. JACK DOESN'T LIKE TO TALK ABOUT IT.
LATER, BACK IN THE FRONT-LINE...
BANDAGING JOB FOR YOU, CHARLEY. THAT FOOL OF A MACHINE-GUNNER WAS TRYING TO TRAIN RATS AND GOT BITTEN ON THE NOSE!
SMITH SEVENTY!
IT IS A FACT, CHARLEY... A SCIENTIFIC PROVEN FACT THAT A PAIR OF RATS, IN IDEAL CONDITIONS, WILL PRODUCE EIGHT-HUNDRED AND EIGHTY OFFSPRING IN A YEAR!
IF YOU DON'T STOP MESSING ABOUT WITH THEM, SMITHY, YOU'LL GET THE BLACK DEATH!
DON'T THINK MUCH OF YOUR BANDAGE, CHARLEY.
HOPE MY NEXT JOB'S BETTER.
Writer PAT MILLS
Artist JOE COLQUHOUN
Letterer MIKE PETERS
BUT...
FUPPING HECK, DAD! WHY HAVE WE GOT TO RUB WHALE OIL INTO THEIR FEET?
BECAUSE THEY FORGET TO DO IT THEMSELVES AND IT STOPS TRENCH FOOT*!
* BADLY SWOLLEN FEET.

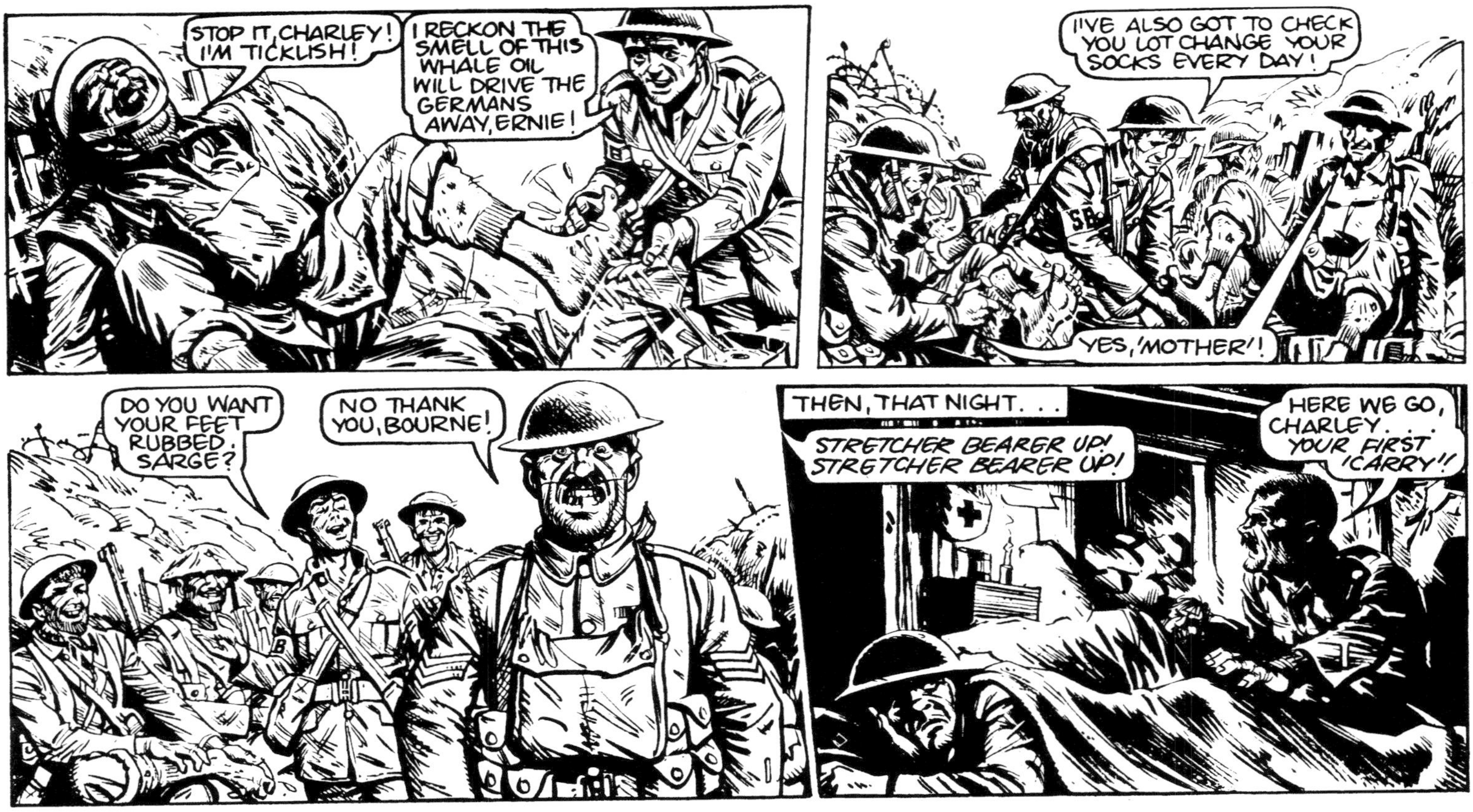
STOP IT, CHARLEY! I'M TICKLISH!
I RECKON THE SMELL OF THIS WHALE OIL WILL DRIVE THE GERMANS AWAY, ERNIE!
I'VE ALSO GOT TO CHECK YOU LOT CHANGE YOUR SOCKS EVERY DAY!
YES, 'MOTHER'!
DO YOU WANT YOUR FEET RUBBED, SARGE?
NO THANK YOU, BOURNE!
THEN, THAT NIGHT...
STRETCHER BEARER UP! STRETCHER BEARER UP!
HERE WE GO, CHARLEY.... YOUR FIRST 'CARRY'!

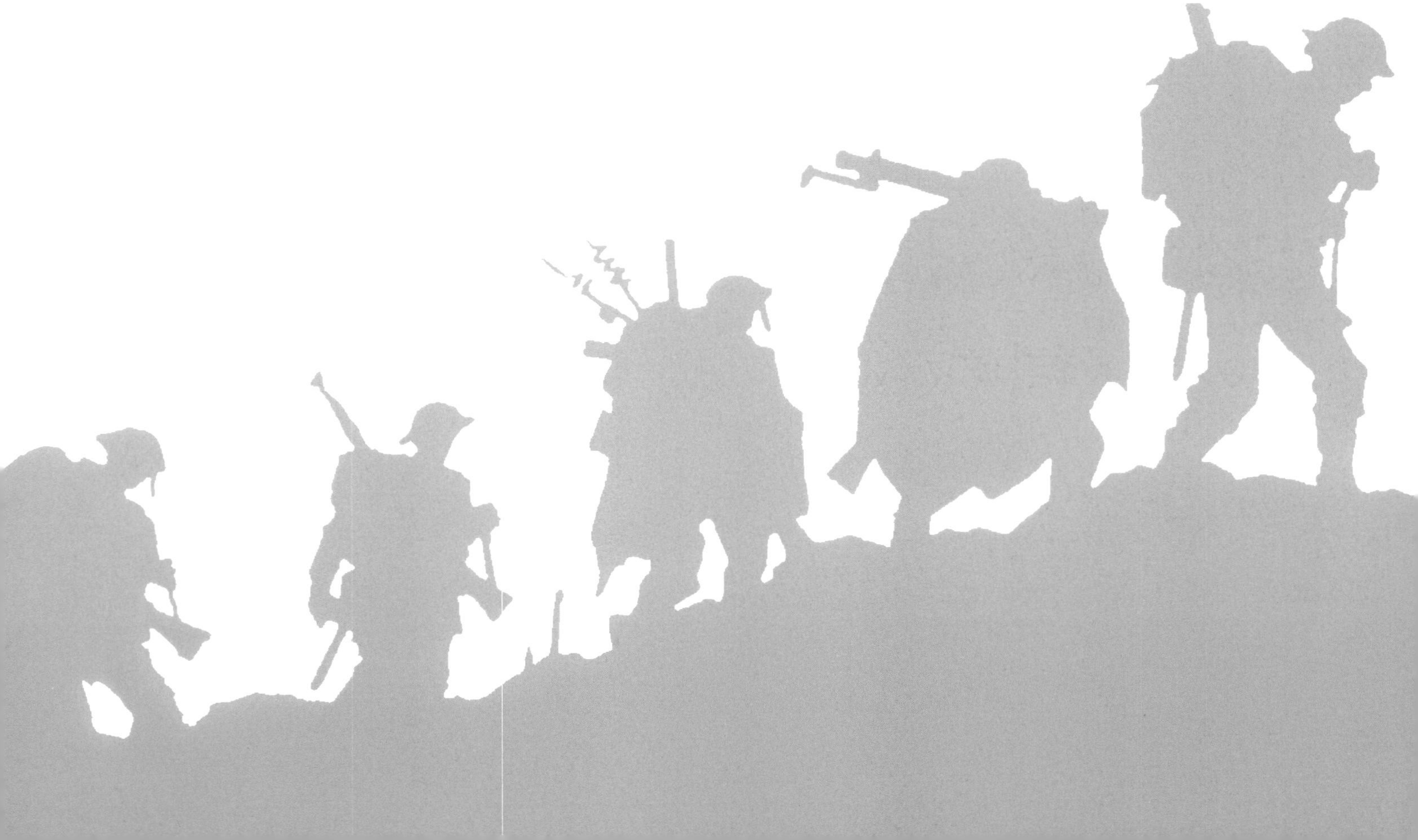

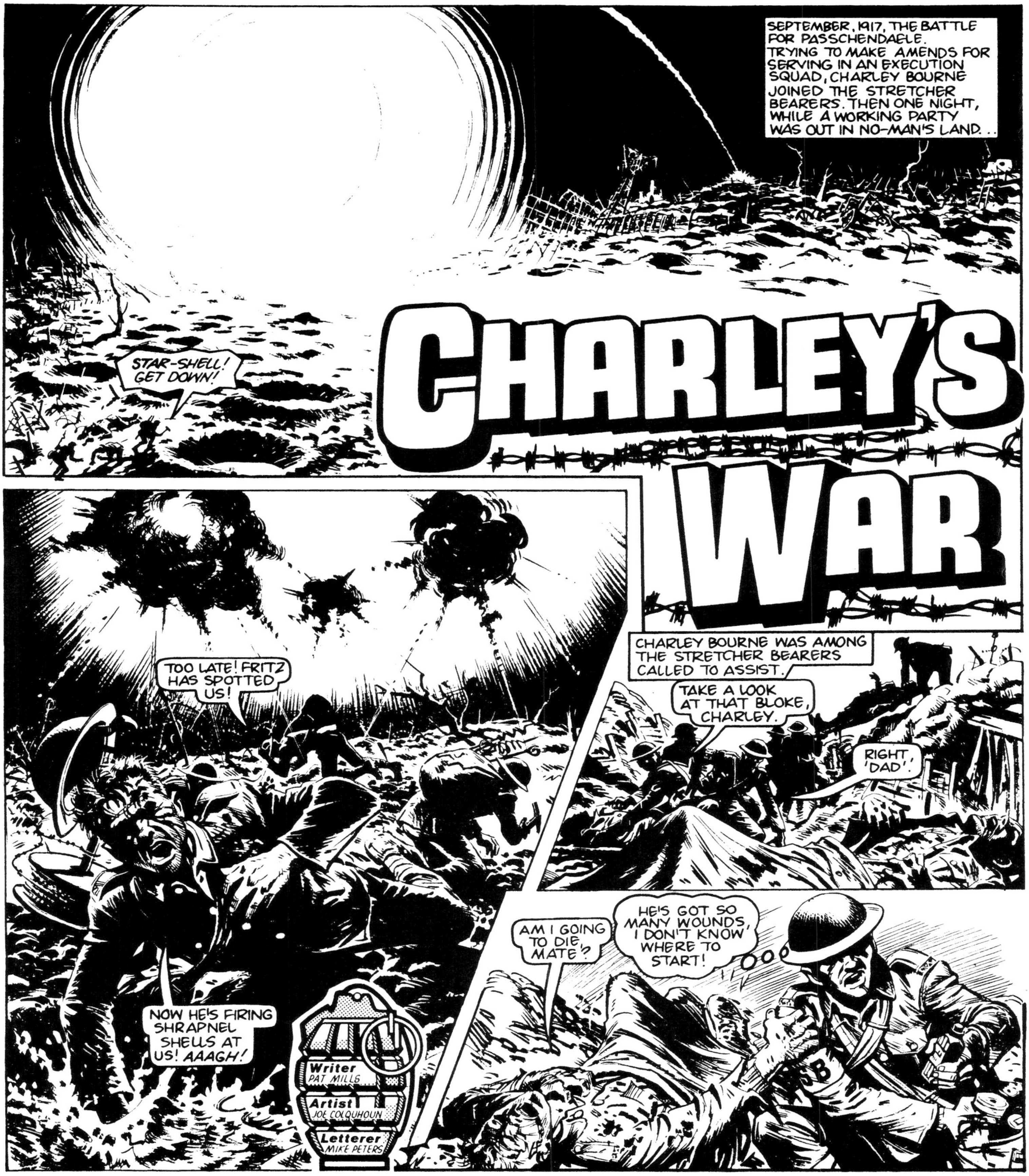
SEPTEMBER, 1917, THE BATTLE FOR PASSCHENDAELE. TRYING TO MAKE AMENDS FOR SERVING IN AN EXECUTION SQUAD, CHARLEY BOURNE JOINED THE STRETCHER BEARERS. THEN ONE NIGHT, WHILE A WORKING PARTY WAS OUT IN NO-MAN'S LAND. . .
STAR-SHELL! GET DOWN!
CHARLEY'S WAR
TOO LATE! FRITZ HAS SPOTTED US!
NOW HE'S FIRING SHRAPNEL SHELLS AT US! AAAGH!
Writer PAT MILLS
Artist JOE COLQUHOUN
Letterer MIKE PETERS
CHARLEY BOURNE WAS AMONG THE STRETCHER BEARERS CALLED TO ASSIST.
TAKE A LOOK AT THAT BLOKE, CHARLEY.
RIGHT, 'DAD'.
AM I GOING TO DIE, MATE?
HE'S GOT SO MANY WOUNDS, I DON'T KNOW WHERE TO START!

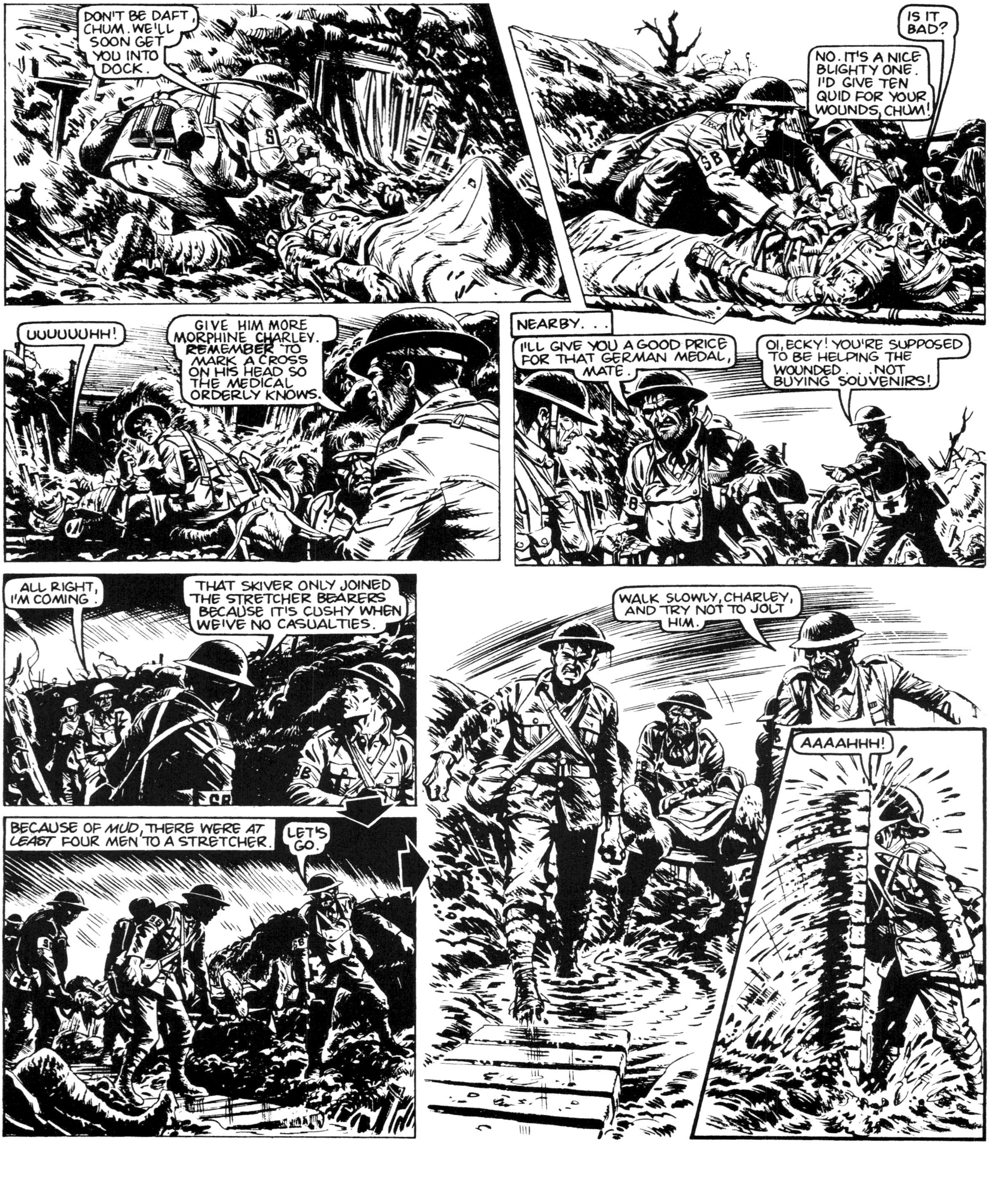
DON'T BE DAFT, CHUM. WE'LL SOON GET YOU INTO DOCK.
IS IT BAD?
NO. IT'S A NICE BLIGHTY ONE. I'D GIVE TEN QUID FOR YOUR WOUNDS, CHUM!
UUUUUUHH!
GIVE HIM MORE MORPHINE CHARLEY. REMEMBER TO MARK A CROSS ON HIS HEAD SO THE MEDICAL ORDERLY KNOWS.
NEARBY. . .
I'LL GIVE YOU A GOOD PRICE FOR THAT GERMAN MEDAL, MATE.
OI, ECKY! YOU'RE SUPPOSED TO BE HELPING THE WOUNDED. . . NOT BUYING SOUVENIRS!
ALL RIGHT, I'M COMING.
THAT SKIVER ONLY JOINED THE STRETCHER BEARERS BECAUSE IT'S CUSHY WHEN WE'VE NO CASUALTIES.
BECAUSE OF MUD, THERE WERE AT LEAST FOUR MEN TO A STRETCHER.
LET'S GO.
WALK SLOWLY, CHARLEY, AND TRY NOT TO JOLT HIM.
AAAAHHH!

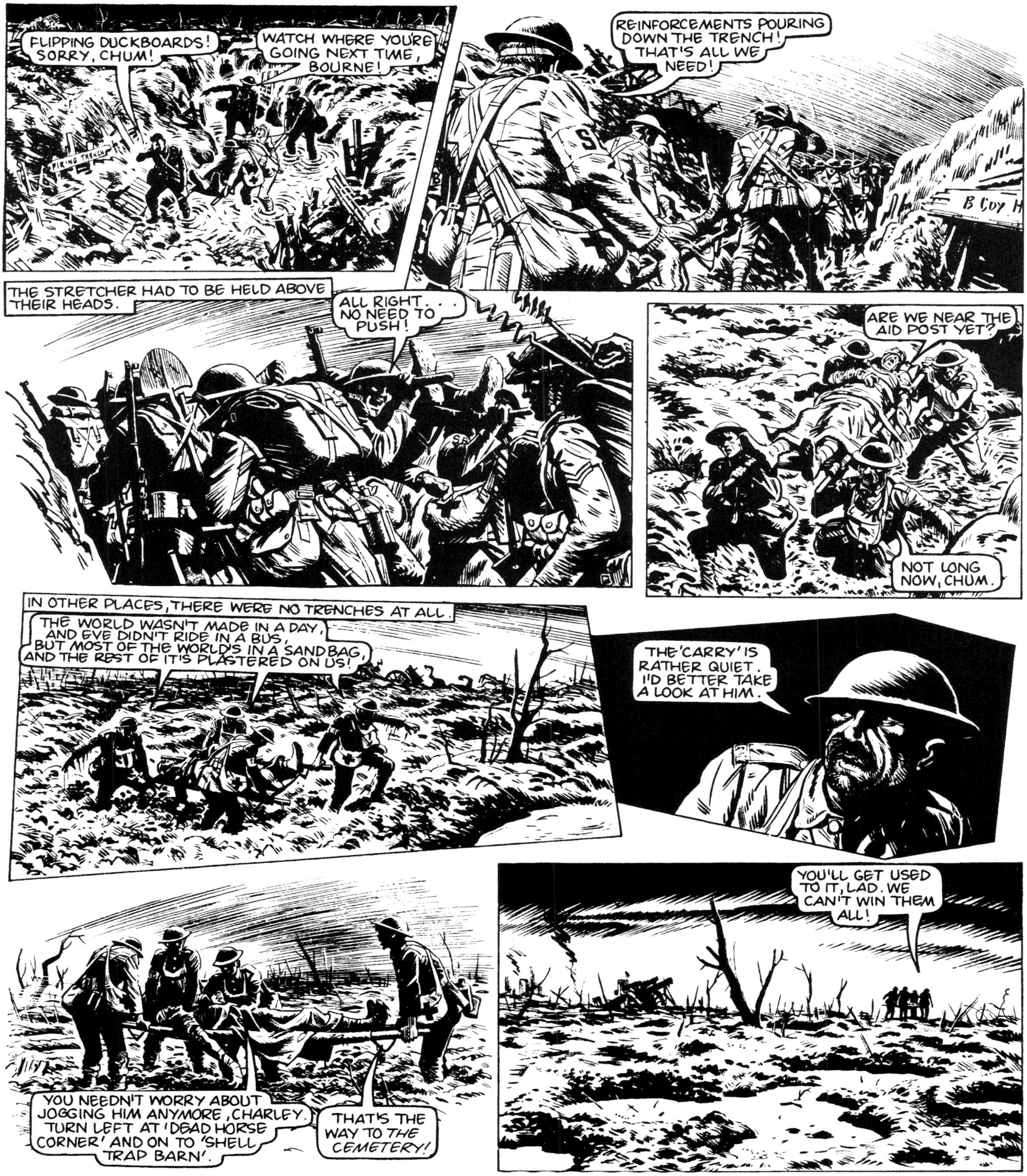
FLIPPING DUCKBOARDS! SORRY, CHUM!
WATCH WHERE YOU'RE GOING NEXT TIME, BOURNE!
FIRING TRENCH
REINFORCEMENTS POURING DOWN THE TRENCH! THAT'S ALL WE NEED!
B COY H
THE STRETCHER HAD TO BE HELD ABOVE THEIR HEADS.
ALL RIGHT. . . NO NEED TO PUSH!
ARE WE NEAR THE AID POST YET?
NOT LONG NOW, CHUM.
IN OTHER PLACES, THERE WERE NO TRENCHES AT ALL.
THE WORLD WASN'T MADE IN A DAY, AND EVE DIDN'T RIDE IN A BUS, BUT MOST OF THE WORLD'S IN A SANDBAG, AND THE REST OF IT'S PLASTERED ON US!
THE 'CARRY' IS RATHER QUIET. I'D BETTER TAKE A LOOK AT HIM.
YOU NEEDN'T WORRY ABOUT JOGGING HIM ANYMORE, CHARLEY. TURN LEFT AT 'DEAD HORSE CORNER' AND ON TO 'SHELL TRAP BARN'.
THAT'S THE WAY TO *THE CEMETERY!*
YOU'LL GET USED TO IT, LAD. WE CAN'T WIN THEM ALL!

CHARLEY'S WAR

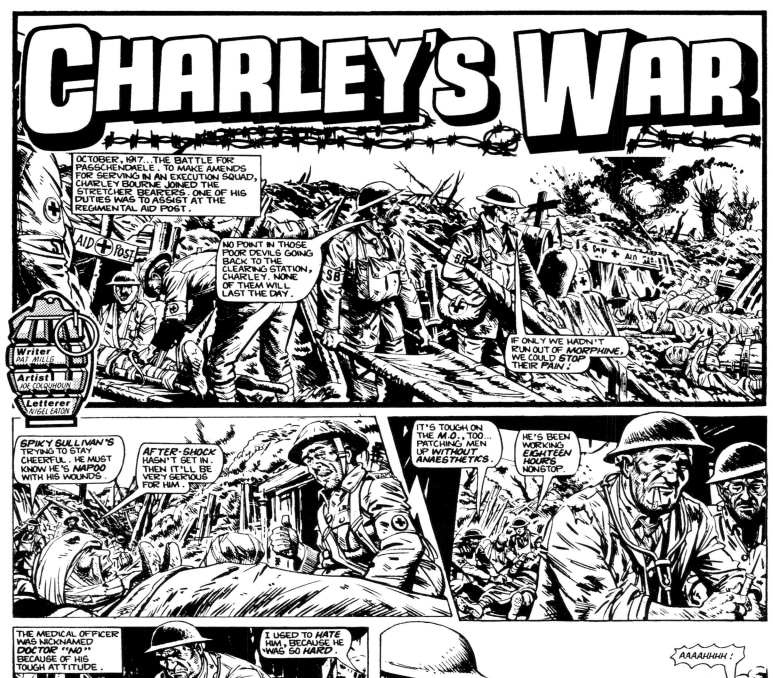

OCTOBER, 1917...THE BATTLE FOR PASSCHENDAELE. TO MAKE AMENDS FOR SERVING IN AN EXECUTION SQUAD, CHARLEY BOURNE JOINED THE STRETCHER BEARERS. ONE OF HIS DUTIES WAS TO ASSIST AT THE REGIMENTAL AID POST.

AID POST

NO POINT IN THOSE POOR DEVILS GOING BACK TO THE CLEARING STATION, CHARLEY. NONE OF THEM WILL LAST THE DAY.

IF ONLY WE HADN'T RUN OUT OF MORPHINE, WE COULD STOP THEIR PAIN!

Writer
PAT MILLS

Artist
JOE COLQUHOUN

Letterer
NIGEL EATON

SPIKY SULLIVAN'S TRYING TO STAY CHEERFUL. HE MUST KNOW HE'S NAPOO WITH HIS WOUNDS.

AFTER-SHOCK HASN'T SET IN. THEN IT'LL BE VERY SERIOUS FOR HIM.

IT'S TOUGH ON THE M.O., TOO... PATCHING MEN UP WITHOUT ANAESTHETICS.

HE'S BEEN WORKING EIGHTEEN HOURS NONSTOP.

THE MEDICAL OFFICER WAS NICKNAMED DOCTOR "NO" BECAUSE OF HIS TOUGH ATTITUDE.

I USED TO HATE HIM, BECAUSE HE WAS SO HARD.

YOU'VE GOT TO BE WHEN YOU'RE A FRONT-LINE M.O., CHARLEY.

AAAAHHHH!

POOR OLD SPIKY.

WATER... WATER...

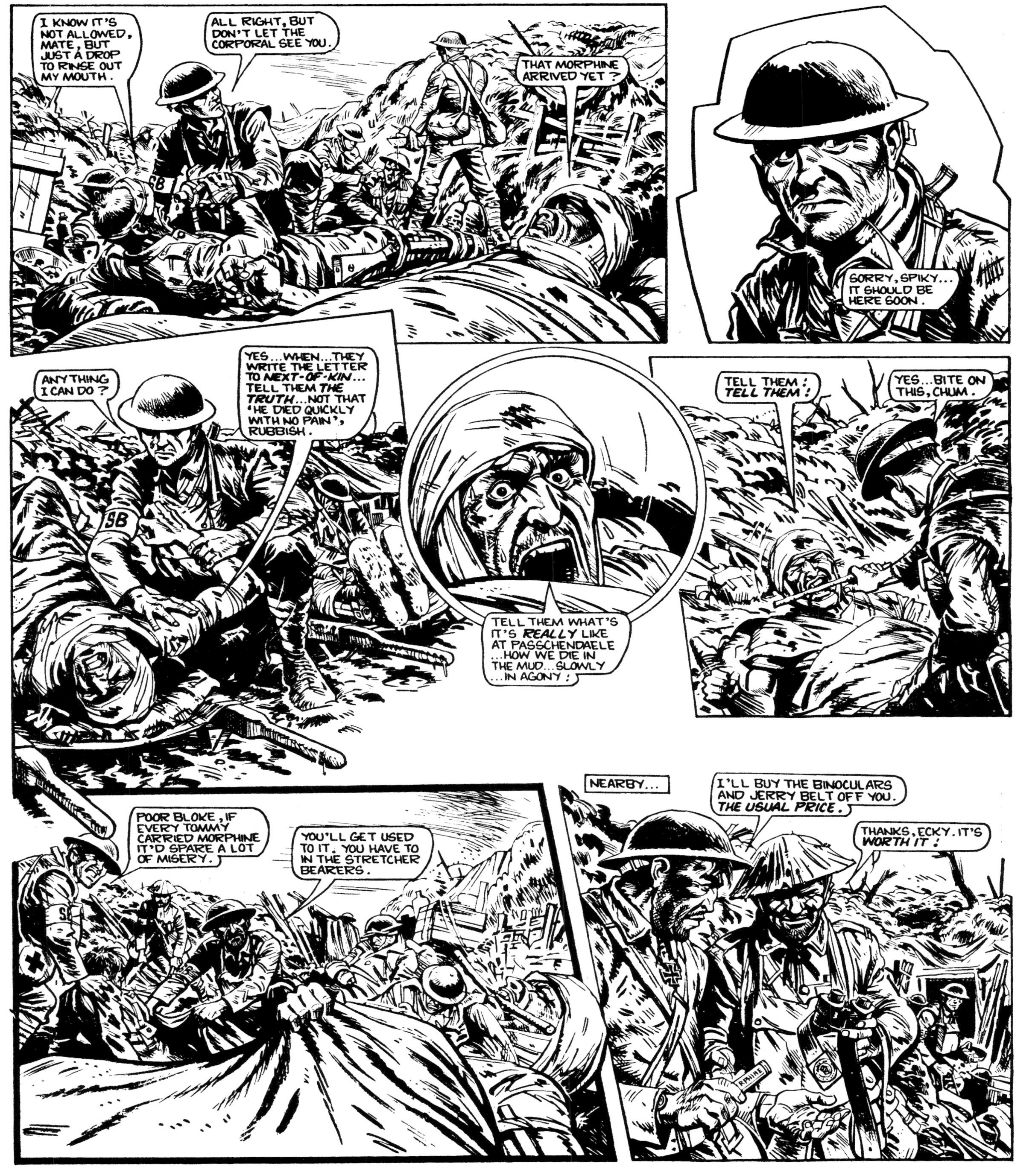
I KNOW IT'S NOT ALLOWED, MATE, BUT JUST A DROP TO RINSE OUT MY MOUTH.
ALL RIGHT, BUT DON'T LET THE CORPORAL SEE YOU.
THAT MORPHINE ARRIVED YET?
SORRY, SPIKY... IT SHOULD BE HERE SOON.
ANYTHING I CAN DO?
YES... WHEN... THEY WRITE THE LETTER TO NEXT-OF-KIN... TELL THEM THE TRUTH... NOT THAT 'HE DIED QUICKLY WITH NO PAIN', RUBBISH.
TELL THEM WHAT'S IT'S REALLY LIKE AT PASSCHENDAELE ...HOW WE DIE IN THE MUD... SLOWLY ...IN AGONY!
TELL THEM! TELL THEM!
YES... BITE ON THIS, CHUM.
POOR BLOKE, IF EVERY TOMMY CARRIED MORPHINE IT'D SPARE A LOT OF MISERY.
YOU'LL GET USED TO IT. YOU HAVE TO IN THE STRETCHER BEARERS.
NEARBY...
I'LL BUY THE BINOCULARS AND JERRY BELT OFF YOU. THE USUAL PRICE.
THANKS, ECKY. IT'S WORTH IT!

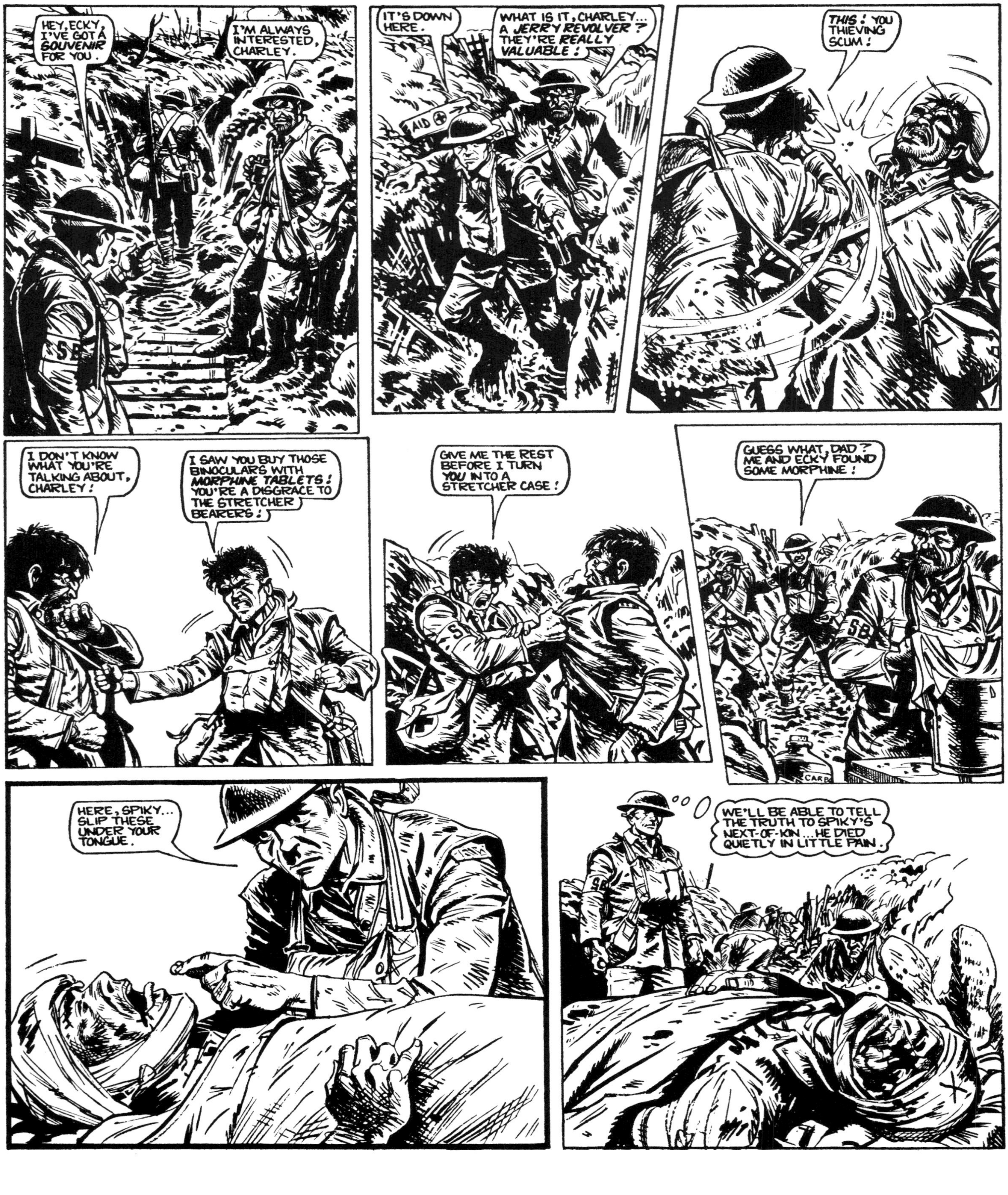
HEY, ECKY, I'VE GOT A SOUVENIR FOR YOU.
I'M ALWAYS INTERESTED, CHARLEY.
IT'S DOWN HERE.
WHAT IS IT, CHARLEY... A JERRY REVOLVER? THEY'RE REALLY VALUABLE!
AID
THIS! YOU THIEVING SCUM!
I DON'T KNOW WHAT YOU'RE TALKING ABOUT, CHARLEY!
I SAW YOU BUY THOSE BINOCULARS WITH MORPHINE TABLETS! YOU'RE A DISGRACE TO THE STRETCHER BEARERS!
GIVE ME THE REST BEFORE I TURN YOU INTO A STRETCHER CASE!
GUESS WHAT, DAD? ME AND ECKY FOUND SOME MORPHINE!
HERE, SPIKY... SLIP THESE UNDER YOUR TONGUE.
WE'LL BE ABLE TO TELL THE TRUTH TO SPIKY'S NEXT-OF-KIN... HE DIED QUIETLY IN LITTLE PAIN.

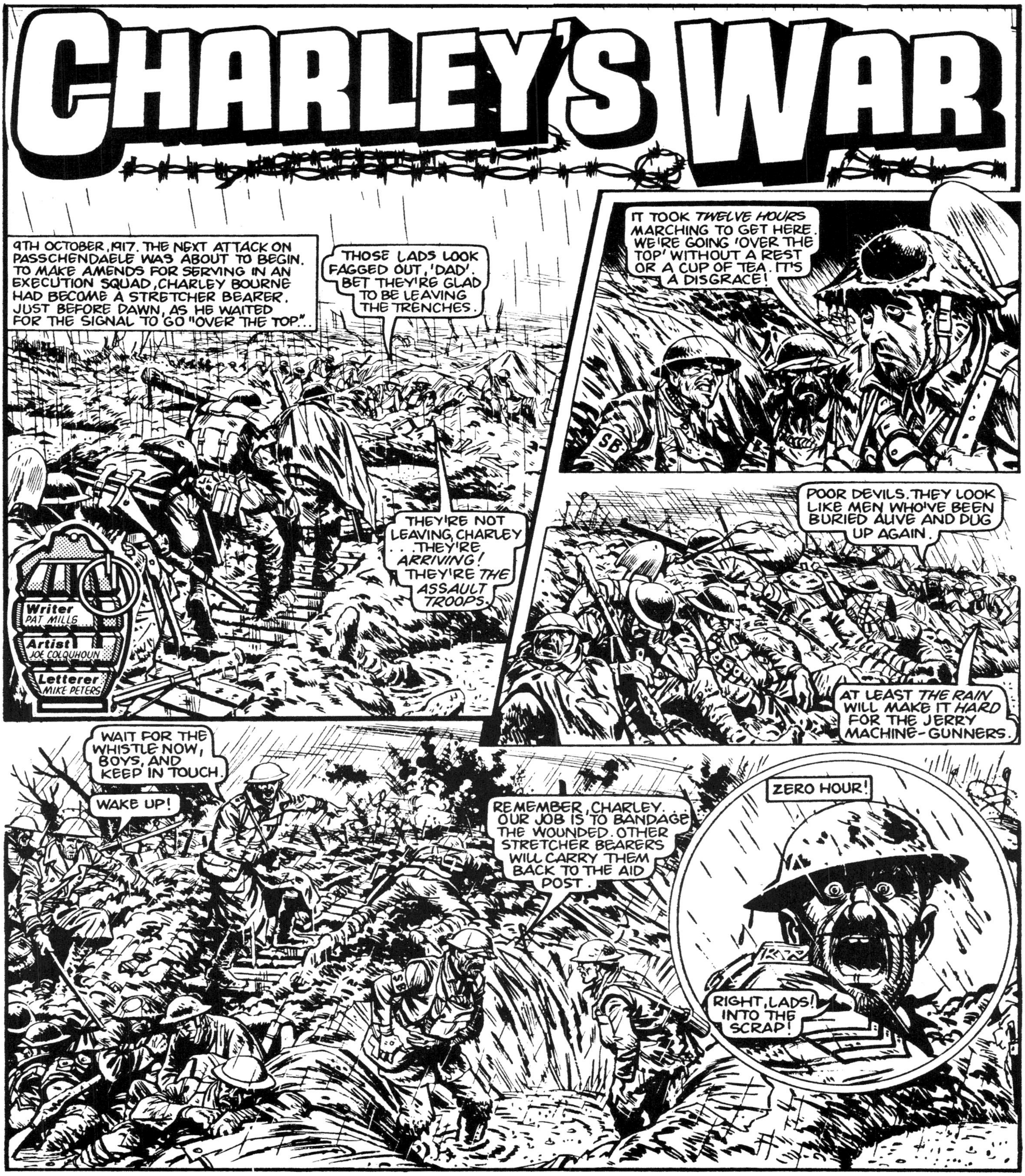
CHARLEY'S WAR
9TH OCTOBER, 1917. THE NEXT ATTACK ON PASSCHENDAELE WAS ABOUT TO BEGIN. TO MAKE AMENDS FOR SERVING IN AN EXECUTION SQUAD, CHARLEY BOURNE HAD BECOME A STRETCHER BEARER. JUST BEFORE DAWN, AS HE WAITED FOR THE SIGNAL TO GO "OVER THE TOP"...
THOSE LADS LOOK FAGGED OUT, 'DAD'. BET THEY'RE GLAD TO BE LEAVING THE TRENCHES.
THEY'RE NOT LEAVING, CHARLEY. THEY'RE ARRIVING! THEY'RE THE ASSAULT TROOPS.
Writer PAT MILLS
Artist JOE COLQUHOUN
Letterer MIKE PETERS
IT TOOK TWELVE HOURS MARCHING TO GET HERE. WE'RE GOING 'OVER THE TOP' WITHOUT A REST OR A CUP OF TEA. IT'S A DISGRACE!
SB
POOR DEVILS. THEY LOOK LIKE MEN WHO'VE BEEN BURIED ALIVE AND DUG UP AGAIN.
AT LEAST THE RAIN WILL MAKE IT HARD FOR THE JERRY MACHINE-GUNNERS.
WAIT FOR THE WHISTLE NOW, BOYS, AND KEEP IN TOUCH.
WAKE UP!
REMEMBER, CHARLEY. OUR JOB IS TO BANDAGE THE WOUNDED. OTHER STRETCHER BEARERS WILL CARRY THEM BACK TO THE AID POST.
ZERO HOUR!
RIGHT, LADS! INTO THE SCRAP!

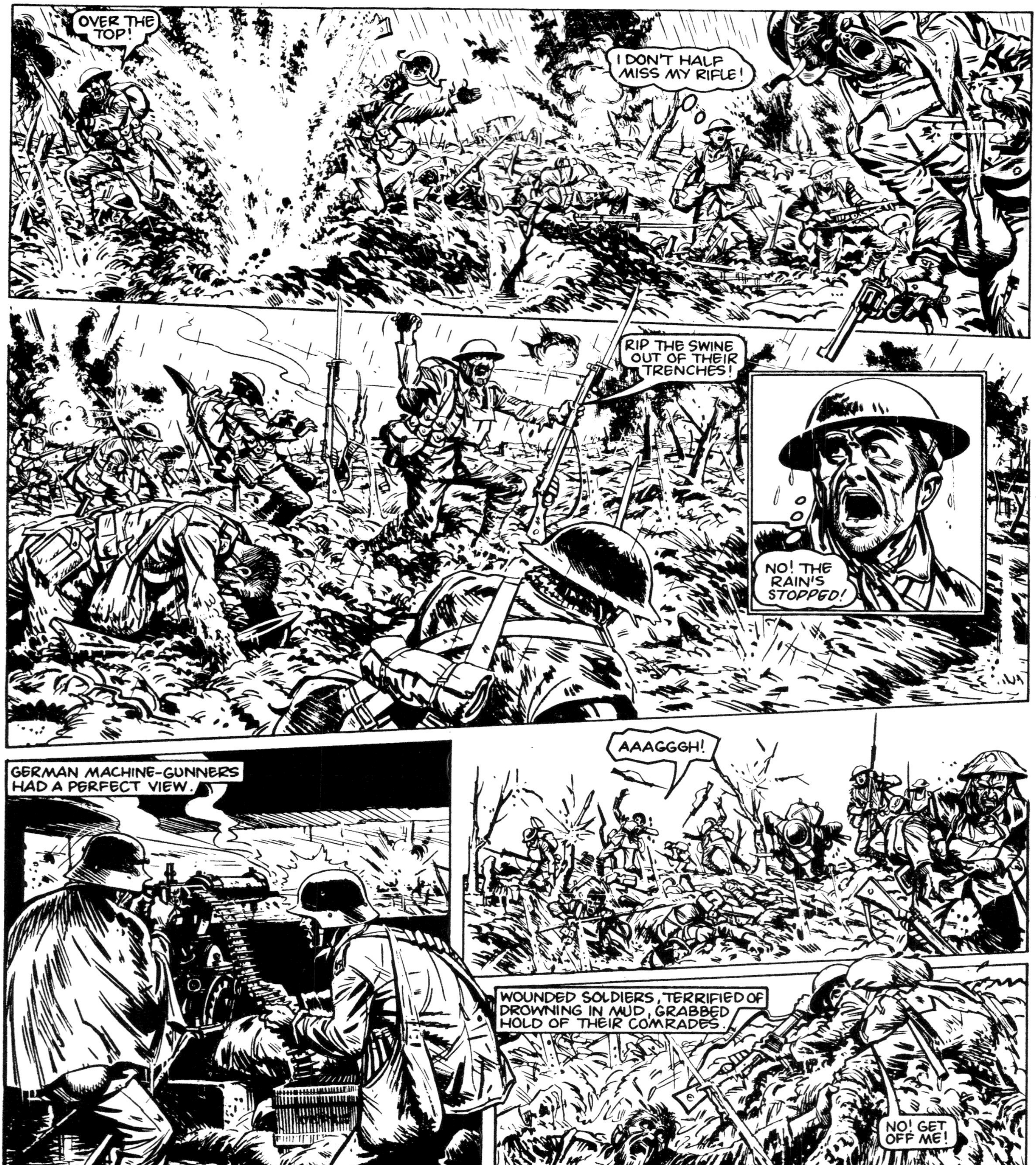
OVER THE TOP!
I DON'T HALF MISS MY RIFLE!
RIP THE SWINE OUT OF THEIR TRENCHES!
NO! THE RAIN'S STOPPED!
GERMAN MACHINE-GUNNERS HAD A PERFECT VIEW.
AAAGGGH!
WOUNDED SOLDIERS, TERRIFIED OF DROWNING IN MUD, GRABBED HOLD OF THEIR COMRADES.
NO! GET OFF ME!

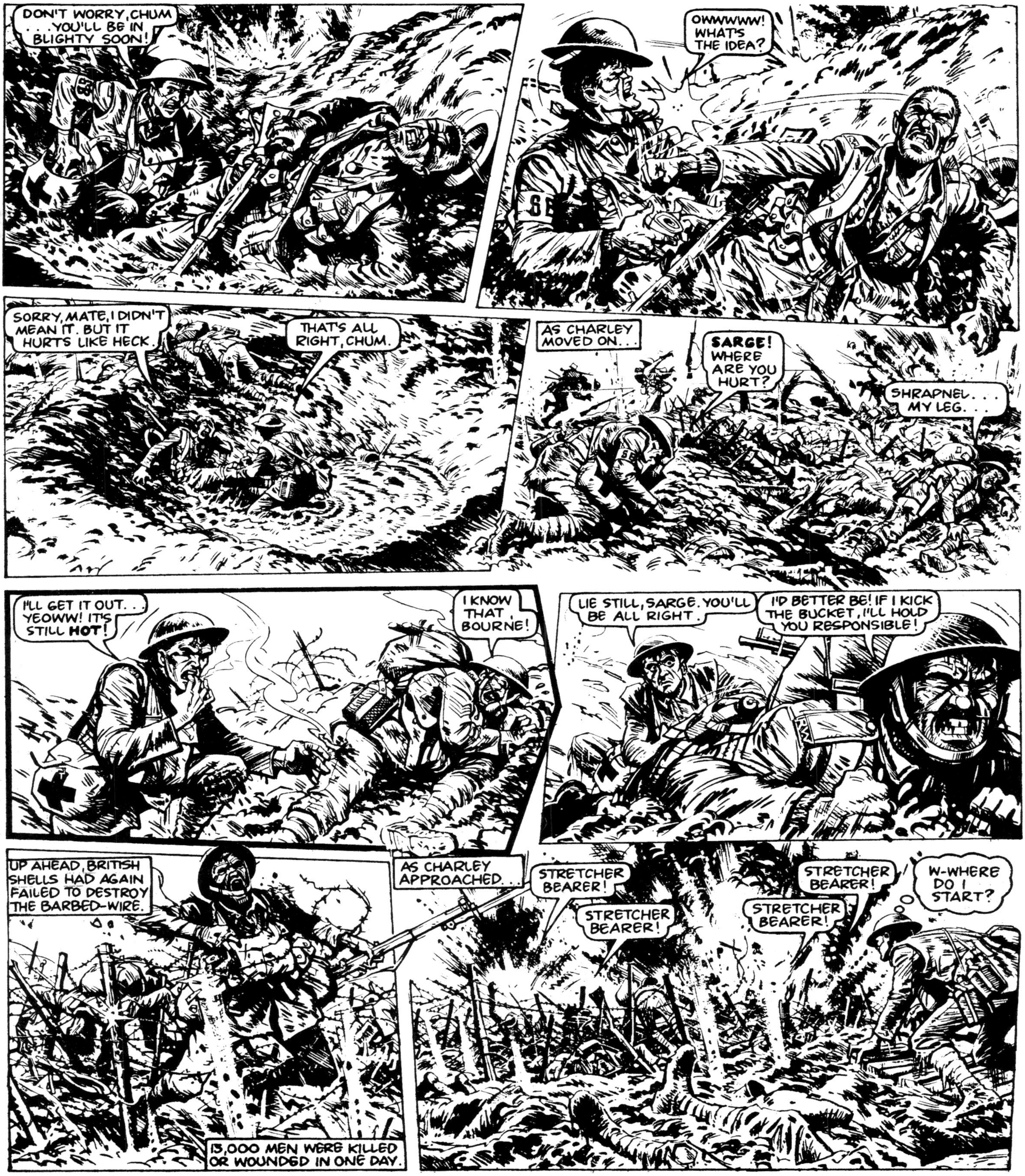
DON'T WORRY, CHUM . . . YOU'LL BE IN BLIGHTY SOON!
OWWWWW! WHAT'S THE IDEA?
SORRY, MATE, I DIDN'T MEAN IT. BUT IT HURTS LIKE HECK.
THAT'S ALL RIGHT, CHUM.
AS CHARLEY MOVED ON. . .
SARGE! WHERE ARE YOU HURT?
SHRAPNEL. . . MY LEG. . .
I'LL GET IT OUT. . . YEOWW! IT'S STILL HOT!
I KNOW THAT, BOURNE!
LIE STILL, SARGE. YOU'LL BE ALL RIGHT.
I'D BETTER BE! IF I KICK THE BUCKET, I'LL HOLD YOU RESPONSIBLE!
UP AHEAD, BRITISH SHELLS HAD AGAIN FAILED TO DESTROY THE BARBED-WIRE.
13,000 MEN WERE KILLED OR WOUNDED IN ONE DAY.
AS CHARLEY APPROACHED. . .
STRETCHER BEARER!
STRETCHER BEARER!
STRETCHER BEARER!
STRETCHER BEARER!
W-WHERE DO I START?

CHARLEY'S WAR

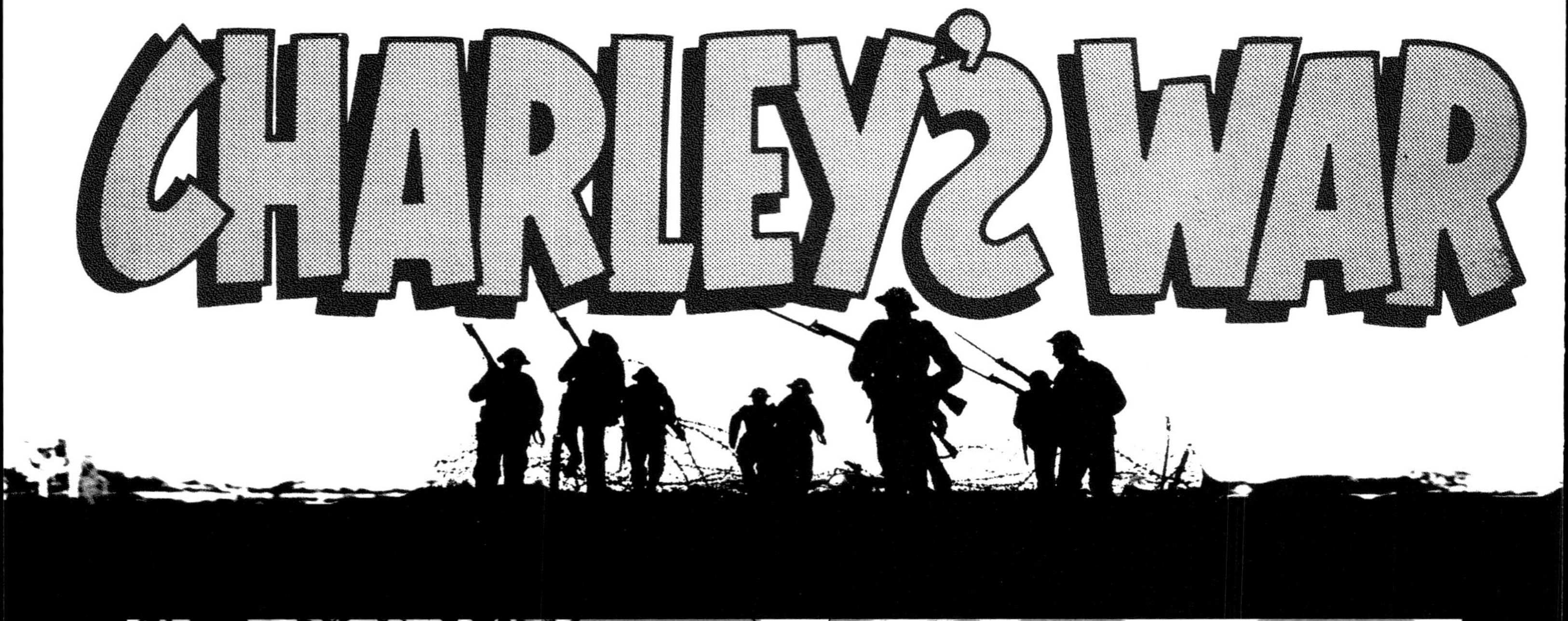

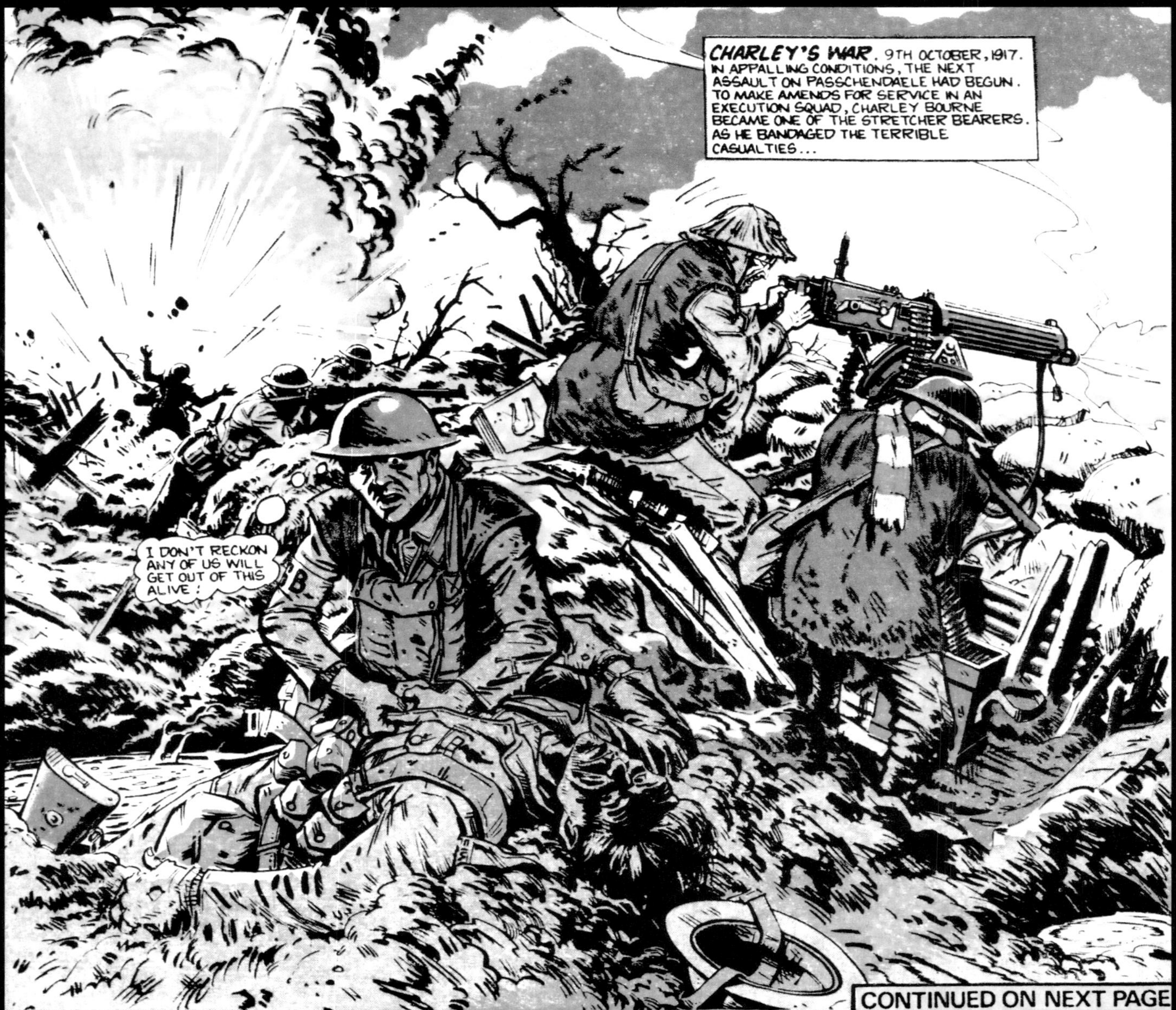
CHARLEY'S WAR. 9TH OCTOBER, 1917. IN APPALLING CONDITIONS, THE NEXT ASSAULT ON PASSCHENDAELE HAD BEGUN. TO MAKE AMENDS FOR SERVICE IN AN EXECUTION SQUAD, CHARLEY BOURNE BECAME ONE OF THE STRETCHER BEARERS. AS HE BANDAGED THE TERRIBLE CASUALTIES...
I DON'T RECKON ANY OF US WILL GET OUT OF THIS ALIVE!

CONTINUED ON NEXT PAGE

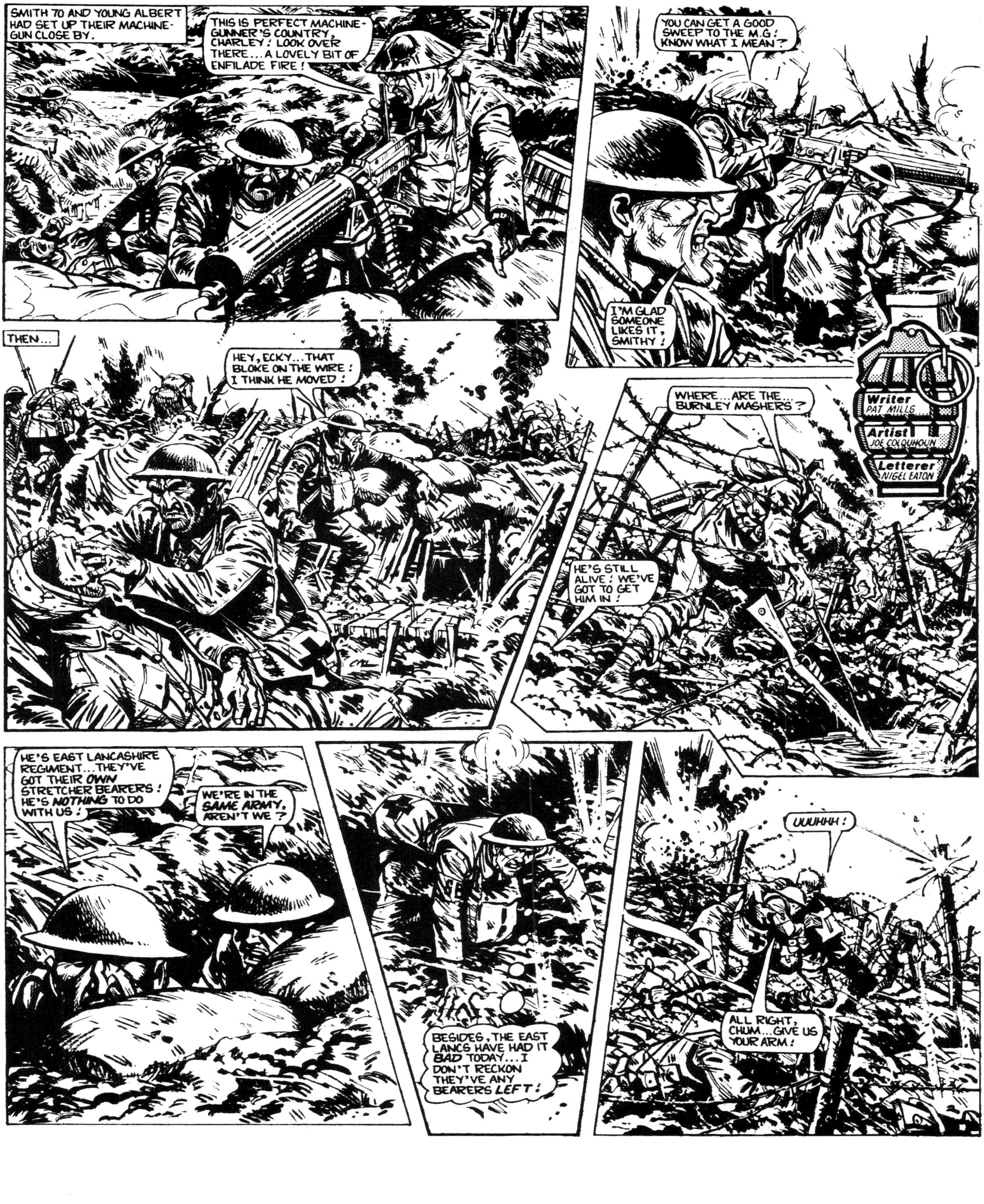
SMITH 70 AND YOUNG ALBERT HAD SET UP THEIR MACHINE-GUN CLOSE BY.
THIS IS PERFECT MACHINE-GUNNER'S COUNTRY, CHARLEY! LOOK OVER THERE... A LOVELY BIT OF ENFILADE FIRE!
YOU CAN GET A GOOD SWEEP TO THE M.G! KNOW WHAT I MEAN?
I'M GLAD SOMEONE LIKES IT, SMITHY!
Writer PAT MILLS
Artist JOE COLQUHOUN
Letterer NIGEL EATON
THEN...
HEY, ECKY... THAT BLOKE ON THE WIRE! I THINK HE MOVED!
WHERE... ARE THE... BURNLEY MASHERS?
HE'S STILL ALIVE! WE'VE GOT TO GET HIM IN!
HE'S EAST LANCASHIRE REGIMENT... THEY'VE GOT THEIR OWN STRETCHER BEARERS! HE'S NOTHING TO DO WITH US!
WE'RE IN THE SAME ARMY, AREN'T WE?
BESIDES, THE EAST LANCS HAVE HAD IT BAD TODAY... I DON'T RECKON THEY'VE ANY BEARERS LEFT!
UUUHHH!
ALL RIGHT, CHUM... GIVE US YOUR ARM!

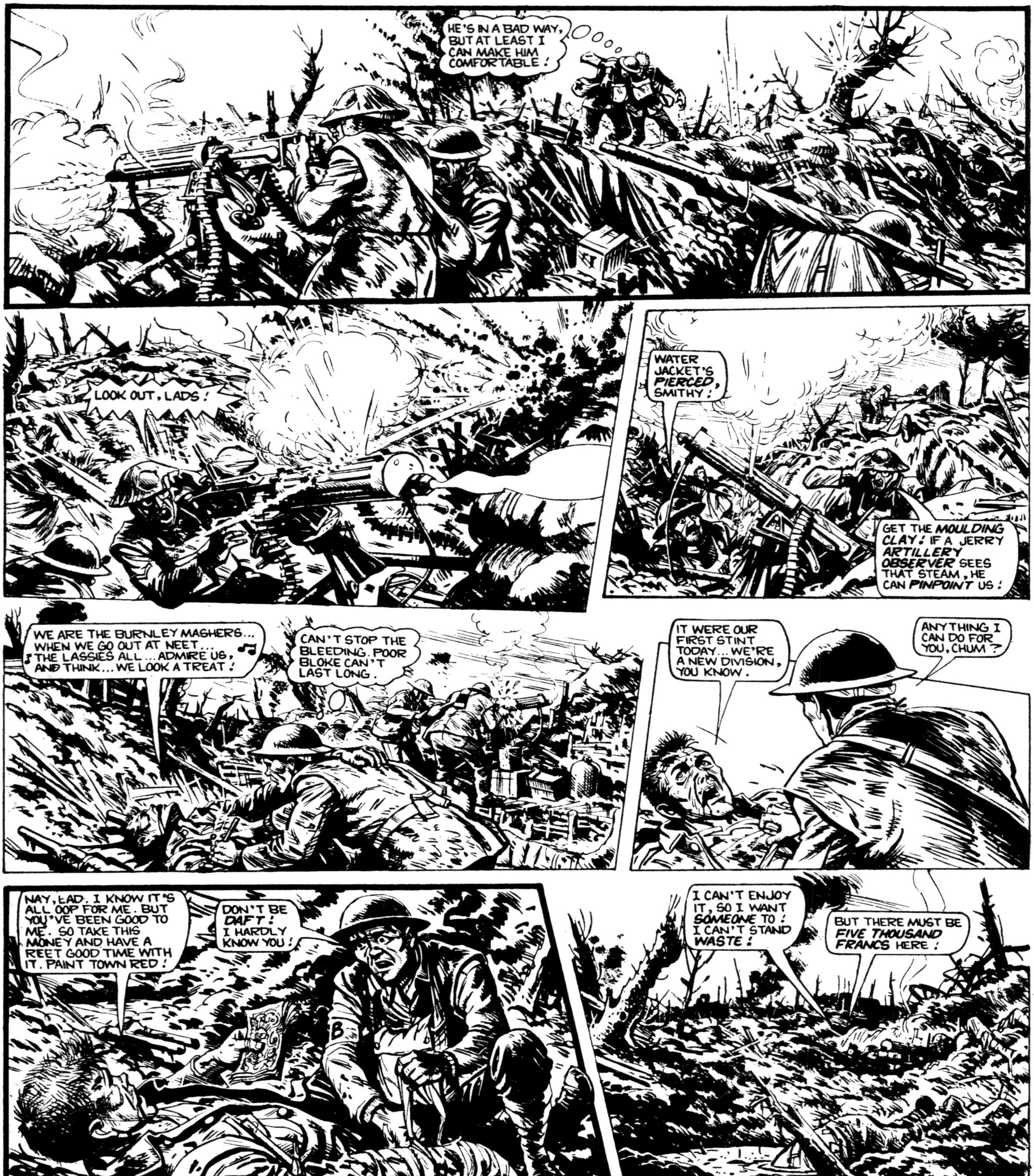
HE'S IN A BAD WAY, BUT AT LEAST I CAN MAKE HIM COMFORTABLE!
LOOK OUT, LADS!
WATER JACKET'S PIERCED, SMITHY!
GET THE MOULDING CLAY! IF A JERRY ARTILLERY OBSERVER SEES THAT STEAM, HE CAN PINPOINT US!
WE ARE THE BURNLEY MASHERS... WHEN WE GO OUT AT NEET... THE LASSIES ALL... ADMIRE US, AND THINK... WE LOOK A TREAT!
CAN'T STOP THE BLEEDING. POOR BLOKE CAN'T LAST LONG.
IT WERE OUR FIRST STINT TODAY... WE'RE A NEW DIVISION, YOU KNOW.
ANYTHING I CAN DO FOR YOU, CHUM?
NAY, LAD. I KNOW IT'S ALL OOP FOR ME. BUT YOU'VE BEEN GOOD TO ME. SO TAKE THIS MONEY AND HAVE A REET GOOD TIME WITH IT. PAINT TOWN RED!
DON'T BE DAFT! I HARDLY KNOW YOU!
I CAN'T ENJOY IT, SO I WANT SOMEONE TO! I CAN'T STAND WASTE!
BUT THERE MUST BE FIVE THOUSAND FRANCS HERE!

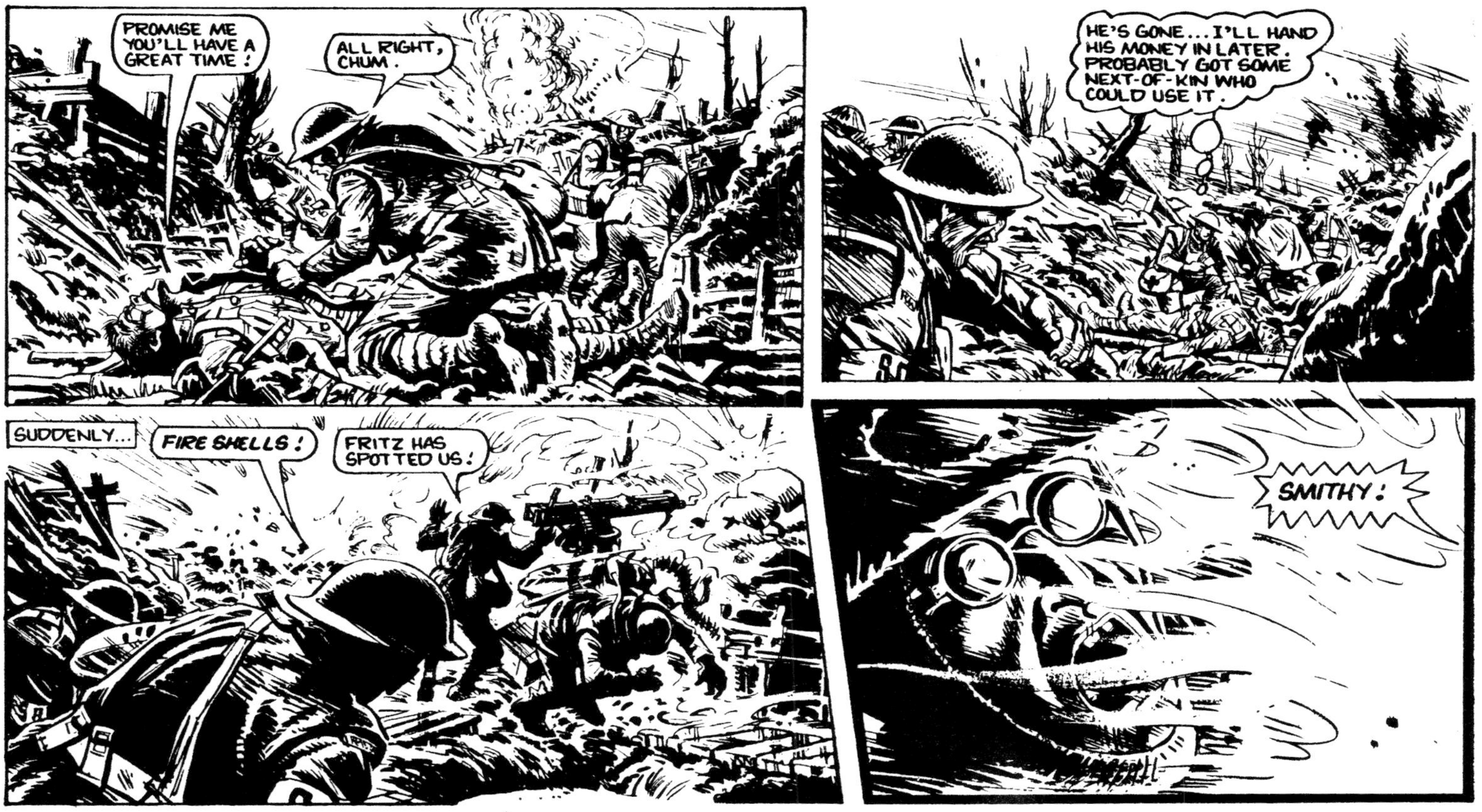
PROMISE ME YOU'LL HAVE A GREAT TIME!
ALL RIGHT, CHUM.
HE'S GONE... I'LL HAND HIS MONEY IN LATER. PROBABLY GOT SOME NEXT-OF-KIN WHO COULD USE IT.
SUDDENLY...
FIRE SHELLS!
FRITZ HAS SPOTTED US!
SMITHY!

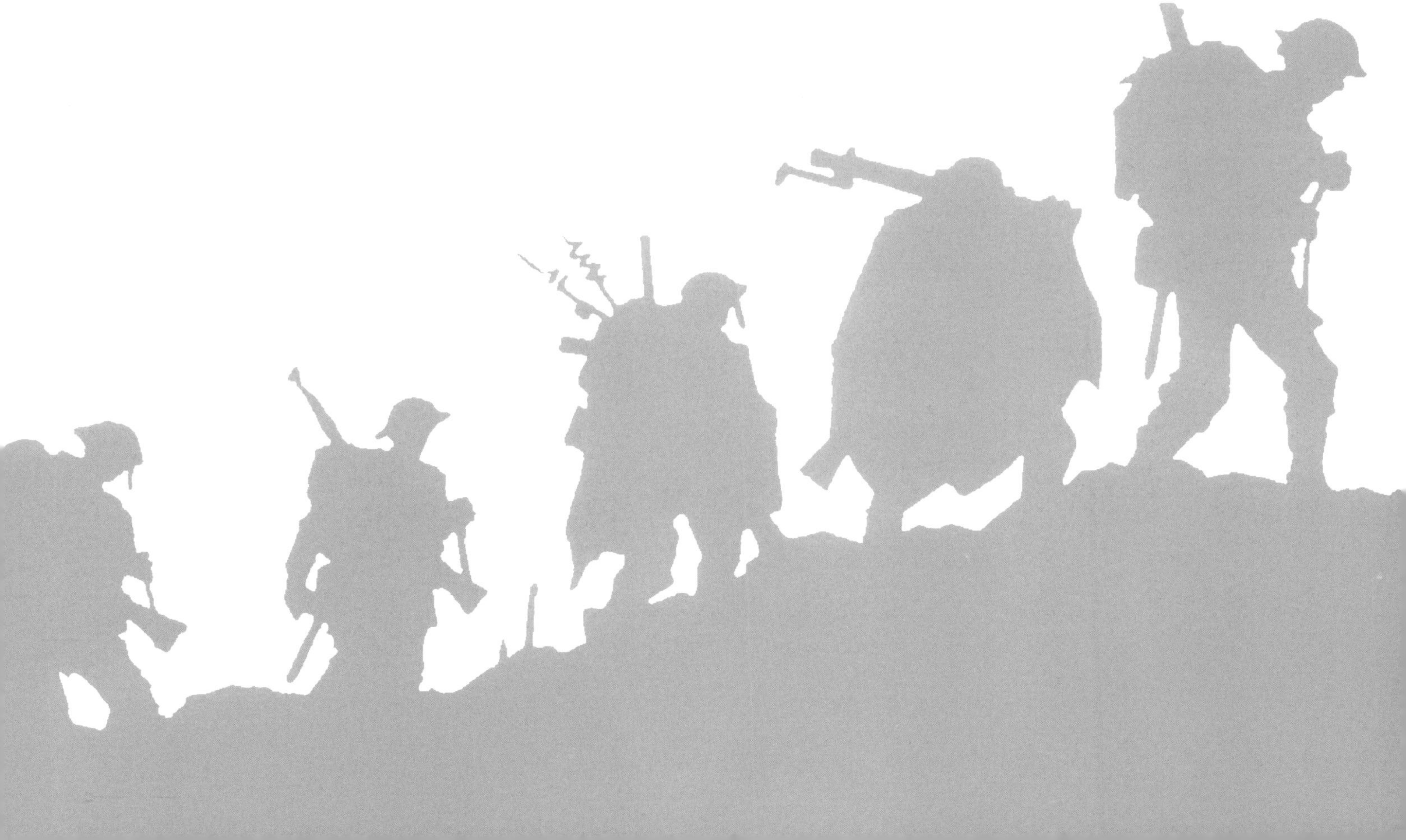

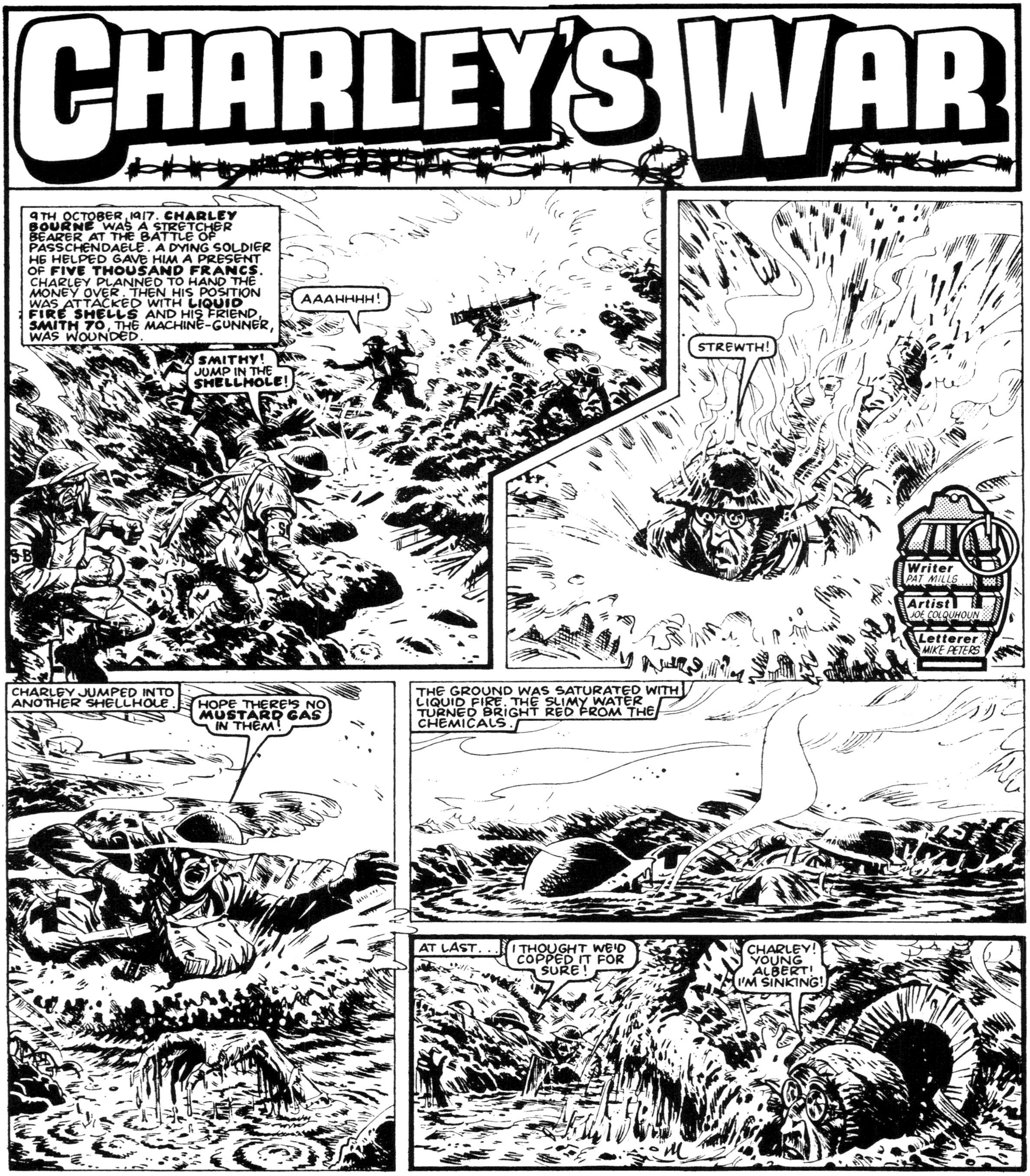
CHARLEY'S WAR
9TH OCTOBER, 1917. CHARLEY BOURNE WAS A STRETCHER BEARER AT THE BATTLE OF PASSCHENDAELE. A DYING SOLDIER HE HELPED GAVE HIM A PRESENT OF FIVE THOUSAND FRANCS. CHARLEY PLANNED TO HAND THE MONEY OVER. THEN HIS POSITION WAS ATTACKED WITH LIQUID FIRE SHELLS AND HIS FRIEND, SMITH 70, THE MACHINE-GUNNER, WAS WOUNDED.
AAAHHHH!
SMITHY! JUMP IN THE SHELLHOLE!
STREWTH!
Writer PAT MILLS
Artist JOE COLQUHOUN
Letterer MIKE PETERS
CHARLEY JUMPED INTO ANOTHER SHELLHOLE.
HOPE THERE'S NO MUSTARD GAS IN THEM!
THE GROUND WAS SATURATED WITH LIQUID FIRE. THE SLIMY WATER TURNED BRIGHT RED FROM THE CHEMICALS.
AT LAST...
I THOUGHT WE'D COPPED IT FOR SURE!
CHARLEY! YOUNG ALBERT! I'M SINKING!

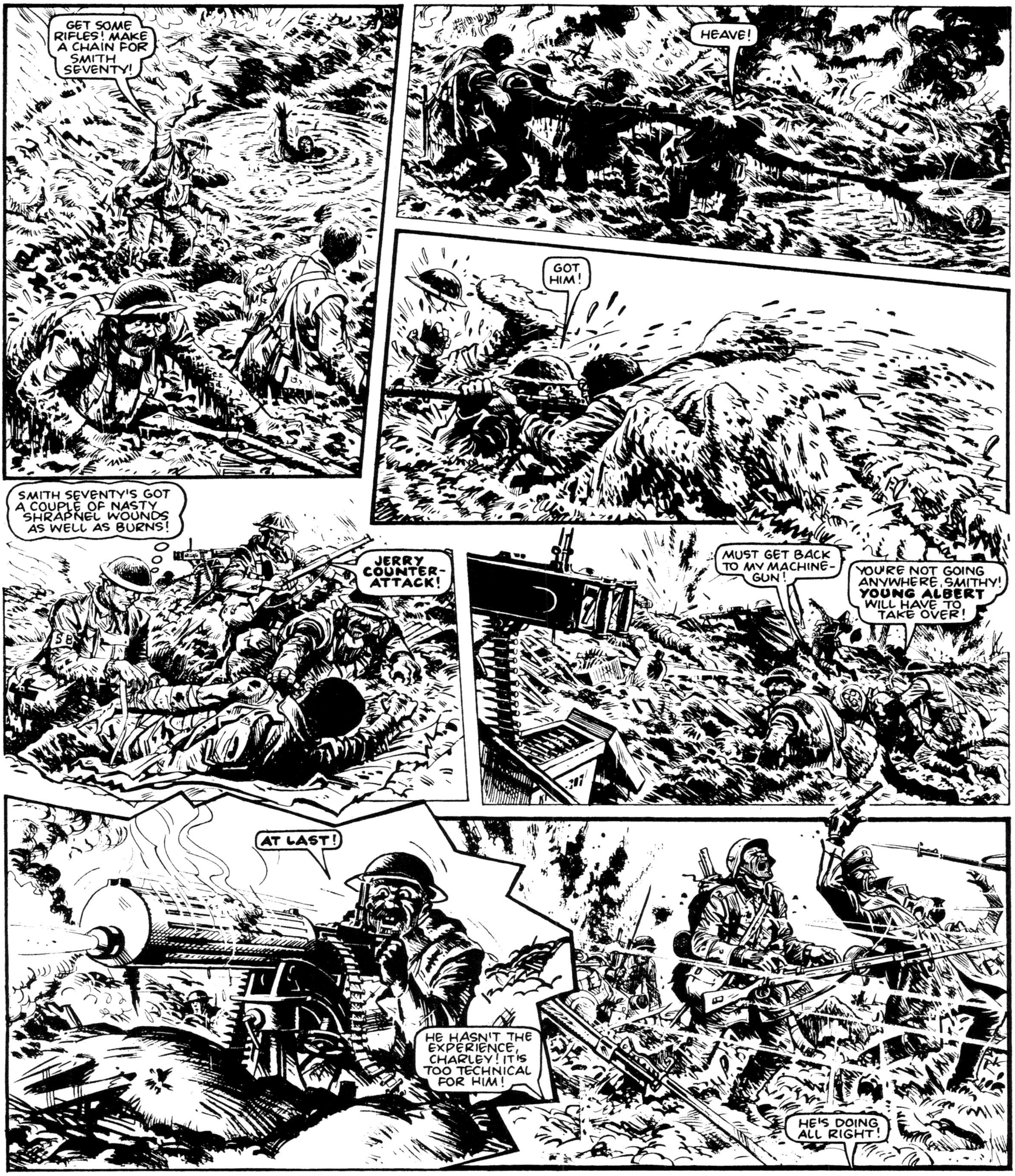
GET SOME RIFLES! MAKE A CHAIN FOR SMITH SEVENTY!
HEAVE!
GOT HIM!
SMITH SEVENTY'S GOT A COUPLE OF NASTY SHRAPNEL WOUNDS AS WELL AS BURNS!
JERRY COUNTER-ATTACK!
MUST GET BACK TO MY MACHINE-GUN!
YOU'RE NOT GOING ANYWHERE, SMITHY! YOUNG ALBERT WILL HAVE TO TAKE OVER!
AT LAST!
HE HASN'T THE EXPERIENCE, CHARLEY! IT'S TOO TECHNICAL FOR HIM!
HE'S DOING ALL RIGHT!

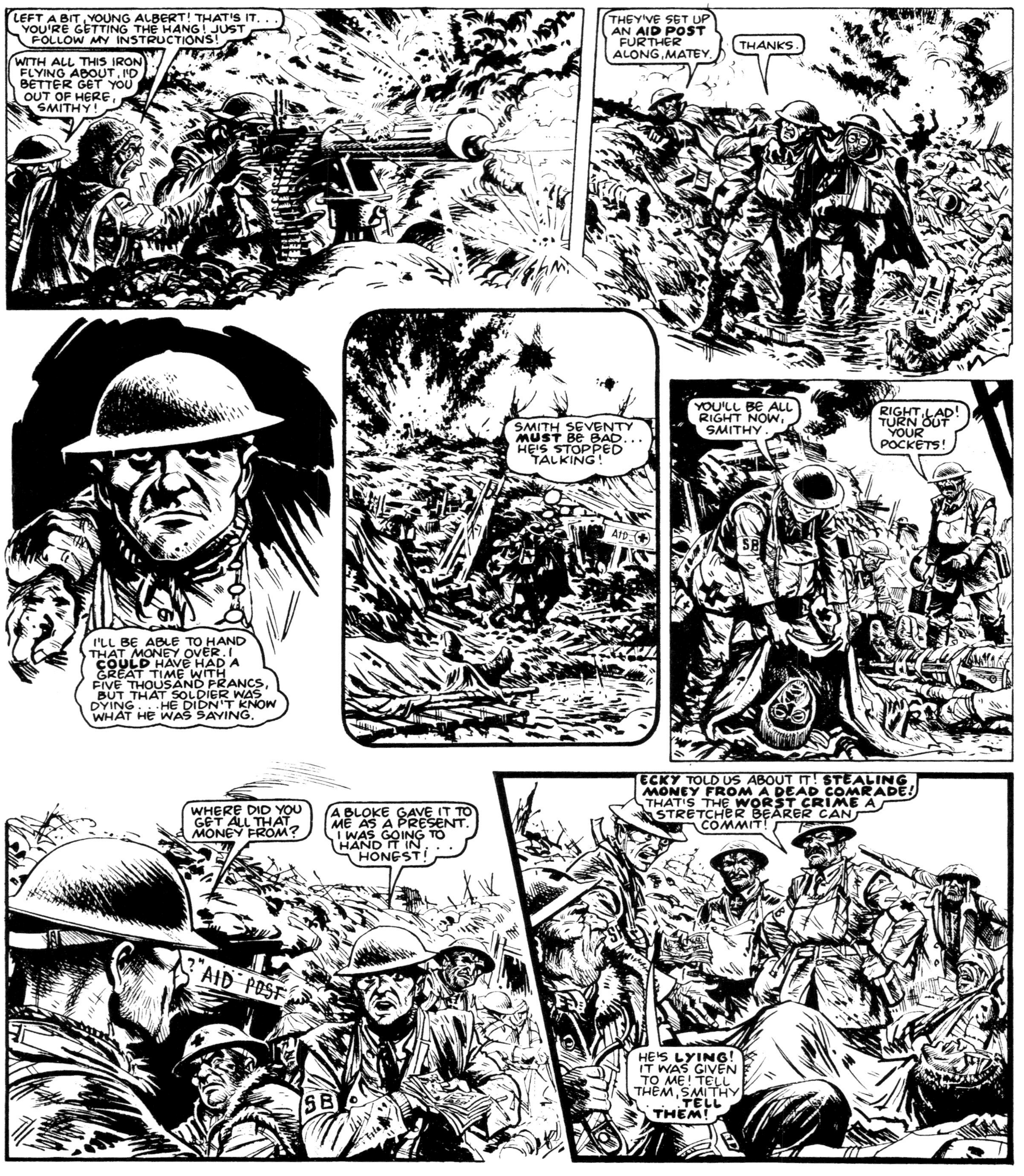
LEFT A BIT, YOUNG ALBERT! THAT'S IT... YOU'RE GETTING THE HANG! JUST FOLLOW MY INSTRUCTIONS!
WITH ALL THIS IRON FLYING ABOUT, I'D BETTER GET YOU OUT OF HERE, SMITHY!
THEY'VE SET UP AN AID POST FURTHER ALONG, MATEY.
THANKS.
I'LL BE ABLE TO HAND THAT MONEY OVER. I COULD HAVE HAD A GREAT TIME WITH FIVE THOUSAND FRANCS, BUT THAT SOLDIER WAS DYING... HE DIDN'T KNOW WHAT HE WAS SAYING.
SMITH SEVENTY MUST BE BAD... HE'S STOPPED TALKING!
AID
YOU'LL BE ALL RIGHT NOW, SMITHY.
RIGHT, LAD! TURN OUT YOUR POCKETS!
WHERE DID YOU GET ALL THAT MONEY FROM?
A BLOKE GAVE IT TO ME AS A PRESENT. I WAS GOING TO HAND IT IN. HONEST!
AID POST
ECKY TOLD US ABOUT IT! STEALING MONEY FROM A DEAD COMRADE! THAT'S THE WORST CRIME A STRETCHER BEARER CAN COMMIT!
HE'S LYING! IT WAS GIVEN TO ME! TELL THEM, SMITHY. TELL THEM!

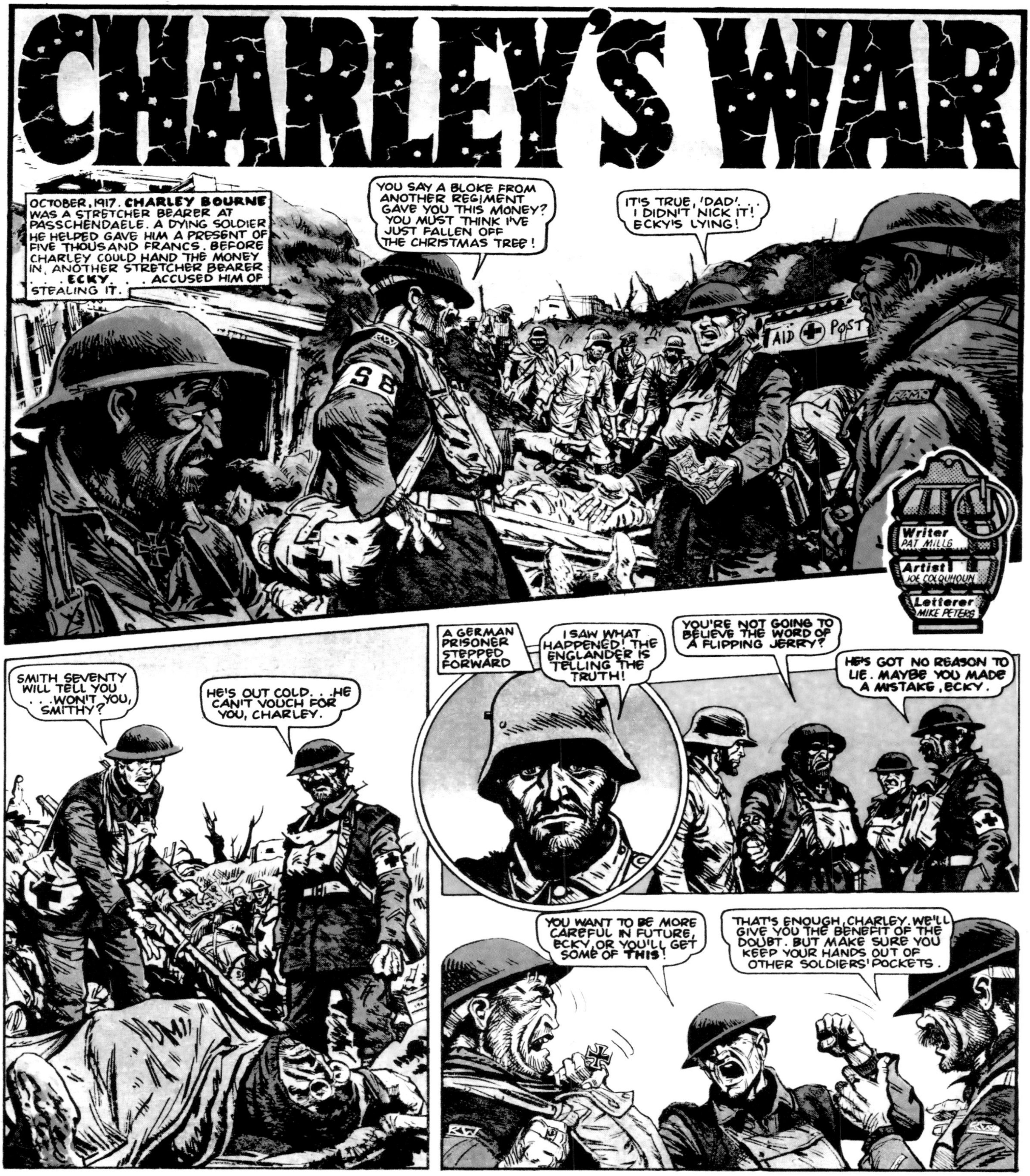
CHARLEY'S WAR
OCTOBER, 1917. CHARLEY BOURNE WAS A STRETCHER BEARER AT PASSCHENDAELE. A DYING SOLDIER HE HELPED GAVE HIM A PRESENT OF FIVE THOUSAND FRANCS. BEFORE CHARLEY COULD HAND THE MONEY IN, ANOTHER STRETCHER BEARER . . . ECKY . . . ACCUSED HIM OF STEALING IT.
YOU SAY A BLOKE FROM ANOTHER REGIMENT GAVE YOU THIS MONEY? YOU MUST THINK I'VE JUST FALLEN OFF THE CHRISTMAS TREE!
IT'S TRUE, 'DAD'. . . I DIDN'T NICK IT! ECKY'S LYING!
AID POST
Writer PAT MILLS
Artist JOE COLQUHOUN
Letterer MIKE PETERS
SMITH SEVENTY WILL TELL YOU . . .WON'T YOU, SMITHY?
HE'S OUT COLD. . .HE CAN'T VOUCH FOR YOU, CHARLEY.
A GERMAN PRISONER STEPPED FORWARD
I SAW WHAT HAPPENED! THE ENGLANDER IS TELLING THE TRUTH!
YOU'RE NOT GOING TO BELIEVE THE WORD OF A FLIPPING JERRY?
HE'S GOT NO REASON TO LIE. MAYBE YOU MADE A MISTAKE, ECKY.
YOU WANT TO BE MORE CAREFUL IN FUTURE, ECKY, OR YOU'LL GET SOME OF THIS!
THAT'S ENOUGH, CHARLEY. WE'LL GIVE YOU THE BENEFIT OF THE DOUBT. BUT MAKE SURE YOU KEEP YOUR HANDS OUT OF OTHER SOLDIERS' POCKETS.

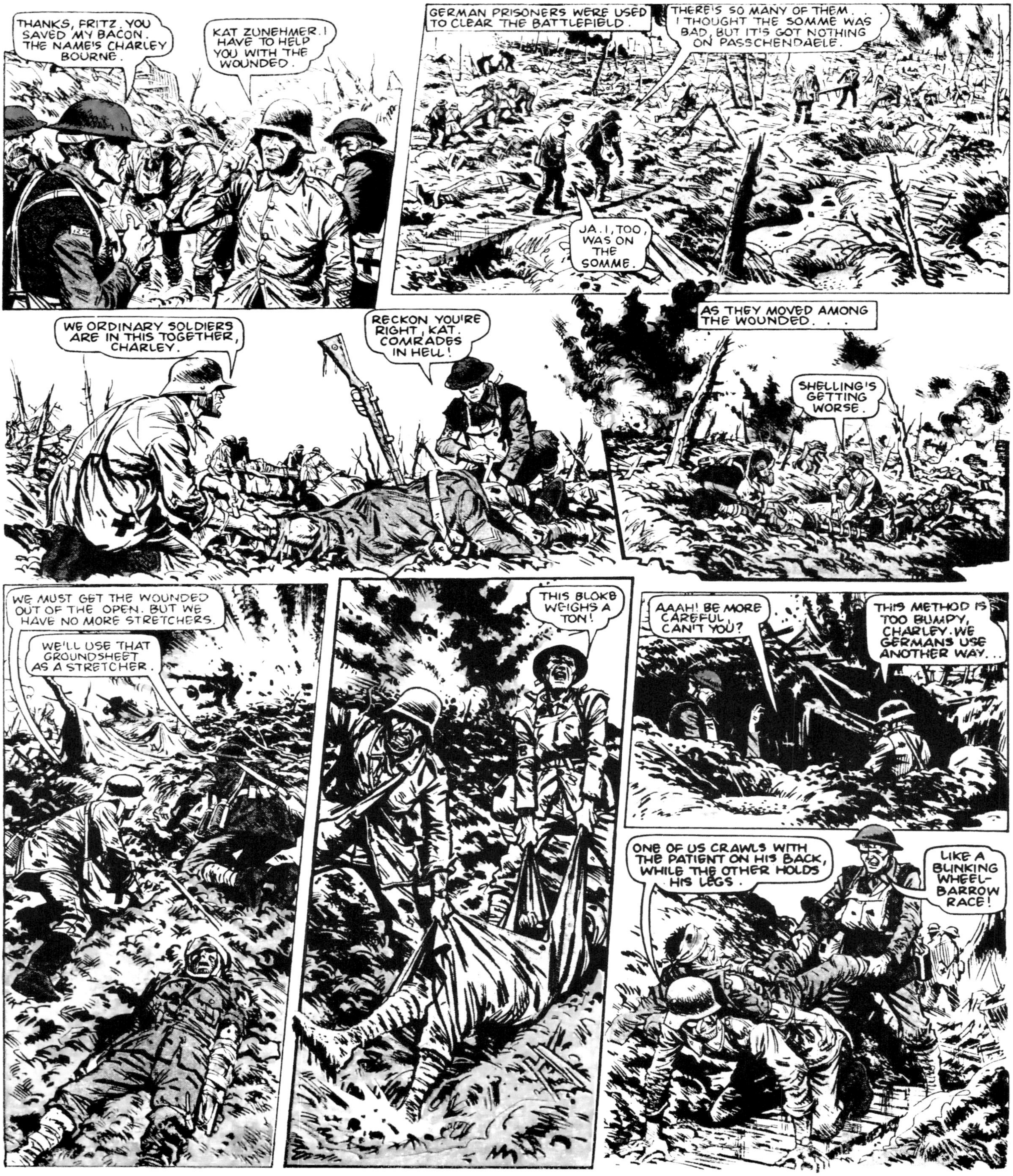
THANKS, FRITZ. YOU SAVED MY BACON. THE NAME'S CHARLEY BOURNE.
KAT ZUNEHMER. I HAVE TO HELP YOU WITH THE WOUNDED.
GERMAN PRISONERS WERE USED TO CLEAR THE BATTLEFIELD.
THERE'S SO MANY OF THEM... I THOUGHT THE SOMME WAS BAD, BUT IT'S GOT NOTHING ON PASSCHENDAELE.
JA. I, TOO, WAS ON THE SOMME.
WE ORDINARY SOLDIERS ARE IN THIS TOGETHER, CHARLEY.
RECKON YOU'RE RIGHT, KAT. COMRADES IN HELL!
AS THEY MOVED AMONG THE WOUNDED...
SHELLING'S GETTING WORSE.
WE MUST GET THE WOUNDED OUT OF THE OPEN. BUT WE HAVE NO MORE STRETCHERS.
WE'LL USE THAT GROUNDSHEET AS A STRETCHER.
THIS BLOKE WEIGHS A TON!
AAAH! BE MORE CAREFUL, CAN'T YOU?
THIS METHOD IS TOO BUMPY, CHARLEY. WE GERMANS USE ANOTHER WAY...
ONE OF US CRAWLS WITH THE PATIENT ON HIS BACK, WHILE THE OTHER HOLDS HIS LEGS.
LIKE A BLINKING WHEEL-BARROW RACE!

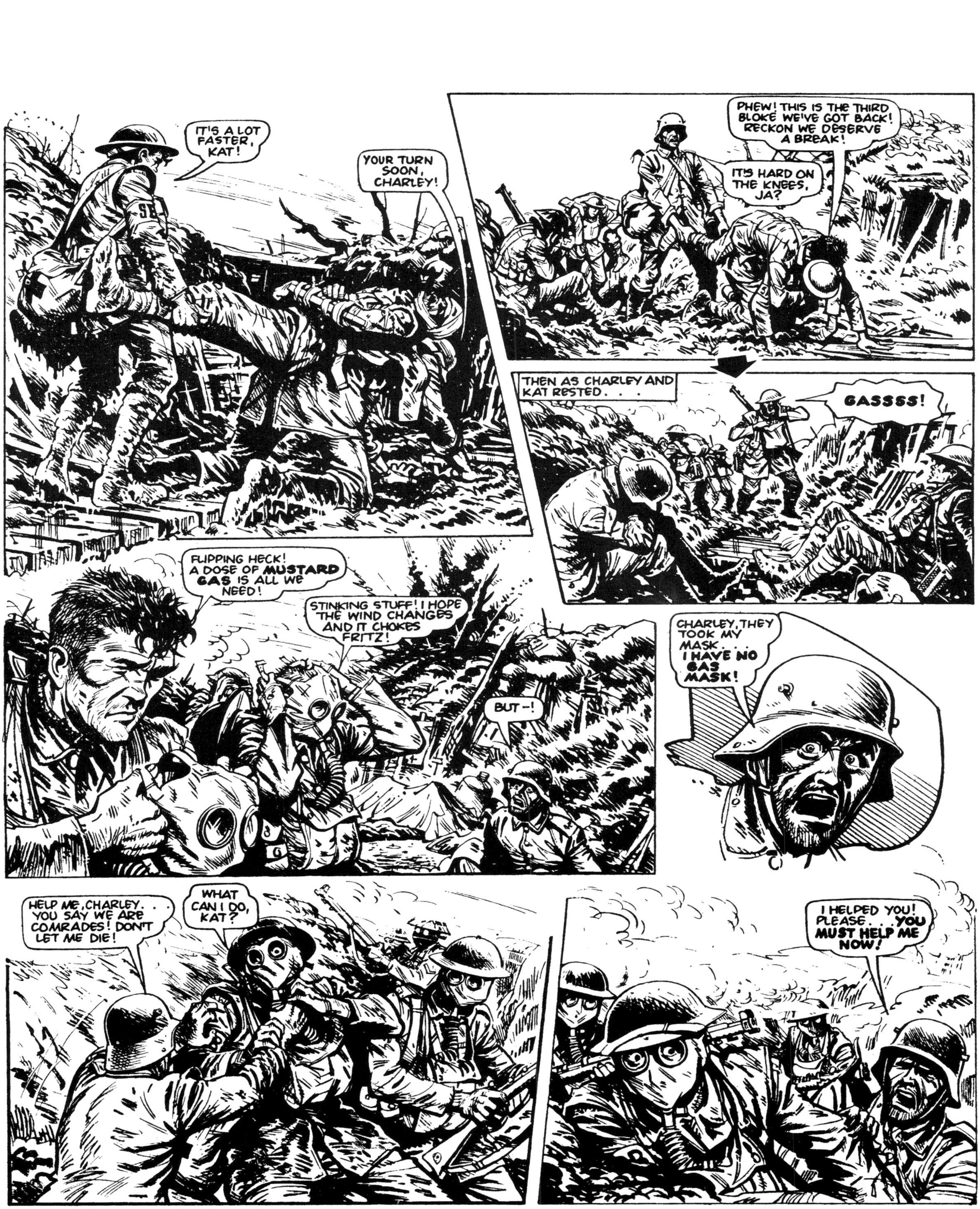
IT'S A LOT FASTER, KAT!
YOUR TURN SOON, CHARLEY!
PHEW! THIS IS THE THIRD BLOKE WE'VE GOT BACK! RECKON WE DESERVE A BREAK!
IT'S HARD ON THE KNEES, JA?
THEN AS CHARLEY AND KAT RESTED . . .
GASSSS!
FLIPPING HECK! A DOSE OF MUSTARD GAS IS ALL WE NEED!
STINKING STUFF! I HOPE THE WIND CHANGES AND IT CHOKES FRITZ!
BUT –!
CHARLEY, THEY TOOK MY MASK . . I HAVE NO GAS MASK!
HELP ME, CHARLEY. . YOU SAY WE ARE COMRADES! DON'T LET ME DIE!
WHAT CAN I DO, KAT?
I HELPED YOU! PLEASE. . . YOU MUST HELP ME NOW!

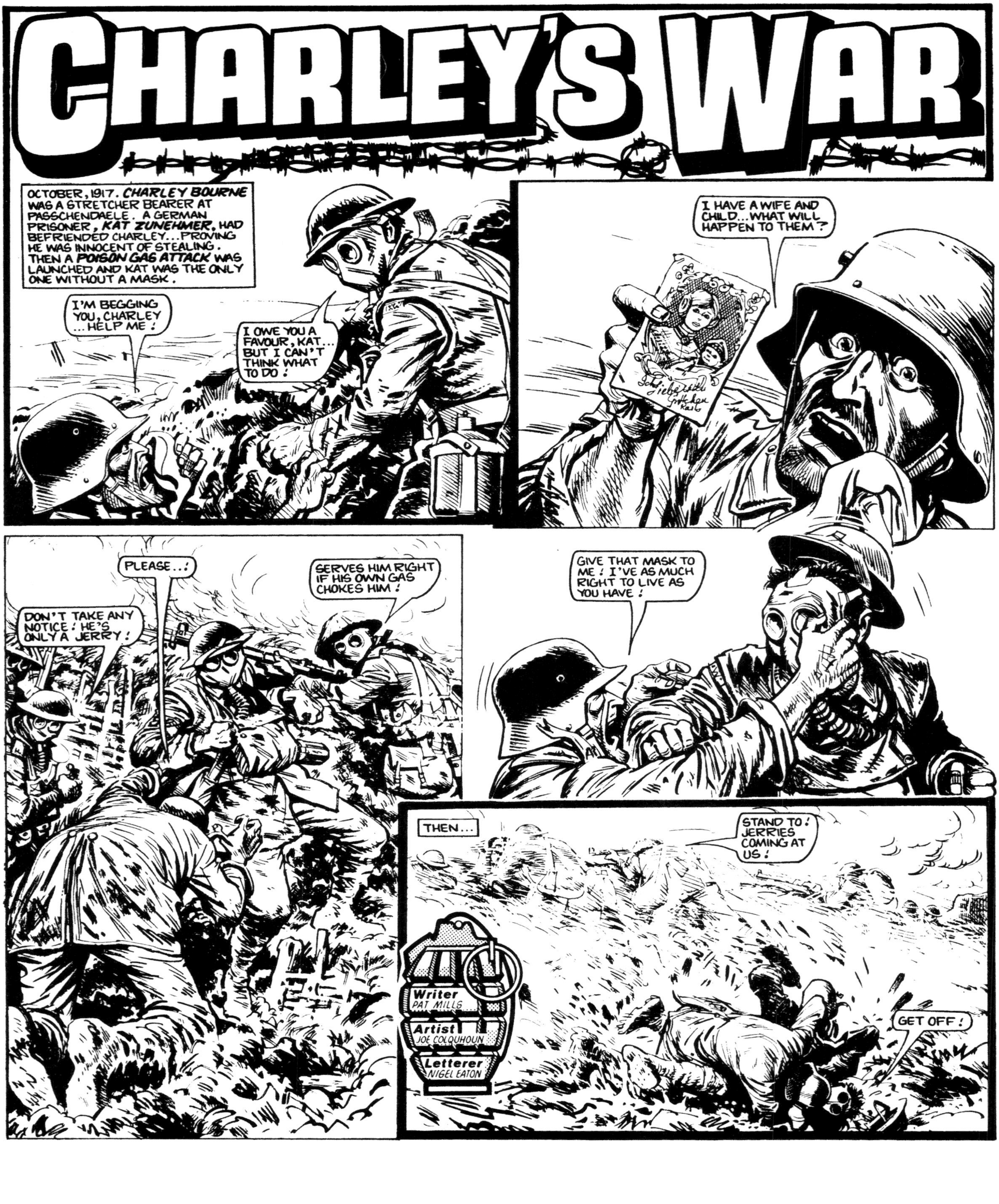
CHARLEY'S WAR
OCTOBER, 1917. CHARLEY BOURNE WAS A STRETCHER BEARER AT PASSCHENDAELE. A GERMAN PRISONER, KAT ZUNEHMER, HAD BEFRIENDED CHARLEY... PROVING HE WAS INNOCENT OF STEALING. THEN A POISON GAS ATTACK WAS LAUNCHED AND KAT WAS THE ONLY ONE WITHOUT A MASK.
I'M BEGGING YOU, CHARLEY ... HELP ME!
I OWE YOU A FAVOUR, KAT... BUT I CAN'T THINK WHAT TO DO!
I HAVE A WIFE AND CHILD... WHAT WILL HAPPEN TO THEM?
PLEASE...!
DON'T TAKE ANY NOTICE! HE'S ONLY A JERRY!
SERVES HIM RIGHT IF HIS OWN GAS CHOKES HIM!
GIVE THAT MASK TO ME! I'VE AS MUCH RIGHT TO LIVE AS YOU HAVE!
THEN...
STAND TO! JERRIES COMING AT US!
Writer PAT MILLS
Artist JOE COLQUHOUN
Letterer NIGEL EATON
GET OFF!

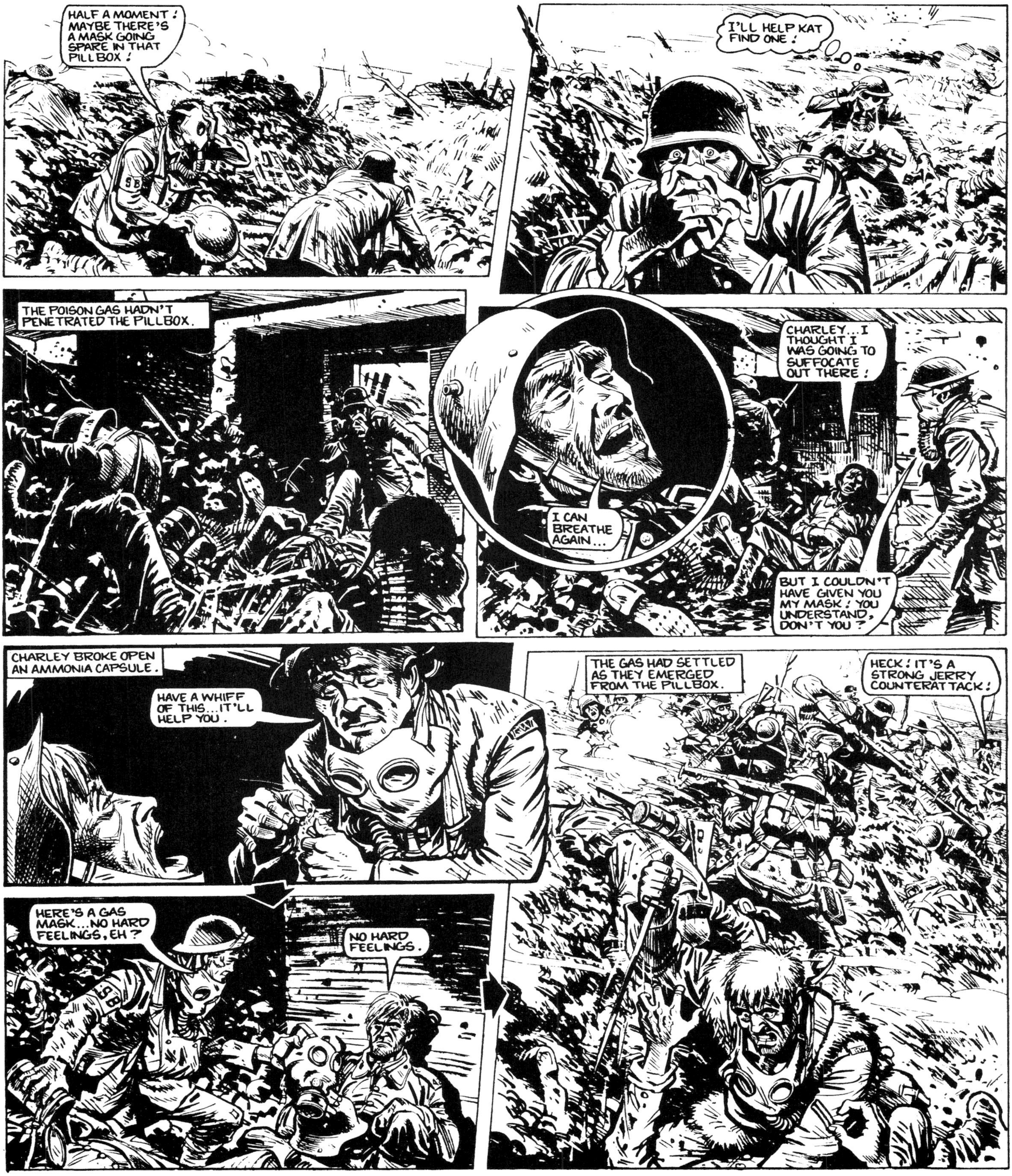

HALF A MOMENT! MAYBE THERE'S A MASK GOING SPARE IN THAT PILLBOX!
I'LL HELP KAT FIND ONE!
THE POISON GAS HADN'T PENETRATED THE PILLBOX.
I CAN BREATHE AGAIN...
CHARLEY... I THOUGHT I WAS GOING TO SUFFOCATE OUT THERE!
BUT I COULDN'T HAVE GIVEN YOU MY MASK! YOU UNDERSTAND, DON'T YOU?
CHARLEY BROKE OPEN AN AMMONIA CAPSULE.
HAVE A WHIFF OF THIS... IT'LL HELP YOU.
HERE'S A GAS MASK... NO HARD FEELINGS, EH?
NO HARD FEELINGS.
THE GAS HAD SETTLED AS THEY EMERGED FROM THE PILLBOX.
HECK! IT'S A STRONG JERRY COUNTERATTACK!

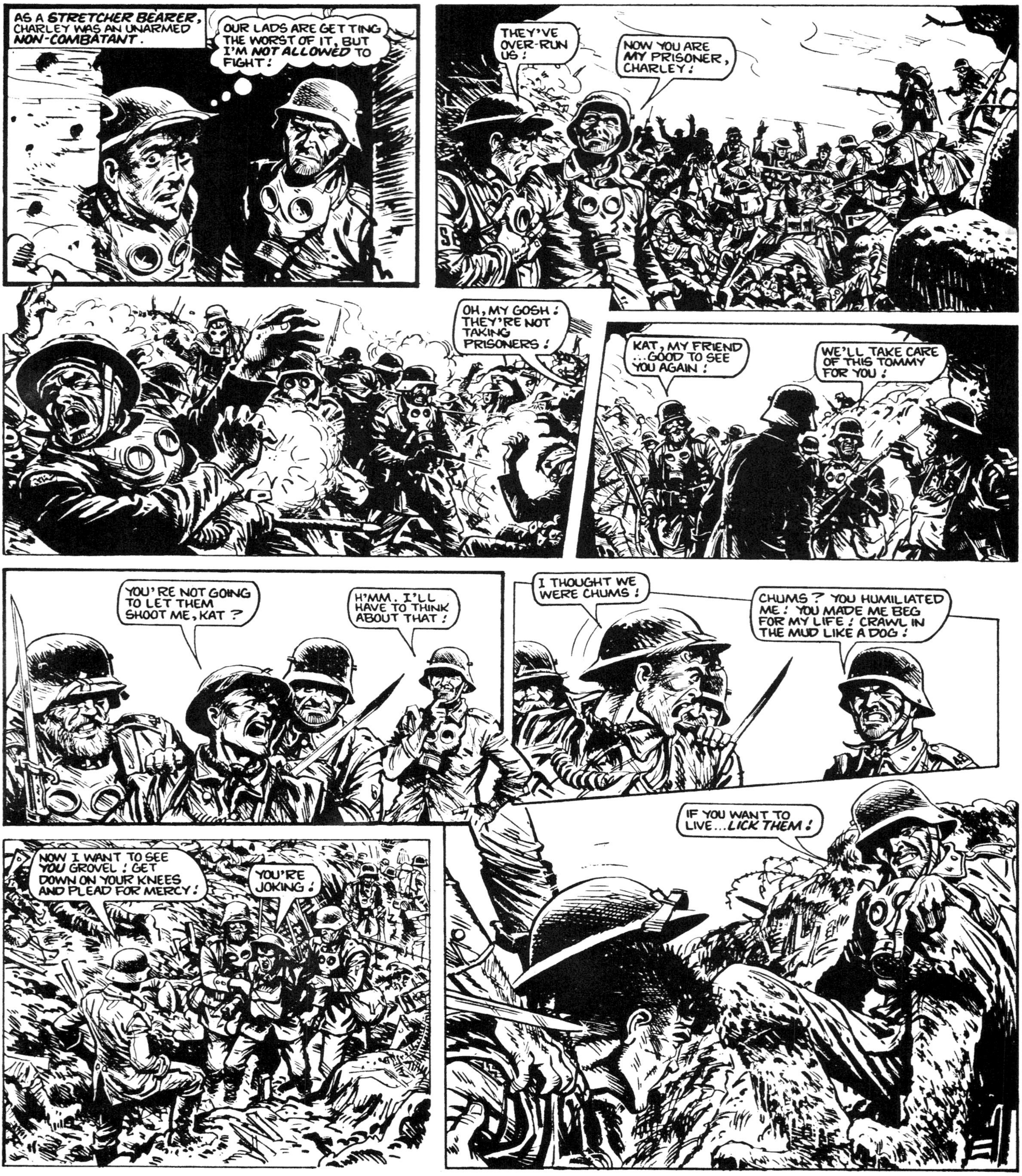
AS A STRETCHER BEARER, CHARLEY WAS AN UNARMED NON-COMBATANT.
OUR LADS ARE GETTING THE WORST OF IT, BUT I'M NOT ALLOWED TO FIGHT!
THEY'VE OVER-RUN US!
NOW YOU ARE MY PRISONER, CHARLEY!
OH, MY GOSH! THEY'RE NOT TAKING PRISONERS!
KAT, MY FRIEND ... GOOD TO SEE YOU AGAIN!
WE'LL TAKE CARE OF THIS TOMMY FOR YOU!
YOU'RE NOT GOING TO LET THEM SHOOT ME, KAT?
H'MM. I'LL HAVE TO THINK ABOUT THAT!
I THOUGHT WE WERE CHUMS!
CHUMS? YOU HUMILIATED ME! YOU MADE ME BEG FOR MY LIFE! CRAWL IN THE MUD LIKE A DOG!
NOW I WANT TO SEE YOU GROVEL! GET DOWN ON YOUR KNEES AND PLEAD FOR MERCY!
YOU'RE JOKING!
IF YOU WANT TO LIVE... LICK THEM!

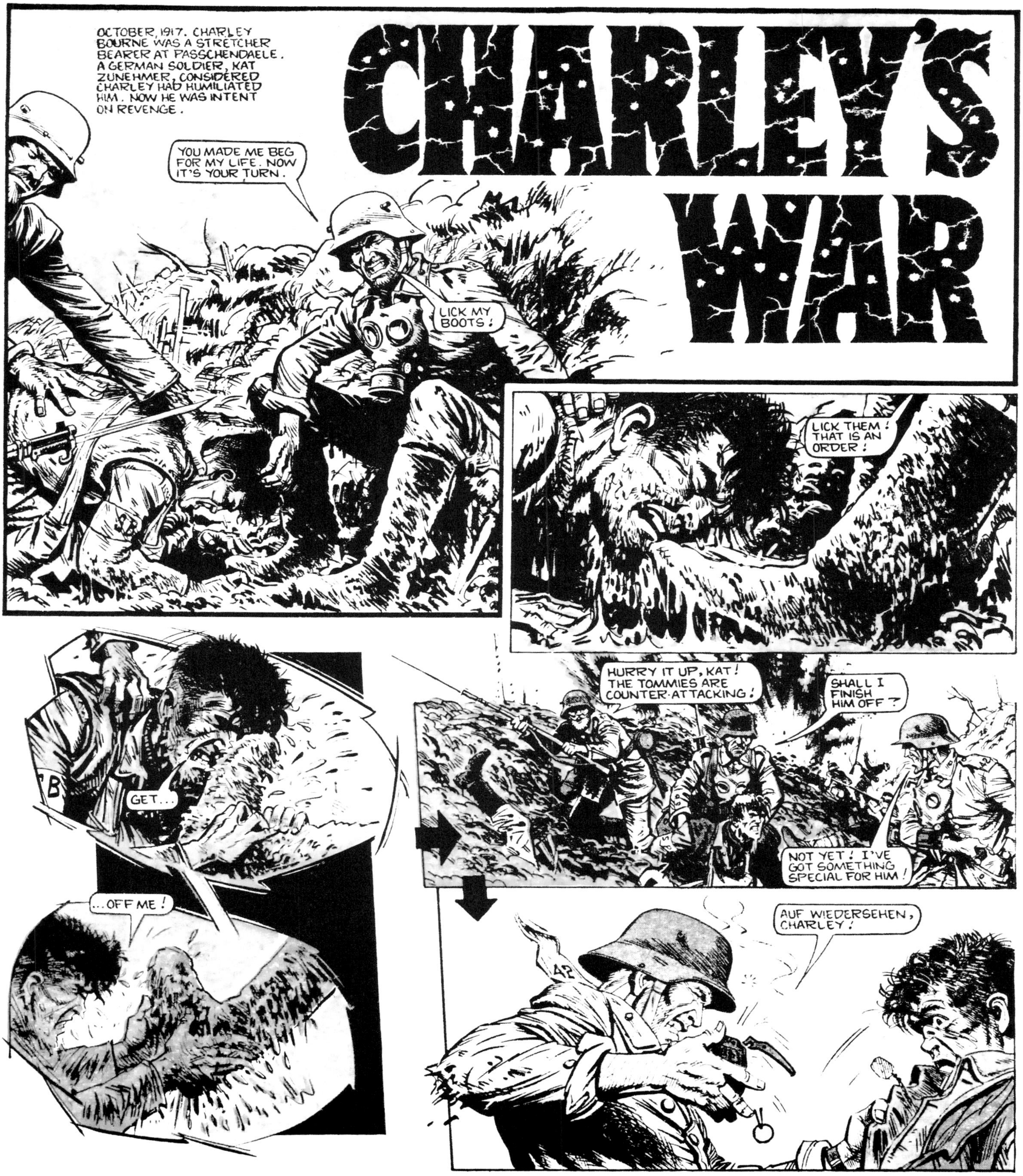
CHARLEY'S WAR
OCTOBER, 1917. CHARLEY BOURNE WAS A STRETCHER BEARER AT PASSCHENDAELE. A GERMAN SOLDIER, KAT ZUNEHMER, CONSIDERED CHARLEY HAD HUMILIATED HIM. NOW HE WAS INTENT ON REVENGE.
YOU MADE ME BEG FOR MY LIFE. NOW IT'S YOUR TURN.
LICK MY BOOTS!
LICK THEM! THAT IS AN ORDER!
GET...
...OFF ME!
HURRY IT UP, KAT! THE TOMMIES ARE COUNTER-ATTACKING!
SHALL I FINISH HIM OFF?
NOT YET! I'VE GOT SOMETHING SPECIAL FOR HIM!
AUF WIEDERSEHEN, CHARLEY!

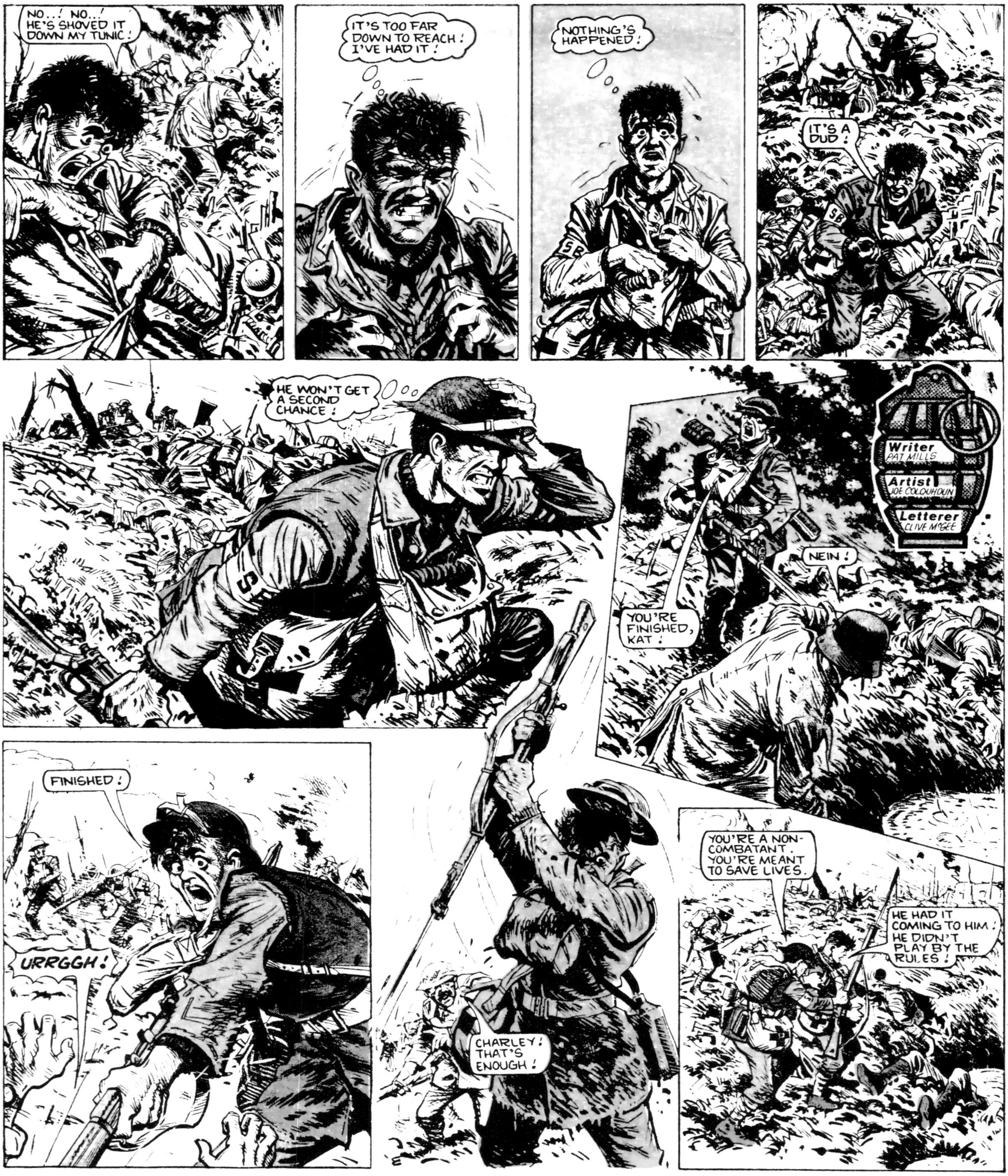
NO..! NO..! HE'S SHOVED IT DOWN MY TUNIC!
IT'S TOO FAR DOWN TO REACH! I'VE HAD IT!
NOTHING'S HAPPENED!
IT'S A DUD!
HE WON'T GET A SECOND CHANCE!
Writer PAT MILLS
Artist JOE COLQUHOUN
Letterer CLIVE McGEE
NEIN!
YOU'RE FINISHED, KAT!
FINISHED!
URRGGH!
CHARLEY! THAT'S ENOUGH!
YOU'RE A NON-COMBATANT. YOU'RE MEANT TO SAVE LIVES.
HE HAD IT COMING TO HIM! HE DIDN'T PLAY BY THE RULES!

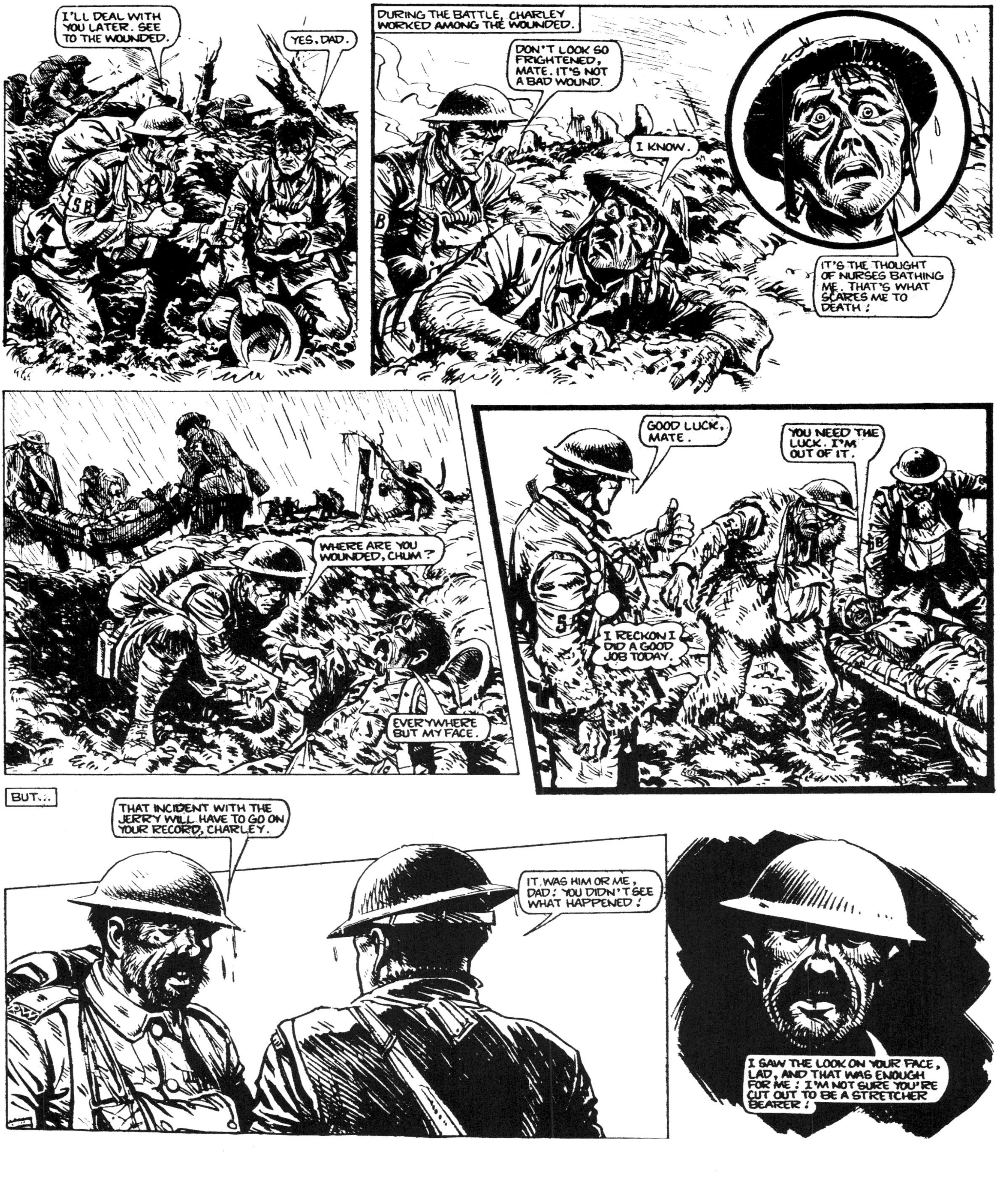
I'LL DEAL WITH YOU LATER. SEE TO THE WOUNDED.
YES, DAD.
DURING THE BATTLE, CHARLEY WORKED AMONG THE WOUNDED.
DON'T LOOK SO FRIGHTENED, MATE. IT'S NOT A BAD WOUND.
I KNOW.
IT'S THE THOUGHT OF NURSES BATHING ME. THAT'S WHAT SCARES ME TO DEATH!
WHERE ARE YOU WOUNDED, CHUM?
EVERYWHERE BUT MY FACE.
GOOD LUCK, MATE.
YOU NEED THE LUCK. I'M OUT OF IT.
I RECKON I DID A GOOD JOB TODAY.
BUT...
THAT INCIDENT WITH THE JERRY WILL HAVE TO GO ON YOUR RECORD, CHARLEY.
IT WAS HIM OR ME, DAD! YOU DIDN'T SEE WHAT HAPPENED!
I SAW THE LOOK ON YOUR FACE, LAD, AND THAT WAS ENOUGH FOR ME! I'M NOT SURE YOU'RE CUT OUT TO BE A STRETCHER BEARER!

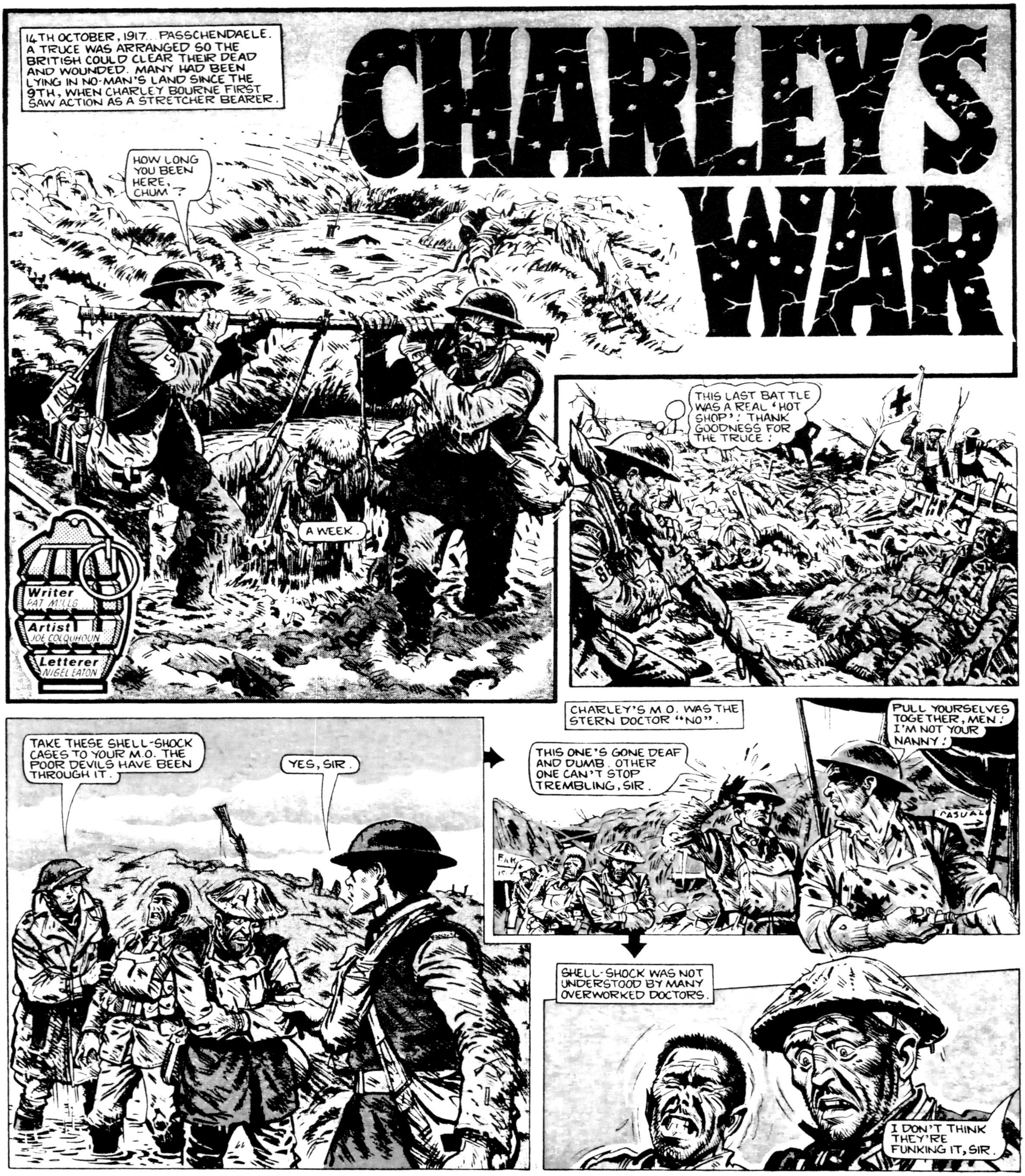
CHARLEY'S WAR
14TH OCTOBER, 1917... PASSCHENDAELE. A TRUCE WAS ARRANGED SO THE BRITISH COULD CLEAR THEIR DEAD AND WOUNDED. MANY HAD BEEN LYING IN NO-MAN'S LAND SINCE THE 9TH, WHEN CHARLEY BOURNE FIRST SAW ACTION AS A STRETCHER BEARER.
HOW LONG YOU BEEN HERE, CHUM ?
A WEEK.
Writer PAT MILLS
Artist JOE COLQUHOUN
Letterer NIGEL EATON
THIS LAST BATTLE WAS A REAL 'HOT SHOP'! THANK GOODNESS FOR THE TRUCE!
TAKE THESE SHELL-SHOCK CASES TO YOUR M.O. THE POOR DEVILS HAVE BEEN THROUGH IT.
YES, SIR.
CHARLEY'S M.O. WAS THE STERN DOCTOR "NO".
THIS ONE'S GONE DEAF AND DUMB. OTHER ONE CAN'T STOP TREMBLING, SIR.
PULL YOURSELVES TOGETHER, MEN! I'M NOT YOUR NANNY!
SHELL-SHOCK WAS NOT UNDERSTOOD BY MANY OVERWORKED DOCTORS.
I DON'T THINK THEY'RE FUNKING IT, SIR.

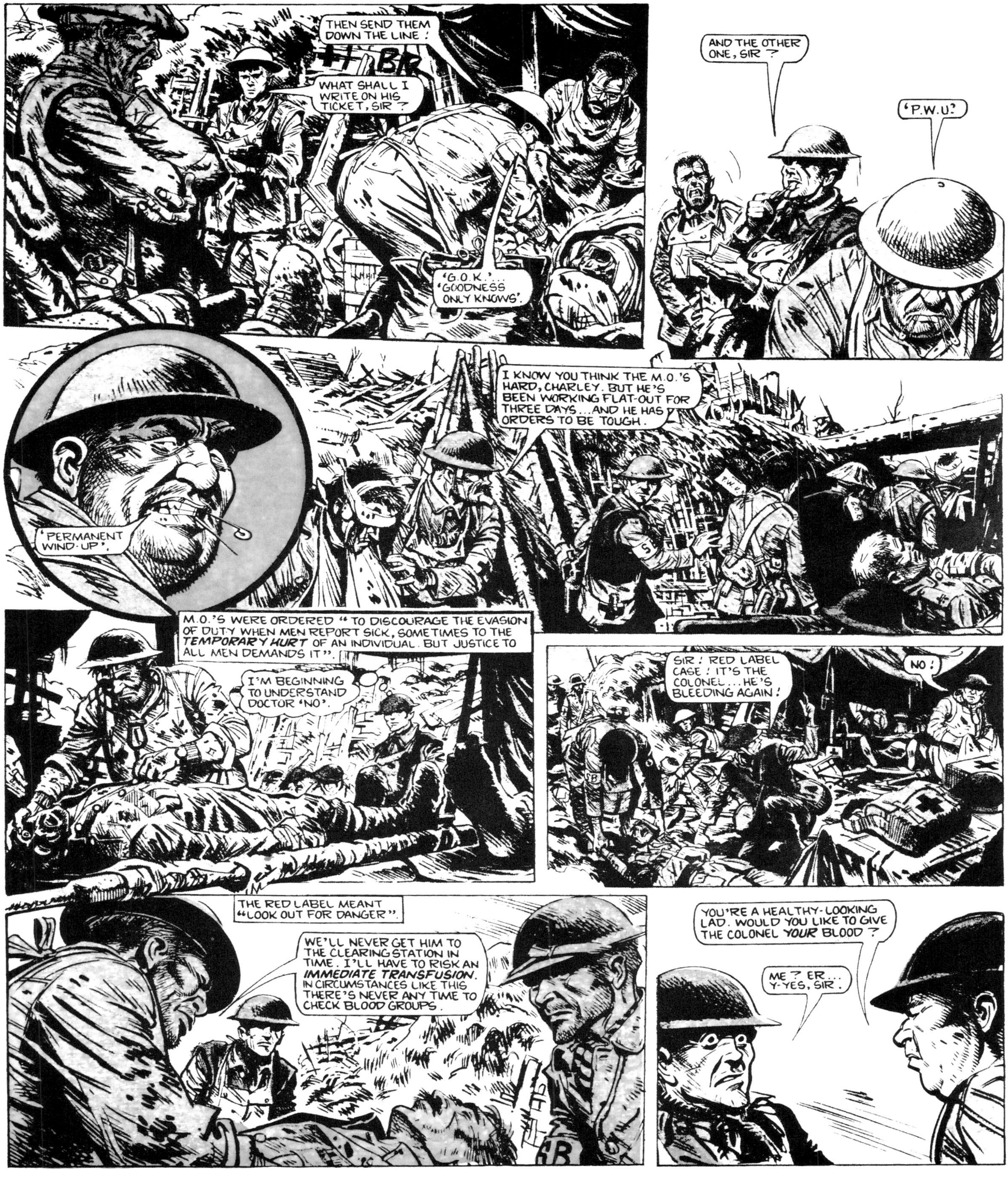
THEN SEND THEM DOWN THE LINE!
WHAT SHALL I WRITE ON HIS TICKET, SIR?
'G.O.K.'... 'GOODNESS ONLY KNOWS'.
AND THE OTHER ONE, SIR?
'P.W.U.'
'PERMANENT WIND-UP'.
I KNOW YOU THINK THE M.O.'S HARD, CHARLEY. BUT HE'S BEEN WORKING FLAT-OUT FOR THREE DAYS... AND HE HAS ORDERS TO BE TOUGH.
M.O.'S WERE ORDERED "TO DISCOURAGE THE EVASION OF DUTY WHEN MEN REPORT SICK, SOMETIMES TO THE TEMPORARY HURT OF AN INDIVIDUAL. BUT JUSTICE TO ALL MEN DEMANDS IT".
I'M BEGINNING TO UNDERSTAND DOCTOR 'NO'.
SIR! RED LABEL CASE! IT'S THE COLONEL... HE'S BLEEDING AGAIN!
NO!
THE RED LABEL MEANT "LOOK OUT FOR DANGER".
WE'LL NEVER GET HIM TO THE CLEARING STATION IN TIME. I'LL HAVE TO RISK AN IMMEDIATE TRANSFUSION. IN CIRCUMSTANCES LIKE THIS THERE'S NEVER ANY TIME TO CHECK BLOOD GROUPS.
YOU'RE A HEALTHY-LOOKING LAD. WOULD YOU LIKE TO GIVE THE COLONEL YOUR BLOOD?
ME? ER... Y-YES, SIR.

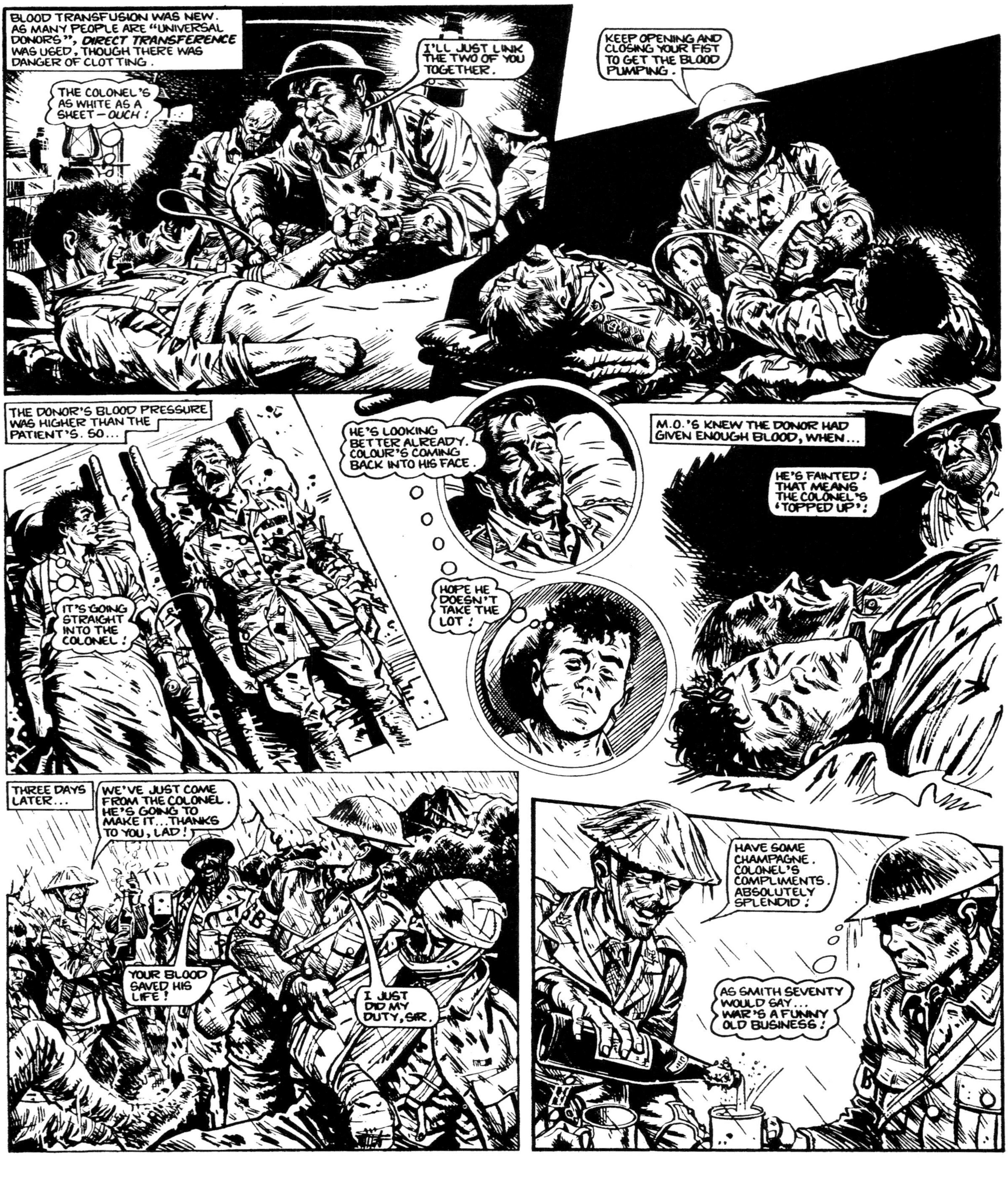

BLOOD TRANSFUSION WAS NEW. AS MANY PEOPLE ARE "UNIVERSAL DONORS", DIRECT TRANSFERENCE WAS USED, THOUGH THERE WAS DANGER OF CLOTTING.
I'LL JUST LINK THE TWO OF YOU TOGETHER.
THE COLONEL'S AS WHITE AS A SHEET—OUCH!
KEEP OPENING AND CLOSING YOUR FIST TO GET THE BLOOD PUMPING.
THE DONOR'S BLOOD PRESSURE WAS HIGHER THAN THE PATIENT'S. SO...
IT'S GOING STRAIGHT INTO THE COLONEL!
HE'S LOOKING BETTER ALREADY. COLOUR'S COMING BACK INTO HIS FACE.
HOPE HE DOESN'T TAKE THE LOT!
M.O.'S KNEW THE DONOR HAD GIVEN ENOUGH BLOOD, WHEN...
HE'S FAINTED! THAT MEANS THE COLONEL'S 'TOPPED UP'!
THREE DAYS LATER...
WE'VE JUST COME FROM THE COLONEL. HE'S GOING TO MAKE IT... THANKS TO YOU, LAD!
YOUR BLOOD SAVED HIS LIFE!
I JUST DID MY DUTY, SIR.
HAVE SOME CHAMPAGNE. COLONEL'S COMPLIMENTS. ABSOLUTELY SPLENDID!
AS SMITH SEVENTY WOULD SAY... WAR'S A FUNNY OLD BUSINESS!

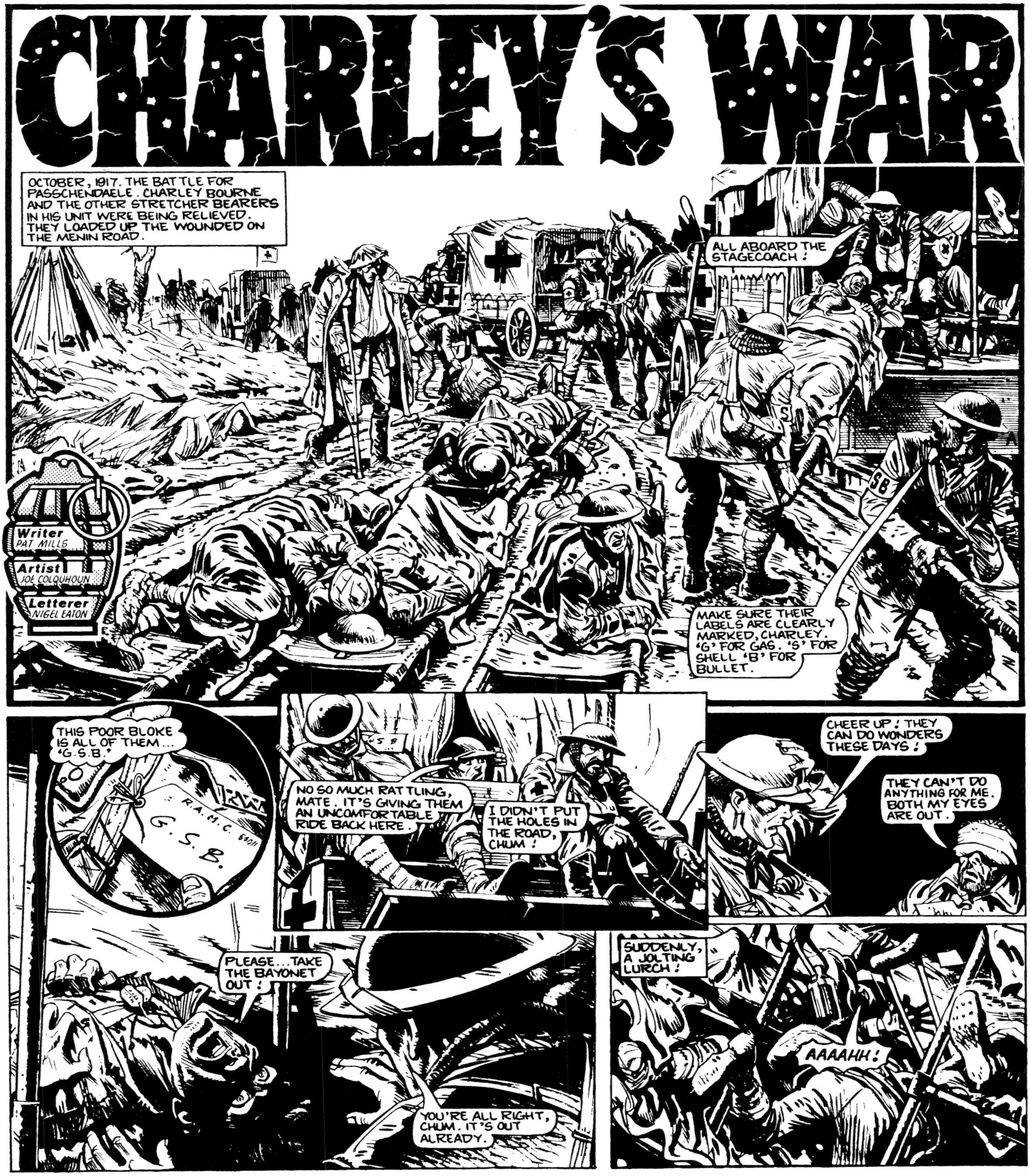
CHARLEY'S WAR
OCTOBER, 1917. THE BATTLE FOR PASSCHENDAELE. CHARLEY BOURNE AND THE OTHER STRETCHER BEARERS IN HIS UNIT WERE BEING RELIEVED. THEY LOADED UP THE WOUNDED ON THE MENIN ROAD.
ALL ABOARD THE STAGECOACH!
Writer PAT MILLS
Artist JOE COLQUHOUN
Letterer NIGEL EATON
MAKE SURE THEIR LABELS ARE CLEARLY MARKED, CHARLEY. 'G' FOR GAS. 'S' FOR SHELL 'B' FOR BULLET.
THIS POOR BLOKE IS ALL OF THEM... 'G.S.B.'
R.A.M.C.
G.S.B.
NO SO MUCH RATTLING, MATE. IT'S GIVING THEM AN UNCOMFORTABLE RIDE BACK HERE.
I DIDN'T PUT THE HOLES IN THE ROAD, CHUM!
CHEER UP! THEY CAN DO WONDERS THESE DAYS!
THEY CAN'T DO ANYTHING FOR ME. BOTH MY EYES ARE OUT.
PLEASE... TAKE THE BAYONET OUT!
YOU'RE ALL RIGHT, CHUM. IT'S OUT ALREADY.
SUDDENLY, A JOLTING LURCH!
AAAAHH!

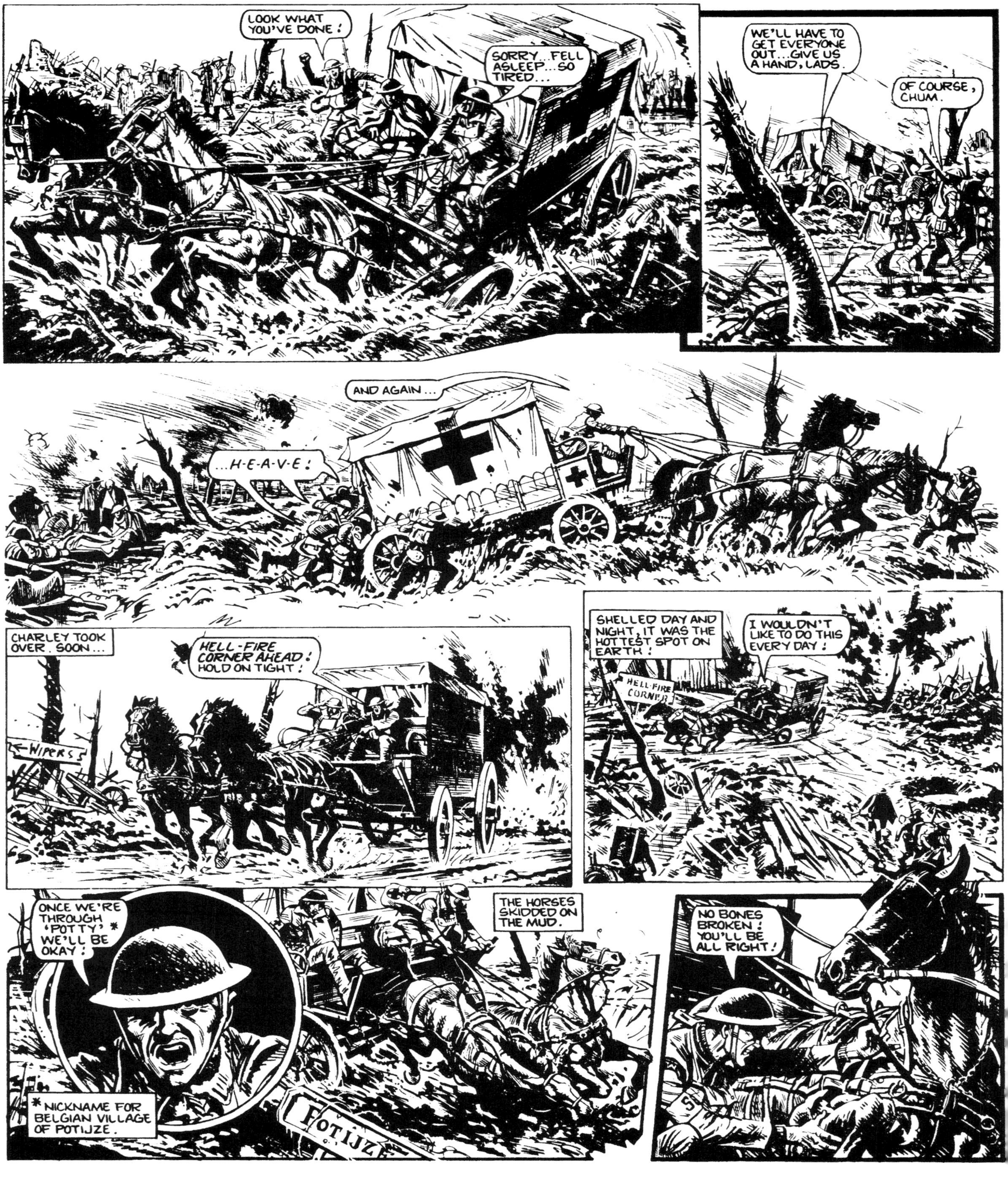
LOOK WHAT YOU'VE DONE!
SORRY...FELL ASLEEP...SO TIRED...
WE'LL HAVE TO GET EVERYONE OUT...GIVE US A HAND, LADS.
OF COURSE, CHUM.
AND AGAIN...
...H-E-A-V-E!
CHARLEY TOOK OVER. SOON...
HELL-FIRE CORNER AHEAD! HOLD ON TIGHT!
WIPERS
SHELLED DAY AND NIGHT, IT WAS THE HOTTEST SPOT ON EARTH!
I WOULDN'T LIKE TO DO THIS EVERY DAY!
HELL-FIRE CORNER
ONCE WE'RE THROUGH 'POTTY'* WE'LL BE OKAY!
THE HORSES SKIDDED ON THE MUD.
*NICKNAME FOR BELGIAN VILLAGE OF POTIJZE.
POTIJZ
NO BONES BROKEN! YOU'LL BE ALL RIGHT!

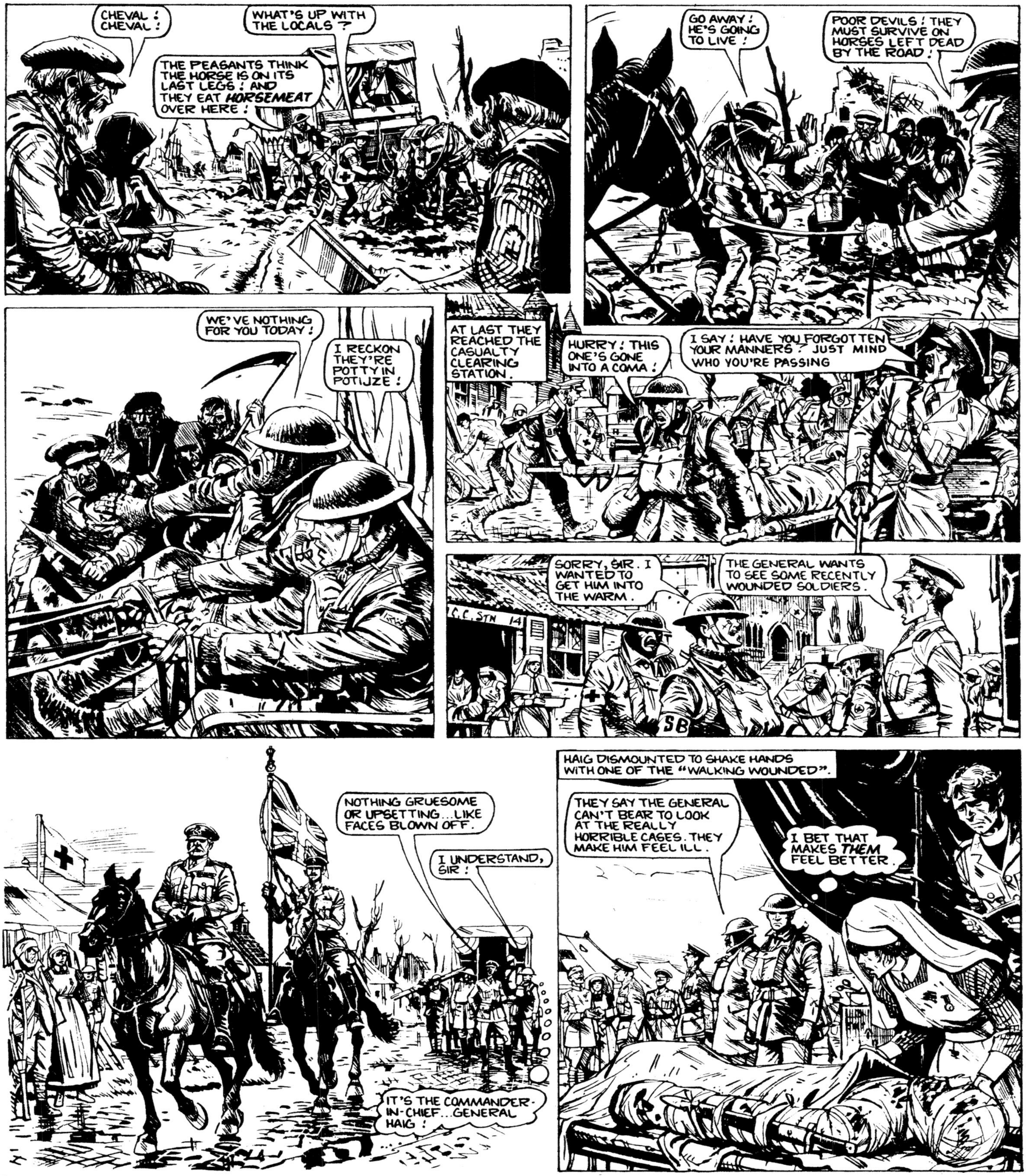
CHEVAL! CHEVAL!
WHAT'S UP WITH THE LOCALS?
THE PEASANTS THINK THE HORSE IS ON ITS LAST LEGS! AND THEY EAT HORSEMEAT OVER HERE!
GO AWAY! HE'S GOING TO LIVE!
POOR DEVILS! THEY MUST SURVIVE ON HORSES LEFT DEAD BY THE ROAD!
WE'VE NOTHING FOR YOU TODAY!
I RECKON THEY'RE POTTY IN POTIJZE!
AT LAST THEY REACHED THE CASUALTY CLEARING STATION.
HURRY! THIS ONE'S GONE INTO A COMA!
I SAY! HAVE YOU FORGOTTEN YOUR MANNERS? JUST MIND WHO YOU'RE PASSING
SORRY, SIR. I WANTED TO GET HIM INTO THE WARM.
THE GENERAL WANTS TO SEE SOME RECENTLY WOUNDED SOLDIERS.
C.C. STN 14
SB
NOTHING GRUESOME OR UPSETTING... LIKE FACES BLOWN OFF.
I UNDERSTAND, SIR!
IT'S THE COMMANDER-IN-CHIEF... GENERAL HAIG!
HAIG DISMOUNTED TO SHAKE HANDS WITH ONE OF THE "WALKING WOUNDED".
THEY SAY THE GENERAL CAN'T BEAR TO LOOK AT THE REALLY HORRIBLE CASES. THEY MAKE HIM FEEL ILL.
I BET THAT MAKES THEM FEEL BETTER.

CHARLEY'S WAR

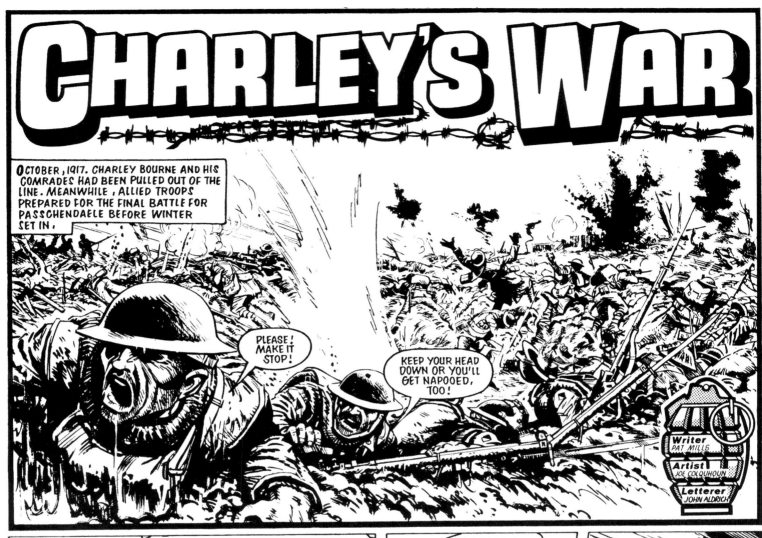

OCTOBER, 1917. CHARLEY BOURNE AND HIS COMRADES HAD BEEN PULLED OUT OF THE LINE. MEANWHILE, ALLIED TROOPS PREPARED FOR THE FINAL BATTLE FOR PASSCHENDAELE BEFORE WINTER SET IN.

PLEASE! MAKE IT STOP!

KEEP YOUR HEAD DOWN OR YOU'LL GET NAPOOED, TOO!

Writer
PAT MILLS

Artist
JOE COLQUHOUN

Letterer
JOHN ALDRICH

AN AMERICAN, DOCTOR FRANKLIN SHOOTER, HAD TAKEN OVER WHILE CHARLEY'S OLD MEDICAL OFFICER WENT ON LEAVE.

THERE'LL BE A FEW CHANGES NOW I'M M.O. WE'LL START WITH THIS EXAM. I WANT TO SEE HOW MUCH YOU BRITISH STRETCHER BEARERS KNOW ABOUT MEDICINE.

HECK! I DON'T UNDERSTAND ANY OF THESE QUESTIONS!

HOW DID YOU GET ON, CHARLEY?

HOPELESS, JACK. I'M NOT GOOD AT TESTS LIKE YOU.

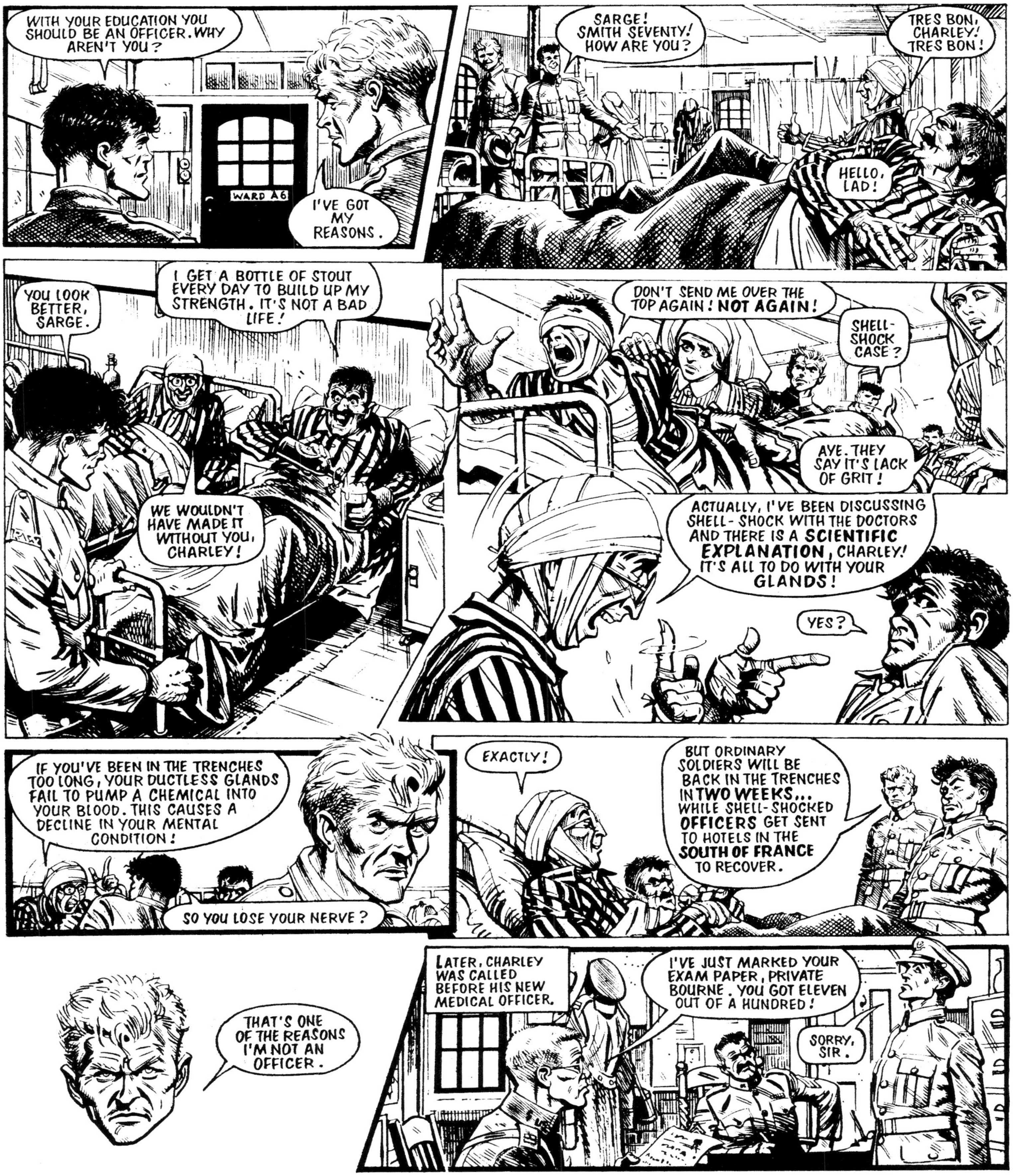

WITH YOUR EDUCATION YOU SHOULD BE AN OFFICER. WHY AREN'T YOU?
WARD A6
I'VE GOT MY REASONS.
SARGE! SMITH SEVENTY! HOW ARE YOU?
TRES BON, CHARLEY! TRES BON!
HELLO, LAD!
YOU LOOK BETTER, SARGE.
I GET A BOTTLE OF STOUT EVERY DAY TO BUILD UP MY STRENGTH. IT'S NOT A BAD LIFE!
WE WOULDN'T HAVE MADE IT WITHOUT YOU, CHARLEY!
DON'T SEND ME OVER THE TOP AGAIN! NOT AGAIN!
SHELL-SHOCK CASE?
AYE. THEY SAY IT'S LACK OF GRIT!
ACTUALLY, I'VE BEEN DISCUSSING SHELL-SHOCK WITH THE DOCTORS AND THERE IS A SCIENTIFIC EXPLANATION, CHARLEY! IT'S ALL TO DO WITH YOUR GLANDS!
YES?
IF YOU'VE BEEN IN THE TRENCHES TOO LONG, YOUR DUCTLESS GLANDS FAIL TO PUMP A CHEMICAL INTO YOUR BLOOD. THIS CAUSES A DECLINE IN YOUR MENTAL CONDITION!
SO YOU LOSE YOUR NERVE?
EXACTLY!
BUT ORDINARY SOLDIERS WILL BE BACK IN THE TRENCHES IN TWO WEEKS... WHILE SHELL-SHOCKED OFFICERS GET SENT TO HOTELS IN THE SOUTH OF FRANCE TO RECOVER.
THAT'S ONE OF THE REASONS I'M NOT AN OFFICER.
LATER, CHARLEY WAS CALLED BEFORE HIS NEW MEDICAL OFFICER.
I'VE JUST MARKED YOUR EXAM PAPER, PRIVATE BOURNE. YOU GOT ELEVEN OUT OF A HUNDRED!
SORRY, SIR.

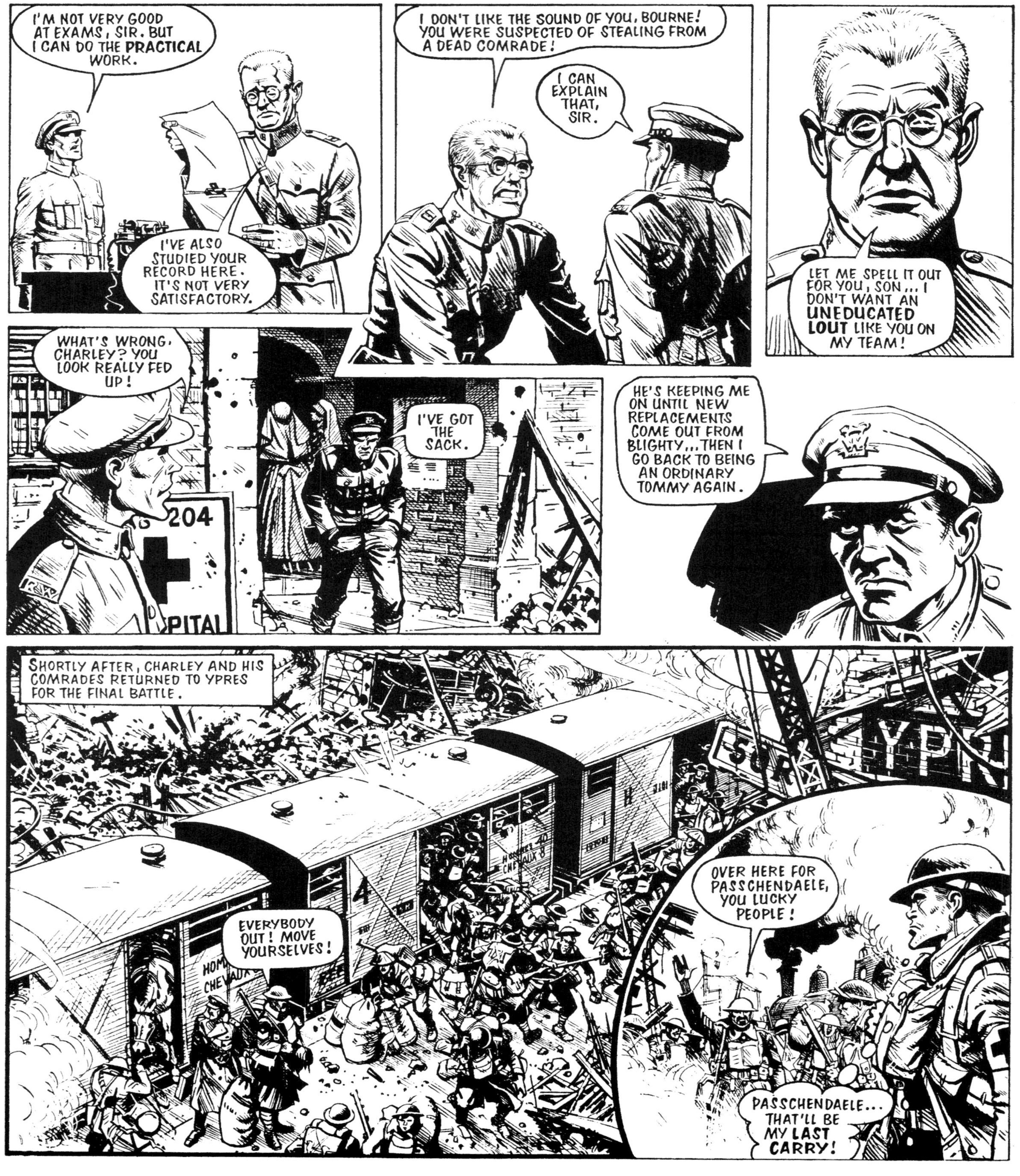
I'M NOT VERY GOOD AT EXAMS, SIR. BUT I CAN DO THE PRACTICAL WORK.
I'VE ALSO STUDIED YOUR RECORD HERE. IT'S NOT VERY SATISFACTORY.
I DON'T LIKE THE SOUND OF YOU, BOURNE! YOU WERE SUSPECTED OF STEALING FROM A DEAD COMRADE!
I CAN EXPLAIN THAT, SIR.
LET ME SPELL IT OUT FOR YOU, SON... I DON'T WANT AN UNEDUCATED LOUT LIKE YOU ON MY TEAM!
WHAT'S WRONG, CHARLEY? YOU LOOK REALLY FED UP!
204
PITAL
I'VE GOT THE SACK.
HE'S KEEPING ME ON UNTIL NEW REPLACEMENTS COME OUT FROM BLIGHTY... THEN I GO BACK TO BEING AN ORDINARY TOMMY AGAIN.
SHORTLY AFTER, CHARLEY AND HIS COMRADES RETURNED TO YPRES FOR THE FINAL BATTLE.
YPR
EVERYBODY OUT! MOVE YOURSELVES!
OVER HERE FOR PASSCHENDAELE, YOU LUCKY PEOPLE!
PASSCHENDAELE... THAT'LL BE MY LAST CARRY!

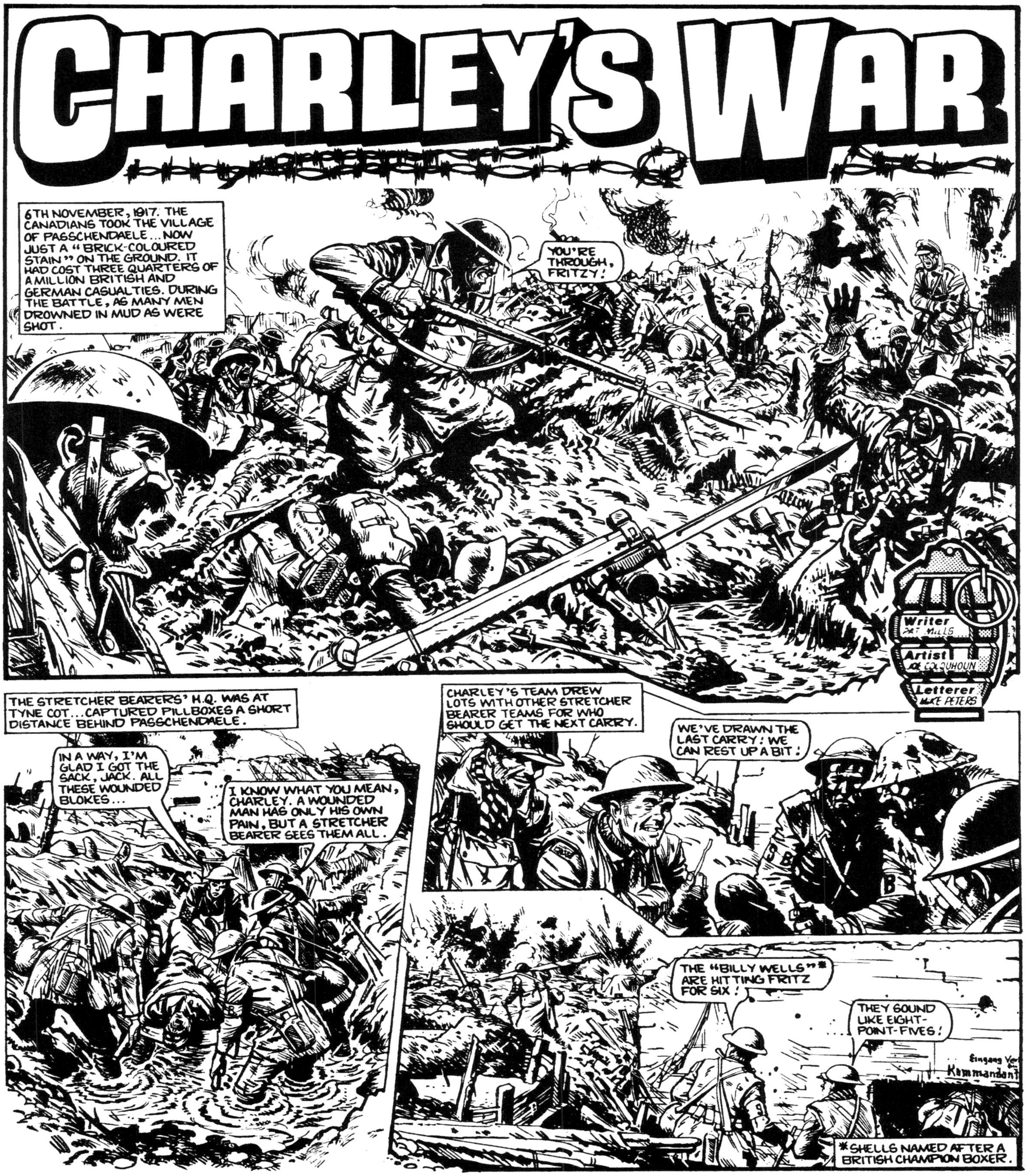
CHARLEY'S WAR
6TH NOVEMBER, 1917. THE CANADIANS TOOK THE VILLAGE OF PASSCHENDAELE... NOW JUST A "BRICK-COLOURED STAIN" ON THE GROUND. IT HAD COST THREE QUARTERS OF A MILLION BRITISH AND GERMAN CASUALTIES. DURING THE BATTLE, AS MANY MEN DROWNED IN MUD AS WERE SHOT.
YOU'RE THROUGH, FRITZY!
Writer
Artist
Letterer
PETERS
THE STRETCHER BEARERS' H.Q. WAS AT TYNE COT... CAPTURED PILLBOXES A SHORT DISTANCE BEHIND PASSCHENDAELE.
IN A WAY, I'M GLAD I GOT THE SACK, JACK. ALL THESE WOUNDED BLOKES...
I KNOW WHAT YOU MEAN, CHARLEY. A WOUNDED MAN HAS ONLY HIS OWN PAIN, BUT A STRETCHER BEARER SEES THEM ALL.
CHARLEY'S TEAM DREW LOTS WITH OTHER STRETCHER BEARER TEAMS FOR WHO SHOULD GET THE NEXT CARRY.
WE'VE DRAWN THE LAST CARRY! WE CAN REST UP A BIT!
THE "BILLY WELLS"* ARE HITTING FRITZ FOR SIX!
THEY SOUND LIKE EIGHT-POINT-FIVES!
Kommandant
*SHELLS NAMED AFTER A BRITISH CHAMPION BOXER.

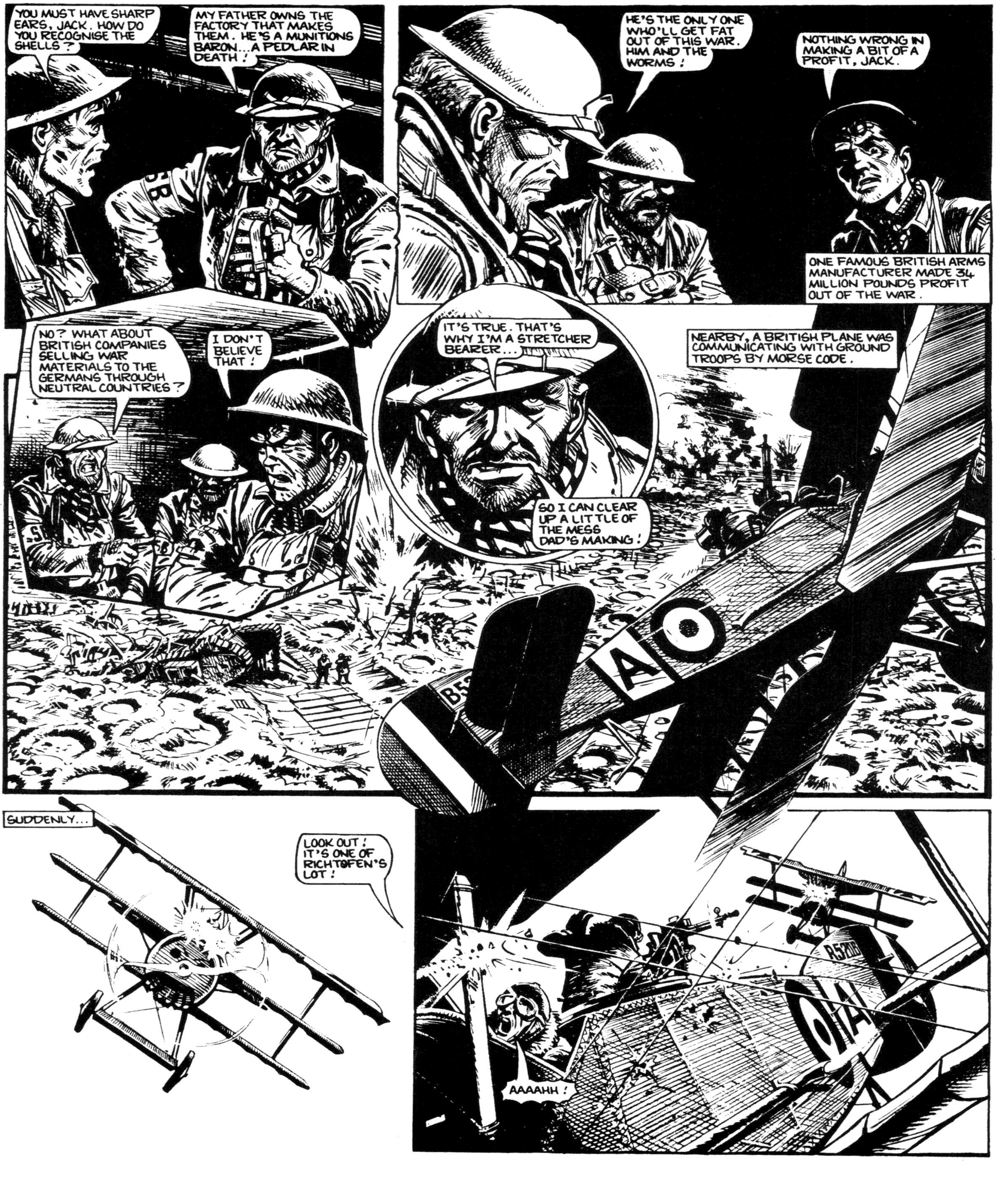
YOU MUST HAVE SHARP EARS, JACK. HOW DO YOU RECOGNISE THE SHELLS?
MY FATHER OWNS THE FACTORY THAT MAKES THEM. HE'S A MUNITIONS BARON... A PEDLAR IN DEATH!
HE'S THE ONLY ONE WHO'LL GET FAT OUT OF THIS WAR. HIM AND THE WORMS!
NOTHING WRONG IN MAKING A BIT OF A PROFIT, JACK.
ONE FAMOUS BRITISH ARMS MANUFACTURER MADE 34 MILLION POUNDS PROFIT OUT OF THE WAR.
NO? WHAT ABOUT BRITISH COMPANIES SELLING WAR MATERIALS TO THE GERMANS THROUGH NEUTRAL COUNTRIES?
I DON'T BELIEVE THAT!
IT'S TRUE. THAT'S WHY I'M A STRETCHER BEARER...
SO I CAN CLEAR UP A LITTLE OF THE MESS DAD'S MAKING!
NEARBY, A BRITISH PLANE WAS COMMUNICATING WITH GROUND TROOPS BY MORSE CODE.
SUDDENLY...
LOOK OUT! IT'S ONE OF RICHTOFEN'S LOT!
AAAAHH!

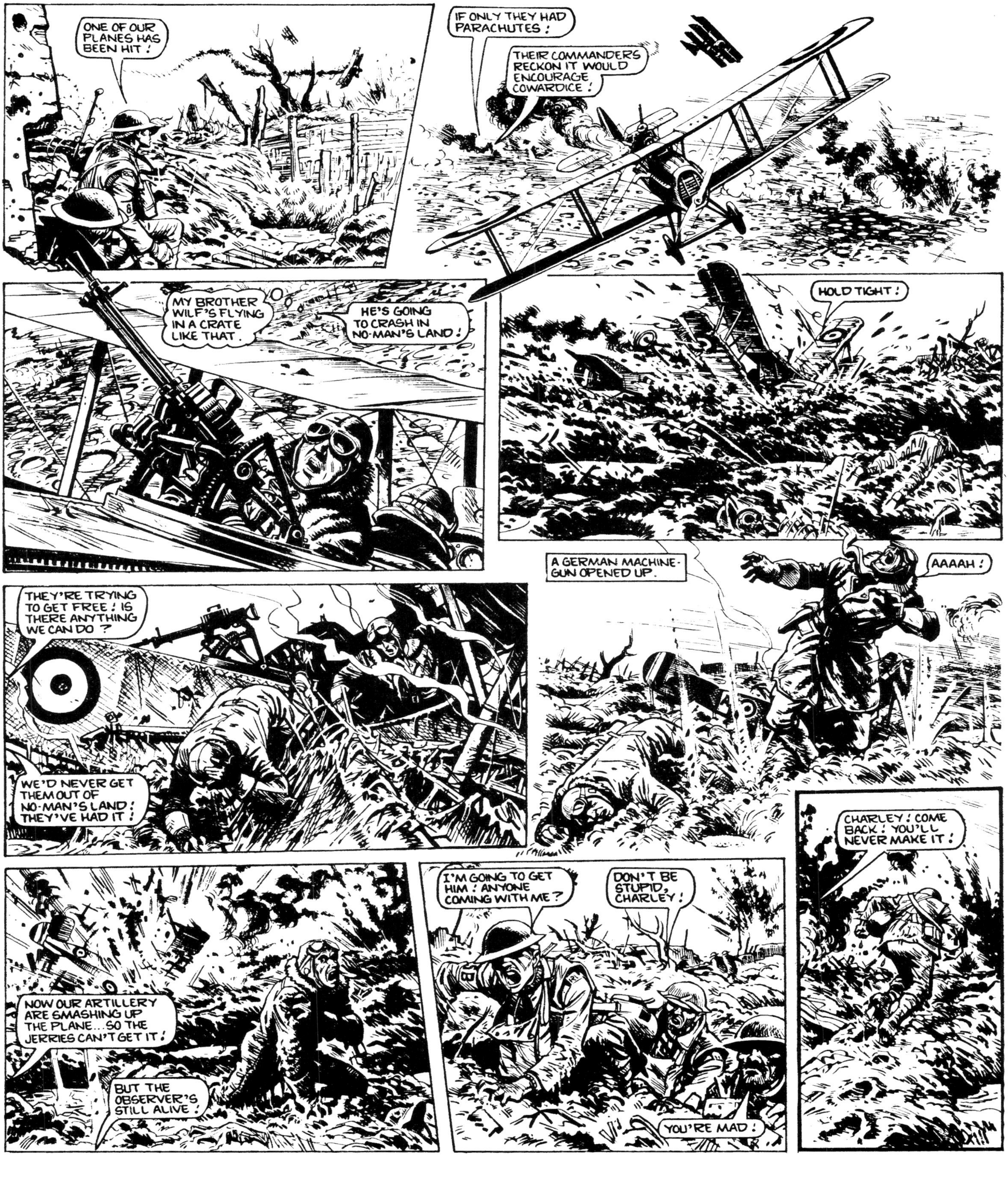

ONE OF OUR PLANES HAS BEEN HIT!
IF ONLY THEY HAD PARACHUTES!
THEIR COMMANDERS RECKON IT WOULD ENCOURAGE COWARDICE!
MY BROTHER WILF'S FLYING IN A CRATE LIKE THAT.
HE'S GOING TO CRASH IN NO-MAN'S LAND!
HOLD TIGHT!
A GERMAN MACHINE-GUN OPENED UP.
AAAAH!
THEY'RE TRYING TO GET FREE! IS THERE ANYTHING WE CAN DO?
WE'D NEVER GET THEM OUT OF NO-MAN'S LAND! THEY'VE HAD IT!
NOW OUR ARTILLERY ARE SMASHING UP THE PLANE... SO THE JERRIES CAN'T GET IT!
BUT THE OBSERVER'S STILL ALIVE!
I'M GOING TO GET HIM! ANYONE COMING WITH ME?
DON'T BE STUPID, CHARLEY!
YOU'RE MAD!
CHARLEY! COME BACK! YOU'LL NEVER MAKE IT!

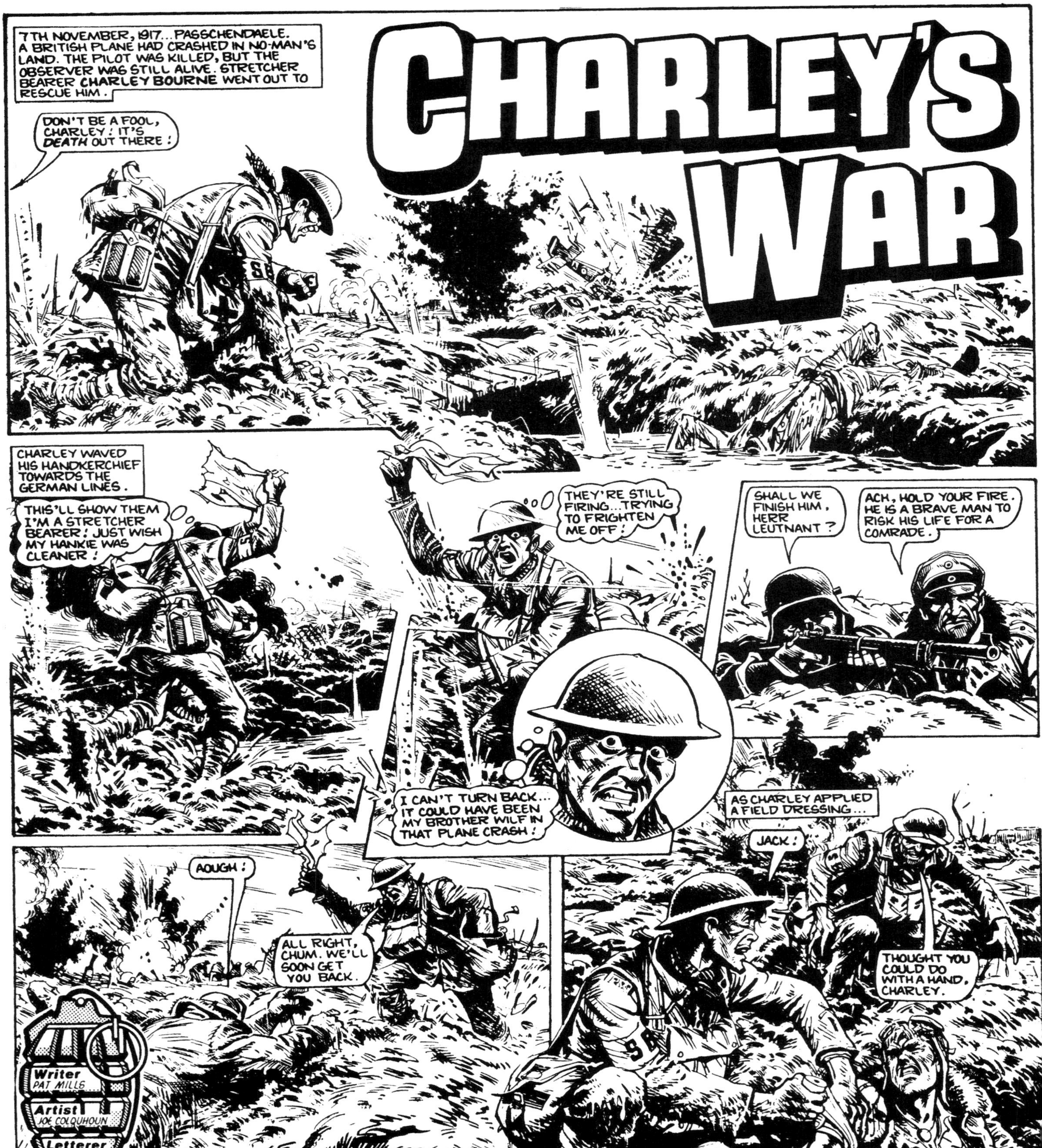

7TH NOVEMBER, 1917... PASSCHENDAELE. A BRITISH PLANE HAD CRASHED IN NO-MAN'S LAND. THE PILOT WAS KILLED, BUT THE OBSERVER WAS STILL ALIVE. STRETCHER BEARER CHARLEY BOURNE WENT OUT TO RESCUE HIM.
CHARLEY'S WAR
DON'T BE A FOOL, CHARLEY: IT'S DEATH OUT THERE!
CHARLEY WAVED HIS HANDKERCHIEF TOWARDS THE GERMAN LINES.
THIS'LL SHOW THEM I'M A STRETCHER BEARER! JUST WISH MY HANKIE WAS CLEANER!
THEY'RE STILL FIRING...TRYING TO FRIGHTEN ME OFF!
I CAN'T TURN BACK... IT COULD HAVE BEEN MY BROTHER WILF IN THAT PLANE CRASH!
SHALL WE FINISH HIM, HERR LEUTNANT?
ACH, HOLD YOUR FIRE. HE IS A BRAVE MAN TO RISK HIS LIFE FOR A COMRADE.
AOUGH!
ALL RIGHT, CHUM. WE'LL SOON GET YOU BACK.
Writer PAT MILLS
Artist JOE COLQUHOUN
Letterer NIGEL EATON
AS CHARLEY APPLIED A FIELD DRESSING...
JACK!
THOUGHT YOU COULD DO WITH A HAND, CHARLEY.

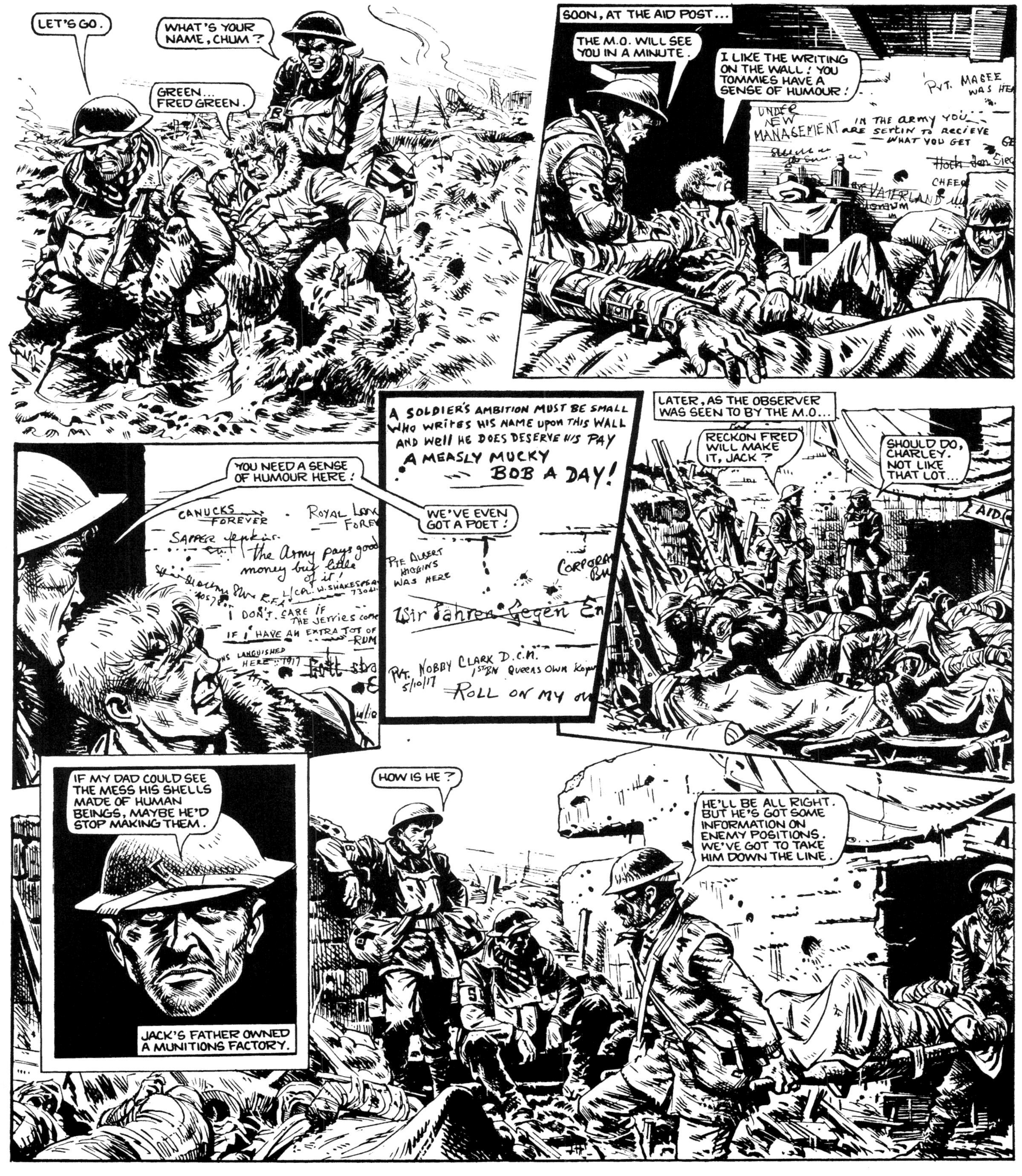
LET'S GO.
WHAT'S YOUR NAME, CHUM ?
GREEN... FRED GREEN.
SOON, AT THE AID POST...
THE M.O. WILL SEE YOU IN A MINUTE.
I LIKE THE WRITING ON THE WALL : YOU TOMMIES HAVE A SENSE OF HUMOUR !
PVT. MAGEE WAS HE
UNDER NEW MANAGEMENT
IN THE ARMY YOU ARE SERTIN TO RECIEVE WHAT YOU GET
YOU NEED A SENSE OF HUMOUR HERE !
WE'VE EVEN GOT A POET !
CANUCKS FOREVER
the Army pays good money but little of it!
I DON'T CARE IF THE JERRIES COME IF I HAVE AN EXTRA TOT OF RUM
A SOLDIER'S AMBITION MUST BE SMALL
WHO WRITES HIS NAME UPON THIS WALL
AND WELL HE DOES DESERVE HIS PAY
A MEASLY MUCKY BOB A DAY!
PTE ALBERT HIGGINS WAS HERE
PVT. NOBBY CLARK D.C.M. 5/10/17
ROLL ON MY
LATER, AS THE OBSERVER WAS SEEN TO BY THE M.O...
RECKON FRED WILL MAKE IT, JACK ?
SHOULD DO, CHARLEY. NOT LIKE THAT LOT...
IF MY DAD COULD SEE THE MESS HIS SHELLS MADE OF HUMAN BEINGS, MAYBE HE'D STOP MAKING THEM.
JACK'S FATHER OWNED A MUNITIONS FACTORY.
HOW IS HE ?
HE'LL BE ALL RIGHT. BUT HE'S GOT SOME INFORMATION ON ENEMY POSITIONS. WE'VE GOT TO TAKE HIM DOWN THE LINE.

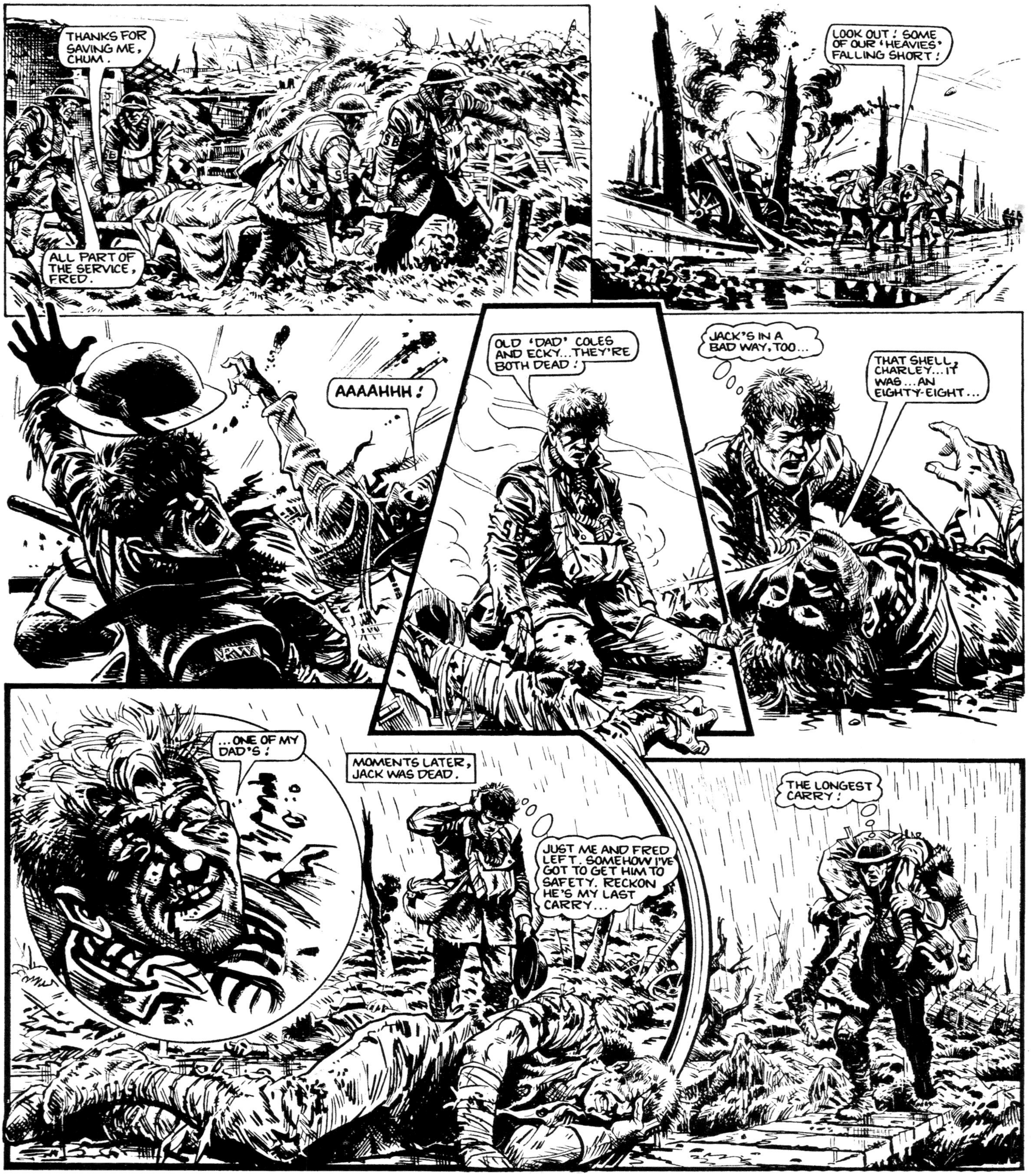
THANKS FOR SAVING ME, CHUM.
ALL PART OF THE SERVICE, FRED.
LOOK OUT! SOME OF OUR 'HEAVIES' FALLING SHORT!
AAAAHHH!
OLD 'DAD' COLES AND ECKY... THEY'RE BOTH DEAD!
JACK'S IN A BAD WAY, TOO...
THAT SHELL, CHARLEY... IT WAS... AN EIGHTY-EIGHT...
...ONE OF MY DAD'S!
MOMENTS LATER, JACK WAS DEAD.
JUST ME AND FRED LEFT. SOMEHOW I'VE GOT TO GET HIM TO SAFETY. RECKON HE'S MY LAST CARRY...
THE LONGEST CARRY!

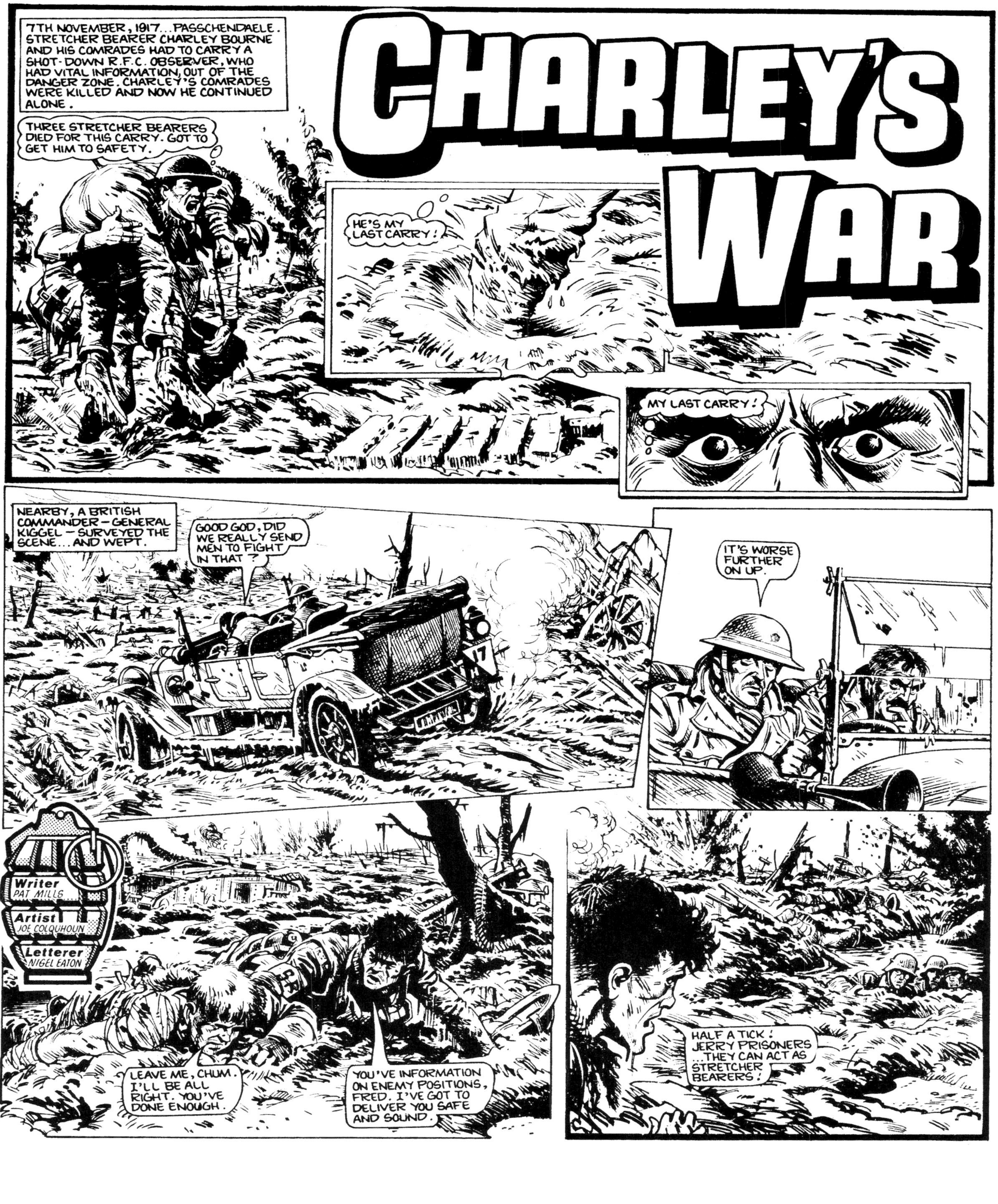

CHARLEY'S WAR
7TH NOVEMBER, 1917... PASSCHENDAELE. STRETCHER BEARER CHARLEY BOURNE AND HIS COMRADES HAD TO CARRY A SHOT-DOWN R.F.C. OBSERVER, WHO HAD VITAL INFORMATION, OUT OF THE DANGER ZONE. CHARLEY'S COMRADES WERE KILLED AND NOW HE CONTINUED ALONE.
THREE STRETCHER BEARERS DIED FOR THIS CARRY. GOT TO GET HIM TO SAFETY.
HE'S MY LAST CARRY!
MY LAST CARRY!
NEARBY, A BRITISH COMMANDER — GENERAL KIGGEL — SURVEYED THE SCENE... AND WEPT.
GOOD GOD, DID WE REALLY SEND MEN TO FIGHT IN THAT?
IT'S WORSE FURTHER ON UP.
Writer PAT MILLS
Artist JOE COLQUHOUN
Letterer NIGEL EATON
LEAVE ME, CHUM. I'LL BE ALL RIGHT. YOU'VE DONE ENOUGH.
YOU'VE INFORMATION ON ENEMY POSITIONS, FRED. I'VE GOT TO DELIVER YOU SAFE AND SOUND.
HALF A TICK! JERRY PRISONERS ...THEY CAN ACT AS STRETCHER BEARERS!

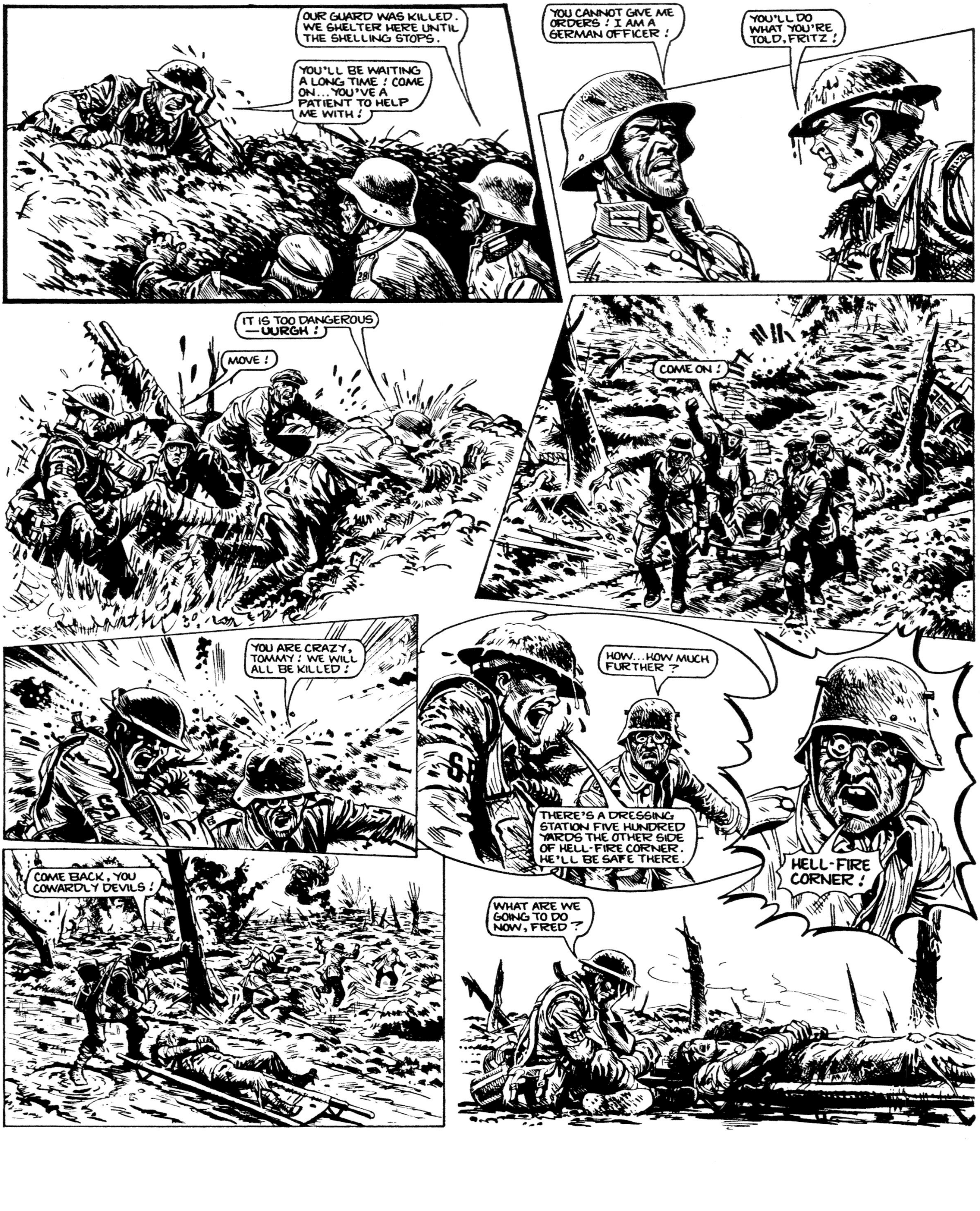
OUR GUARD WAS KILLED. WE SHELTER HERE UNTIL THE SHELLING STOPS.
YOU'LL BE WAITING A LONG TIME! COME ON... YOU'VE A PATIENT TO HELP ME WITH!
YOU CANNOT GIVE ME ORDERS! I AM A GERMAN OFFICER!
YOU'LL DO WHAT YOU'RE TOLD, FRITZ!
MOVE!
IT IS TOO DANGEROUS —UURGH!
COME ON!
YOU ARE CRAZY, TOMMY! WE WILL ALL BE KILLED!
HOW...HOW MUCH FURTHER?
THERE'S A DRESSING STATION FIVE HUNDRED YARDS THE OTHER SIDE OF HELL-FIRE CORNER. HE'LL BE SAFE THERE.
HELL-FIRE CORNER!
COME BACK, YOU COWARDLY DEVILS!
WHAT ARE WE GOING TO DO NOW, FRED?

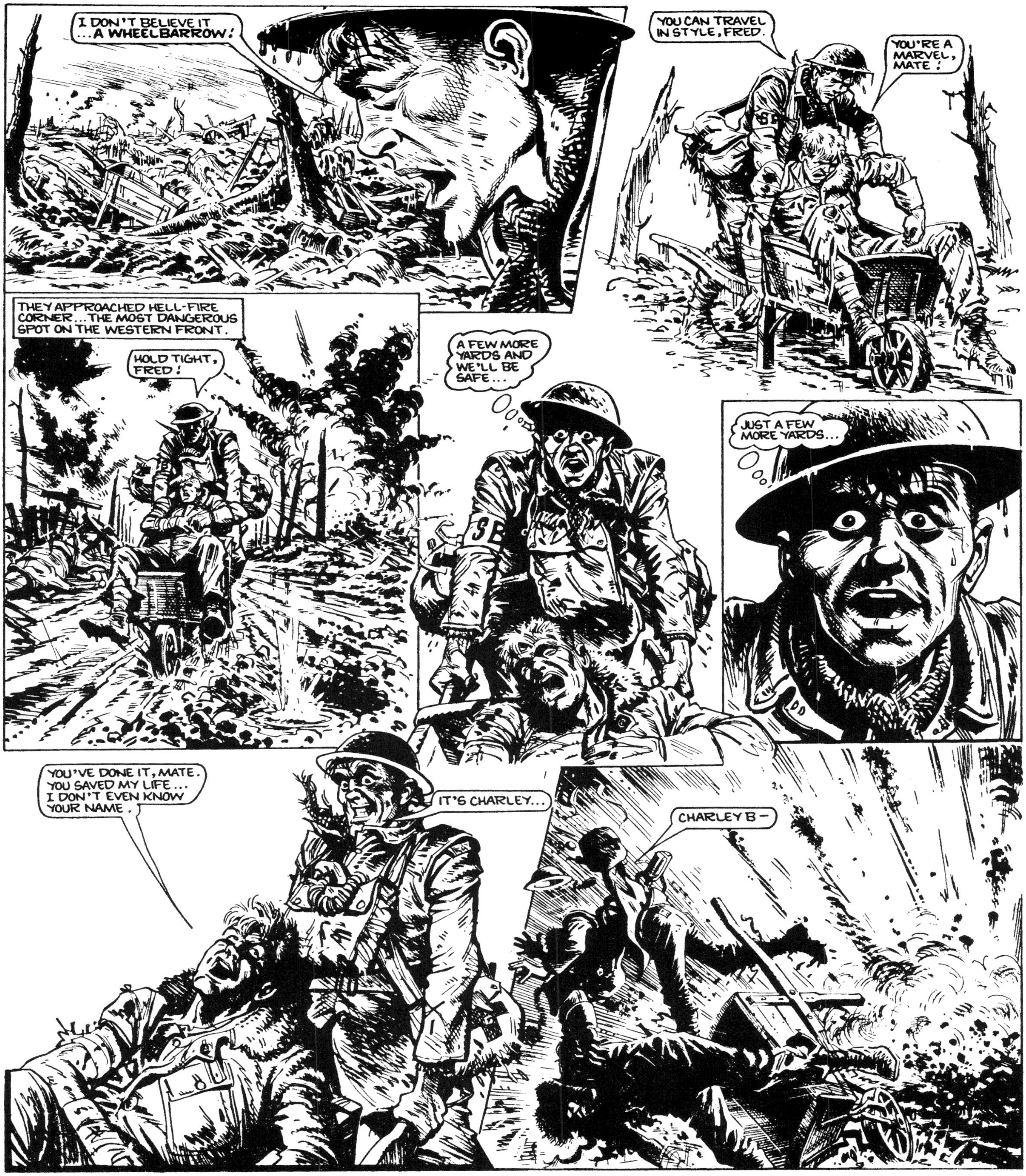
I DON'T BELIEVE IT ...A WHEELBARROW!
YOU CAN TRAVEL IN STYLE, FRED.
YOU'RE A MARVEL, MATE!
THEY APPROACHED HELL-FIRE CORNER...THE MOST DANGEROUS SPOT ON THE WESTERN FRONT.
HOLD TIGHT, FRED!
A FEW MORE YARDS AND WE'LL BE SAFE...
JUST A FEW MORE YARDS...
YOU'VE DONE IT, MATE. YOU SAVED MY LIFE... I DON'T EVEN KNOW YOUR NAME.
IT'S CHARLEY...
CHARLEY B—

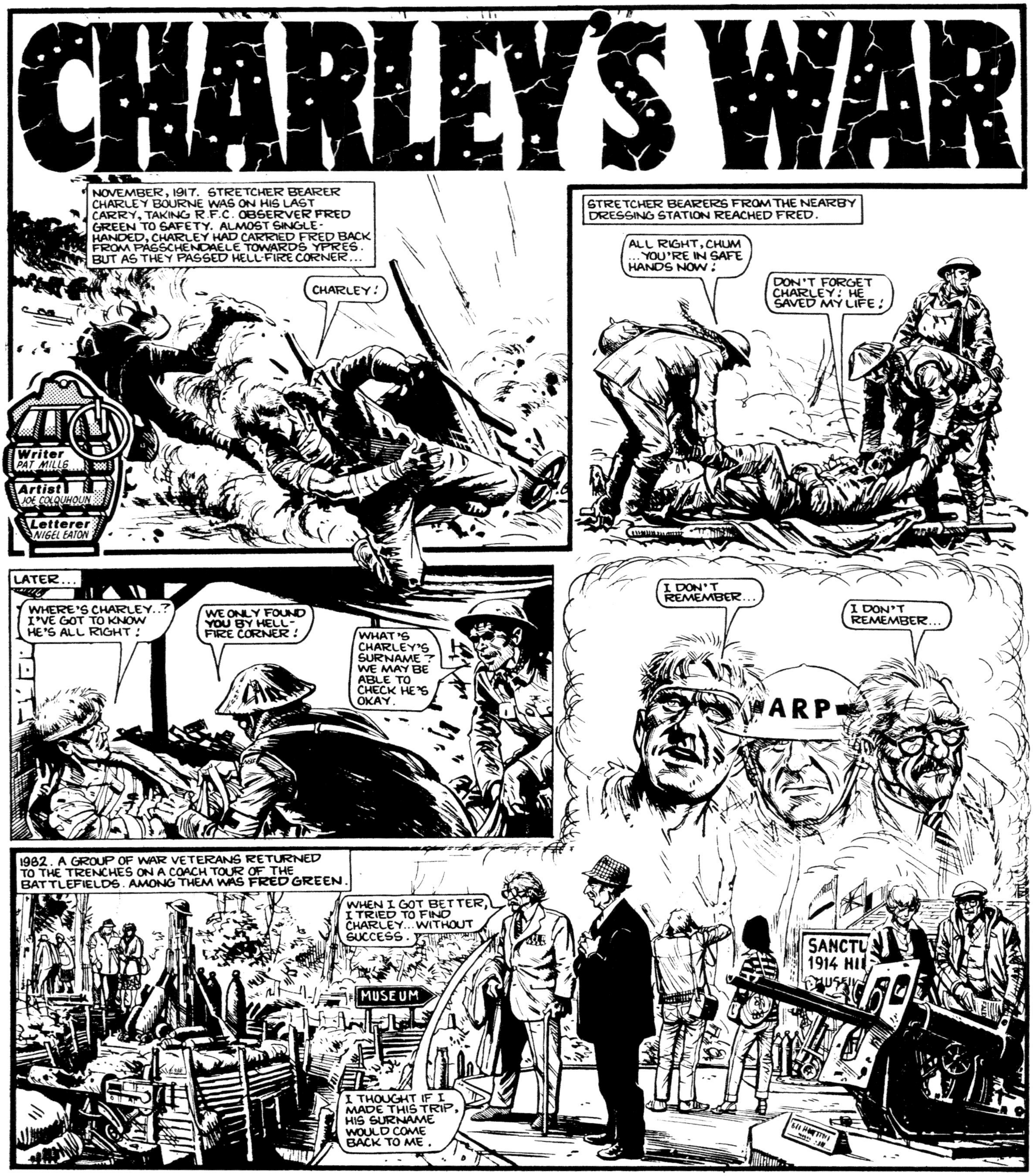
CHARLEY'S WAR
NOVEMBER, 1917. STRETCHER BEARER CHARLEY BOURNE WAS ON HIS LAST CARRY, TAKING R.F.C. OBSERVER FRED GREEN TO SAFETY. ALMOST SINGLE-HANDED, CHARLEY HAD CARRIED FRED BACK FROM PASSCHENDAELE TOWARDS YPRES. BUT AS THEY PASSED HELL-FIRE CORNER...
CHARLEY!
Writer PAT MILLS
Artist JOE COLQUHOUN
Letterer NIGEL EATON
STRETCHER BEARERS FROM THE NEARBY DRESSING STATION REACHED FRED.
ALL RIGHT, CHUM ...YOU'RE IN SAFE HANDS NOW!
DON'T FORGET CHARLEY! HE SAVED MY LIFE!
LATER...
WHERE'S CHARLEY..? I'VE GOT TO KNOW HE'S ALL RIGHT!
WE ONLY FOUND YOU BY HELL-FIRE CORNER!
WHAT'S CHARLEY'S SURNAME? WE MAY BE ABLE TO CHECK HE'S OKAY.
I DON'T REMEMBER...
I DON'T REMEMBER...
ARP
1982. A GROUP OF WAR VETERANS RETURNED TO THE TRENCHES ON A COACH TOUR OF THE BATTLEFIELDS. AMONG THEM WAS FRED GREEN.
WHEN I GOT BETTER, I TRIED TO FIND CHARLEY... WITHOUT SUCCESS.
MUSEUM
I THOUGHT IF I MADE THIS TRIP, HIS SURNAME WOULD COME BACK TO ME.

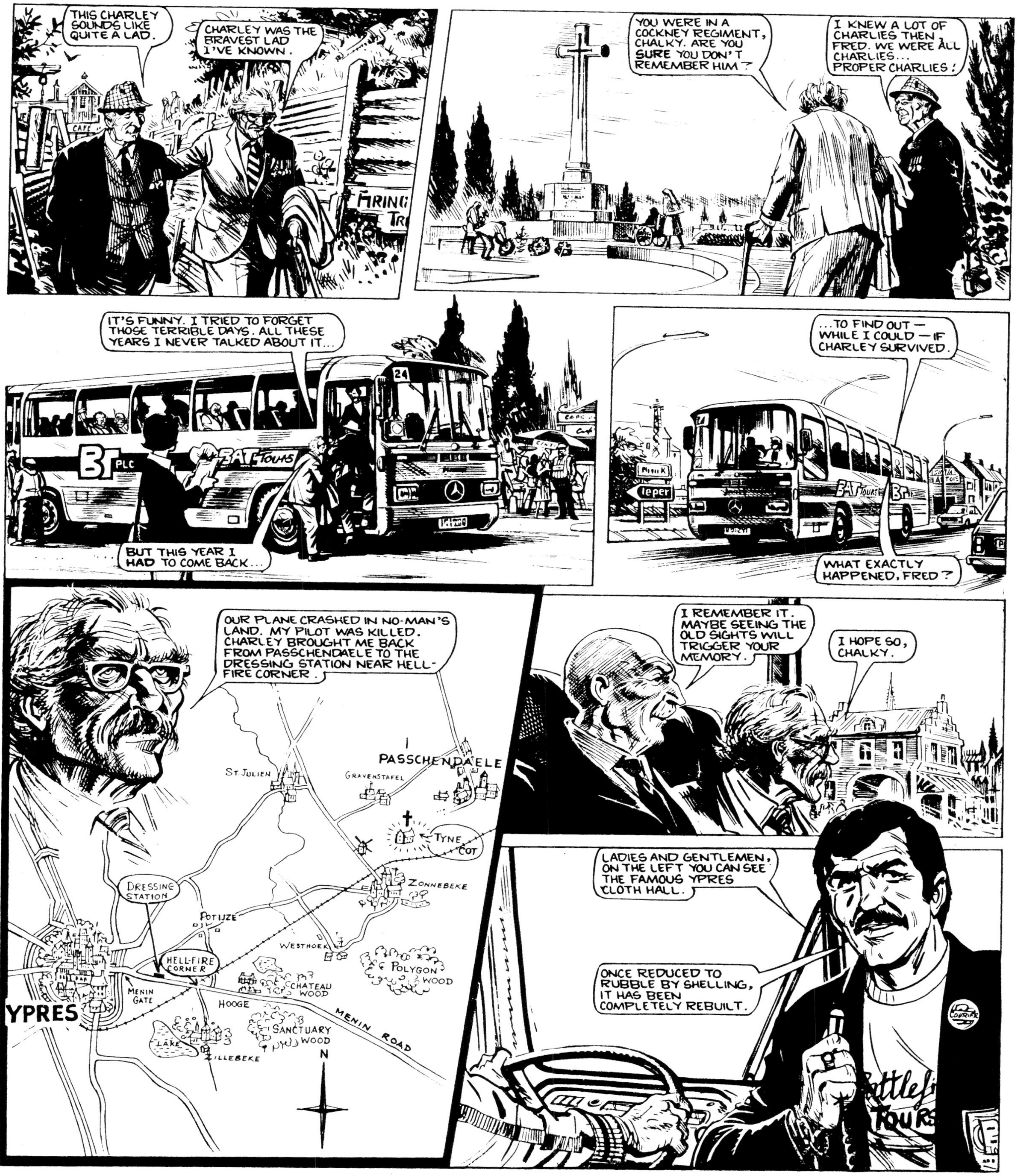
THIS CHARLEY SOUNDS LIKE QUITE A LAD.
CHARLEY WAS THE BRAVEST LAD I'VE KNOWN.
CAFE
YOU WERE IN A COCKNEY REGIMENT, CHALKY. ARE YOU SURE YOU DON'T REMEMBER HIM?
I KNEW A LOT OF CHARLIES THEN, FRED. WE WERE ALL CHARLIES... PROPER CHARLIES!
IT'S FUNNY. I TRIED TO FORGET THOSE TERRIBLE DAYS. ALL THESE YEARS I NEVER TALKED ABOUT IT...
24
BUT THIS YEAR I HAD TO COME BACK...
...TO FIND OUT — WHILE I COULD — IF CHARLEY SURVIVED.
Ieper
WHAT EXACTLY HAPPENED, FRED?
OUR PLANE CRASHED IN NO-MAN'S LAND. MY PILOT WAS KILLED. CHARLEY BROUGHT ME BACK FROM PASSCHENDAELE TO THE DRESSING STATION NEAR HELL-FIRE CORNER.
PASSCHENDAELE
ST. JULIEN
GRAVENSTAFEL
TYNE COT
DRESSING STATION
ZONNEBEKE
POTIJZE
WESTHOEK
POLYGON WOOD
HELL-FIRE CORNER
CHATEAU WOOD
MENIN GATE
HOOGE
YPRES
SANCTUARY WOOD
LAKE
ZILLEBEKE
MENIN ROAD
N
I REMEMBER IT. MAYBE SEEING THE OLD SIGHTS WILL TRIGGER YOUR MEMORY.
I HOPE SO, CHALKY.
LADIES AND GENTLEMEN, ON THE LEFT YOU CAN SEE THE FAMOUS YPRES CLOTH HALL.
ONCE REDUCED TO RUBBLE BY SHELLING, IT HAS BEEN COMPLETELY REBUILT.

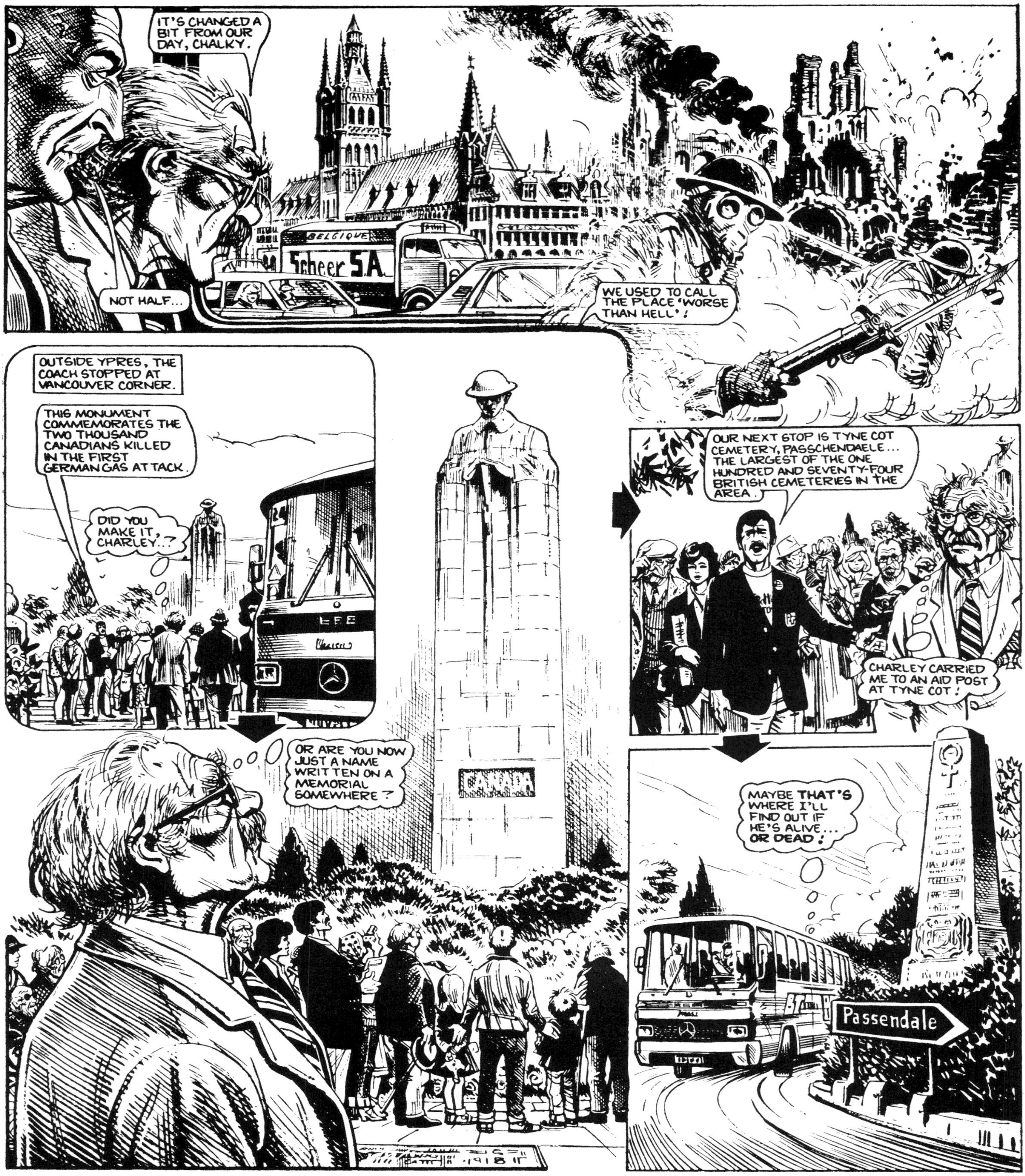
IT'S CHANGED A BIT FROM OUR DAY, CHALKY.
BELGIQUE
Scheer S.A.
NOT HALF...
WE USED TO CALL THE PLACE 'WORSE THAN HELL'!
OUTSIDE YPRES, THE COACH STOPPED AT VANCOUVER CORNER.
THIS MONUMENT COMMEMORATES THE TWO THOUSAND CANADIANS KILLED IN THE FIRST GERMAN GAS ATTACK.
DID YOU MAKE IT, CHARLEY...?
CANADA
OR ARE YOU NOW JUST A NAME WRITTEN ON A MEMORIAL SOMEWHERE?
OUR NEXT STOP IS TYNE COT CEMETERY, PASSCHENDAELE... THE LARGEST OF THE ONE HUNDRED AND SEVENTY-FOUR BRITISH CEMETERIES IN THE AREA.
CHARLEY CARRIED ME TO AN AID POST AT TYNE COT!
MAYBE **THAT'S** WHERE I'LL FIND OUT IF HE'S ALIVE... **OR DEAD**!
Passendale

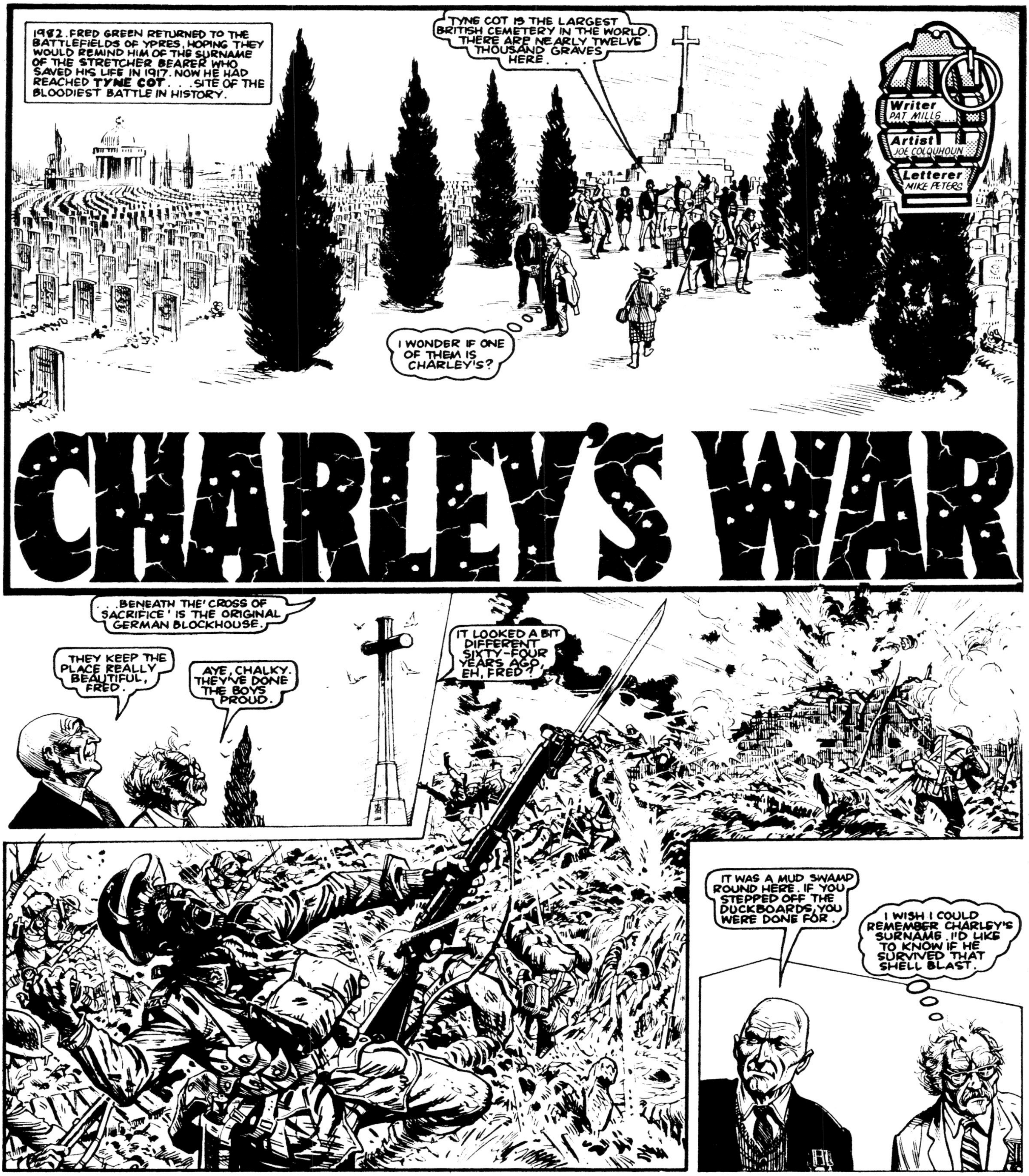
1982. FRED GREEN RETURNED TO THE BATTLEFIELDS OF YPRES, HOPING THEY WOULD REMIND HIM OF THE SURNAME OF THE STRETCHER BEARER WHO SAVED HIS LIFE IN 1917. NOW HE HAD REACHED TYNE COT . . . SITE OF THE BLOODIEST BATTLE IN HISTORY.
TYNE COT IS THE LARGEST BRITISH CEMETERY IN THE WORLD. THERE ARE NEARLY TWELVE THOUSAND GRAVES HERE . . .
I WONDER IF ONE OF THEM IS CHARLEY'S?
Writer PAT MILLS
Artist JOE COLQUHOUN
Letterer MIKE PETERS
CHARLEY'S WAR
. . BENEATH THE 'CROSS OF SACRIFICE' IS THE ORIGINAL GERMAN BLOCKHOUSE.
THEY KEEP THE PLACE REALLY BEAUTIFUL, FRED.
AYE, CHALKY. THEY'VE DONE THE BOYS PROUD.
IT LOOKED A BIT DIFFERENT SIXTY-FOUR YEARS AGO, EH, FRED?
IT WAS A MUD SWAMP ROUND HERE. IF YOU STEPPED OFF THE DUCKBOARDS, YOU WERE DONE FOR.
I WISH I COULD REMEMBER CHARLEY'S SURNAME. I'D LIKE TO KNOW IF HE SURVIVED THAT SHELL BLAST.

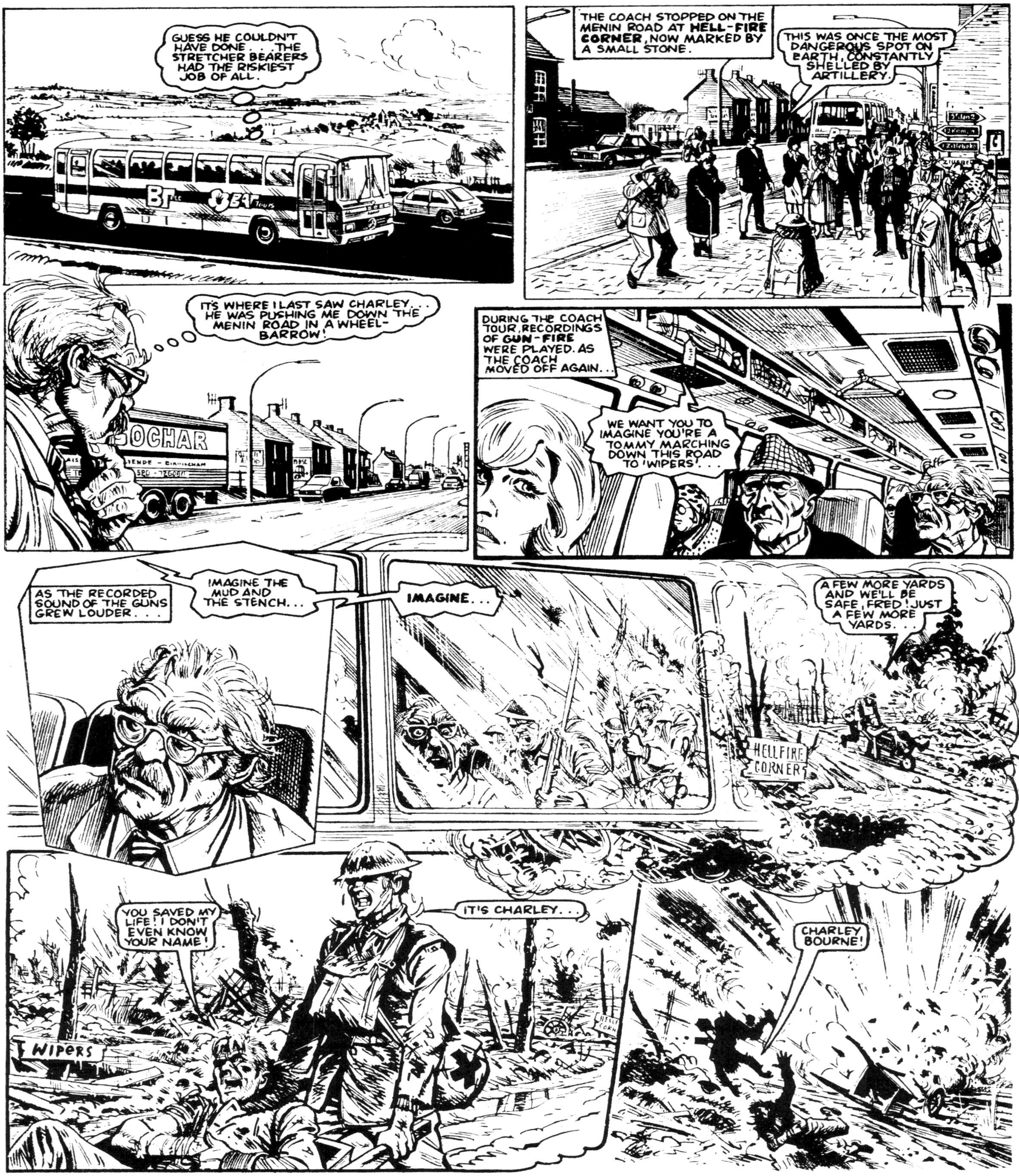

GUESS HE COULDN'T HAVE DONE . . . THE STRETCHER BEARERS HAD THE RISKIEST JOB OF ALL.
THE COACH STOPPED ON THE MENIN ROAD AT **HELL-FIRE CORNER**, NOW MARKED BY A SMALL STONE.
THIS WAS ONCE THE MOST DANGEROUS SPOT ON EARTH, CONSTANTLY SHELLED BY ARTILLERY.
IT'S WHERE I LAST SAW CHARLEY... HE WAS PUSHING ME DOWN THE MENIN ROAD IN A WHEEL-BARROW!
DURING THE COACH TOUR, RECORDINGS OF **GUN-FIRE** WERE PLAYED. AS THE COACH MOVED OFF AGAIN...
WE WANT YOU TO IMAGINE YOU'RE A TOMMY MARCHING DOWN THIS ROAD TO 'WIPERS'...
AS THE RECORDED SOUND OF THE GUNS GREW LOUDER...
IMAGINE THE MUD AND THE STENCH...
IMAGINE...
A FEW MORE YARDS AND WE'LL BE SAFE, FRED! JUST A FEW MORE YARDS...
HELLFIRE CORNER
YOU SAVED MY LIFE! I DON'T EVEN KNOW YOUR NAME!
IT'S CHARLEY...
WIPERS
CHARLEY BOURNE!

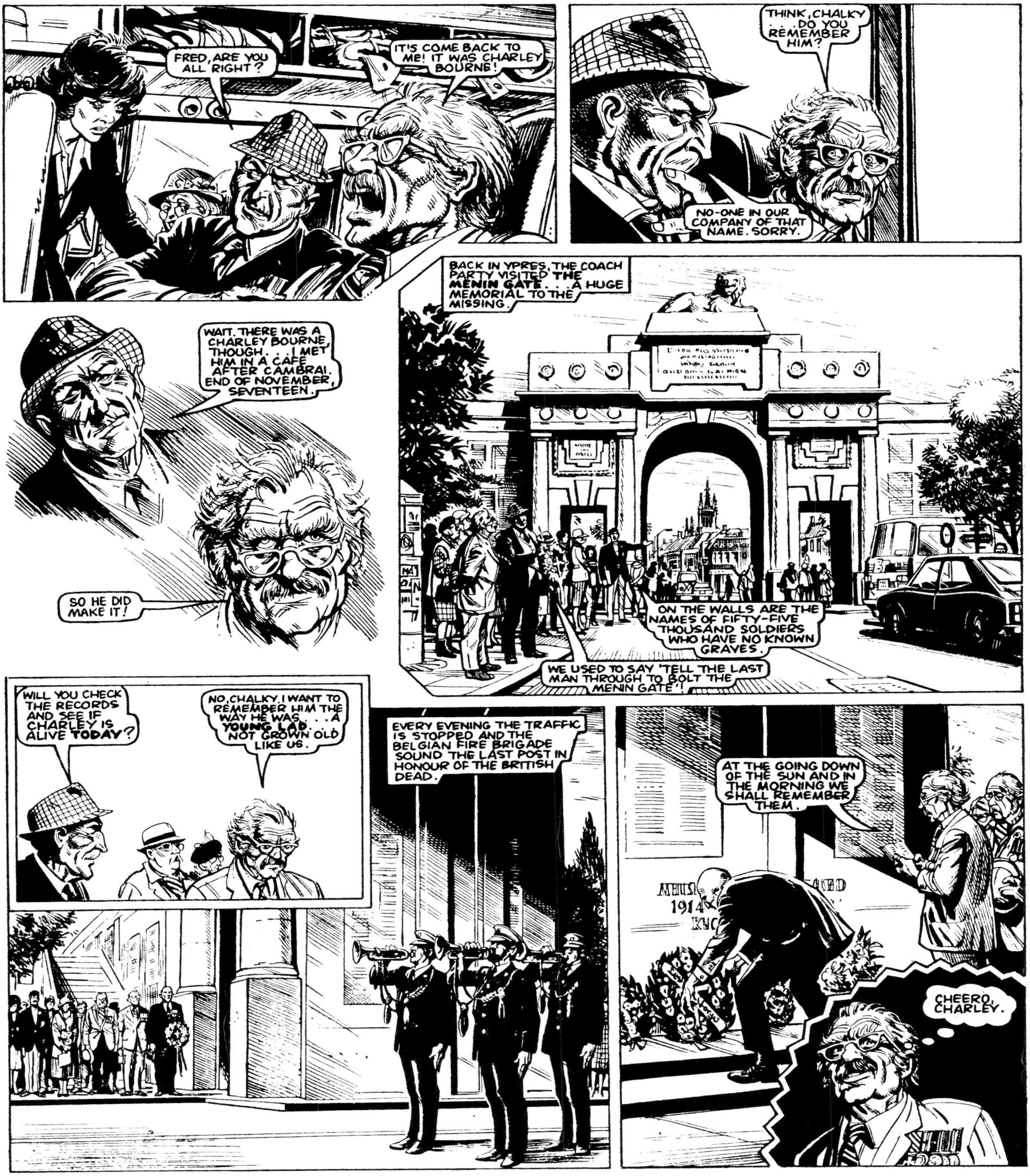
FRED, ARE YOU ALL RIGHT?
IT'S COME BACK TO ME! IT WAS CHARLEY BOURNE!
THINK, CHALKY . . . DO YOU REMEMBER HIM?
NO-ONE IN OUR COMPANY OF THAT NAME. SORRY.
WAIT. THERE WAS A CHARLEY BOURNE, THOUGH. . . I MET HIM IN A CAFÉ AFTER CAMBRAI. END OF NOVEMBER, SEVENTEEN.
SO HE DID MAKE IT!
BACK IN YPRES, THE COACH PARTY VISITED THE MENIN GATE . . . A HUGE MEMORIAL TO THE MISSING.
ON THE WALLS ARE THE NAMES OF FIFTY-FIVE THOUSAND SOLDIERS WHO HAVE NO KNOWN GRAVES.
WE USED TO SAY 'TELL THE LAST MAN THROUGH TO BOLT THE MENIN GATE'!
WILL YOU CHECK THE RECORDS AND SEE IF CHARLEY IS ALIVE TODAY?
NO, CHALKY. I WANT TO REMEMBER HIM THE WAY HE WAS . . . A YOUNG LAD . . . NOT GROWN OLD LIKE US.
EVERY EVENING THE TRAFFIC IS STOPPED AND THE BELGIAN FIRE BRIGADE SOUND THE LAST POST IN HONOUR OF THE BRITISH DEAD.
AT THE GOING DOWN OF THE SUN AND IN THE MORNING WE SHALL REMEMBER THEM.
CHEERO, CHARLEY.

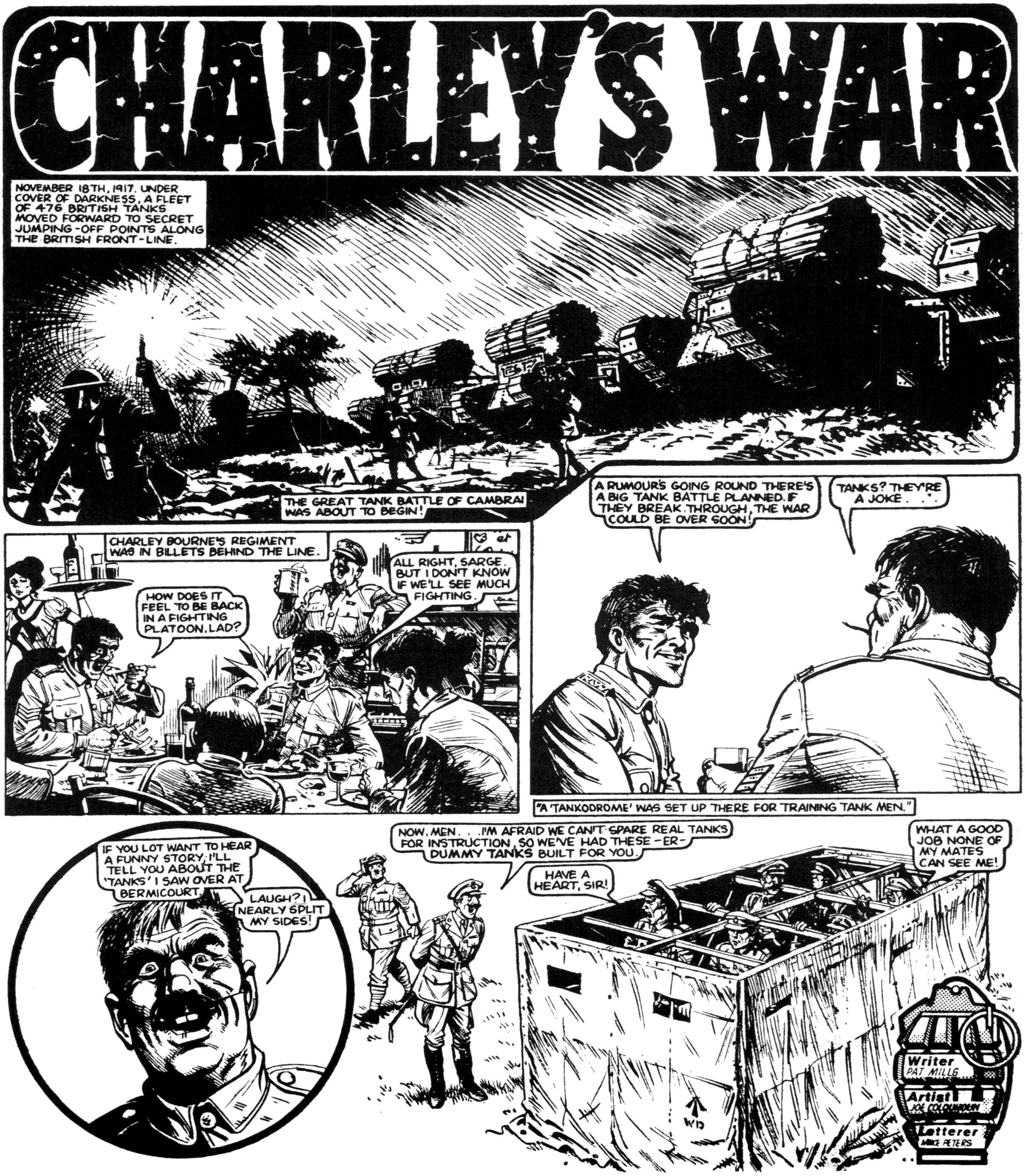
CHARLEY'S WAR
NOVEMBER 18TH, 1917. UNDER COVER OF DARKNESS, A FLEET OF 476 BRITISH TANKS MOVED FORWARD TO SECRET JUMPING-OFF POINTS ALONG THE BRITISH FRONT-LINE.
THE GREAT TANK BATTLE OF CAMBRAI WAS ABOUT TO BEGIN!
CHARLEY BOURNE'S REGIMENT WAS IN BILLETS BEHIND THE LINE.
HOW DOES IT FEEL TO BE BACK IN A FIGHTING PLATOON, LAD?
ALL RIGHT, SARGE. BUT I DON'T KNOW IF WE'LL SEE MUCH FIGHTING.
A RUMOUR'S GOING ROUND THERE'S A BIG TANK BATTLE PLANNED. IF THEY BREAK THROUGH, THE WAR COULD BE OVER SOON!
TANKS? THEY'RE A JOKE . . .
IF YOU LOT WANT TO HEAR A FUNNY STORY, I'LL TELL YOU ABOUT THE 'TANKS' I SAW OVER AT BERMICOURT.
LAUGH? I NEARLY SPLIT MY SIDES!
"A 'TANKODROME' WAS SET UP THERE FOR TRAINING TANK MEN."
NOW, MEN. . . I'M AFRAID WE CAN'T SPARE REAL TANKS FOR INSTRUCTION, SO WE'VE HAD THESE - ER - DUMMY TANKS BUILT FOR YOU.
HAVE A HEART, SIR!
WHAT A GOOD JOB NONE OF MY MATES CAN SEE ME!
Writer PAT MILLS
Artist JOE COLQUHOUN
Letterer MIKE PETERS

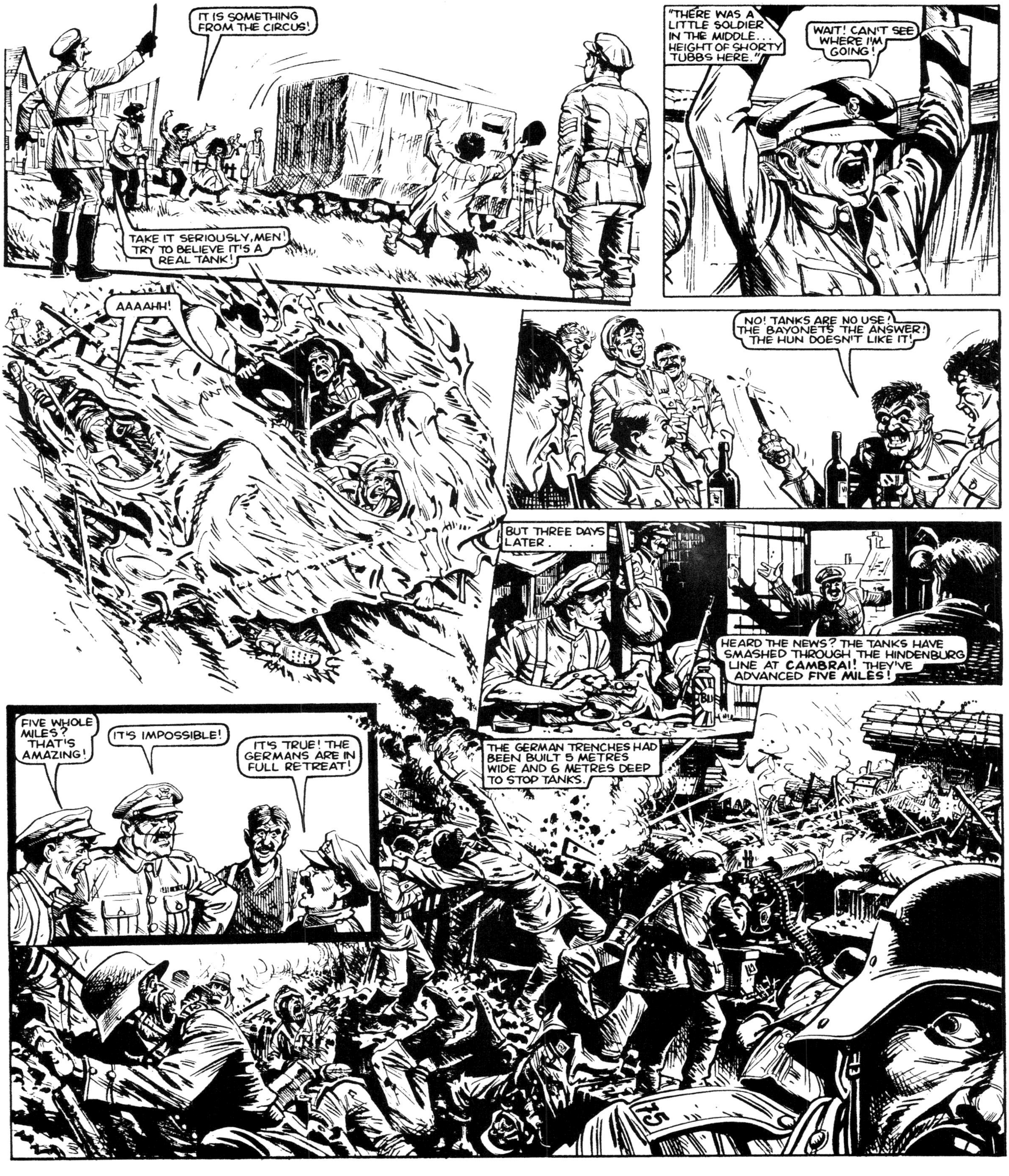
IT IS SOMETHING FROM THE CIRCUS!
TAKE IT SERIOUSLY, MEN! TRY TO BELIEVE IT'S A REAL TANK!
"THERE WAS A LITTLE SOLDIER IN THE MIDDLE... HEIGHT OF SHORTY TUBBS HERE."
WAIT! CAN'T SEE WHERE I'M GOING!
AAAAHH!
NO! TANKS ARE NO USE! THE BAYONET'S THE ANSWER! THE HUN DOESN'T LIKE IT!
BUT THREE DAYS LATER . . .
HEARD THE NEWS? THE TANKS HAVE SMASHED THROUGH THE HINDENBURG LINE AT CAMBRAI! THEY'VE ADVANCED FIVE MILES!
FIVE WHOLE MILES? THAT'S AMAZING!
IT'S IMPOSSIBLE!
IT'S TRUE! THE GERMANS ARE IN FULL RETREAT!
THE GERMAN TRENCHES HAD BEEN BUILT 5 METRES WIDE AND 6 METRES DEEP TO STOP TANKS.

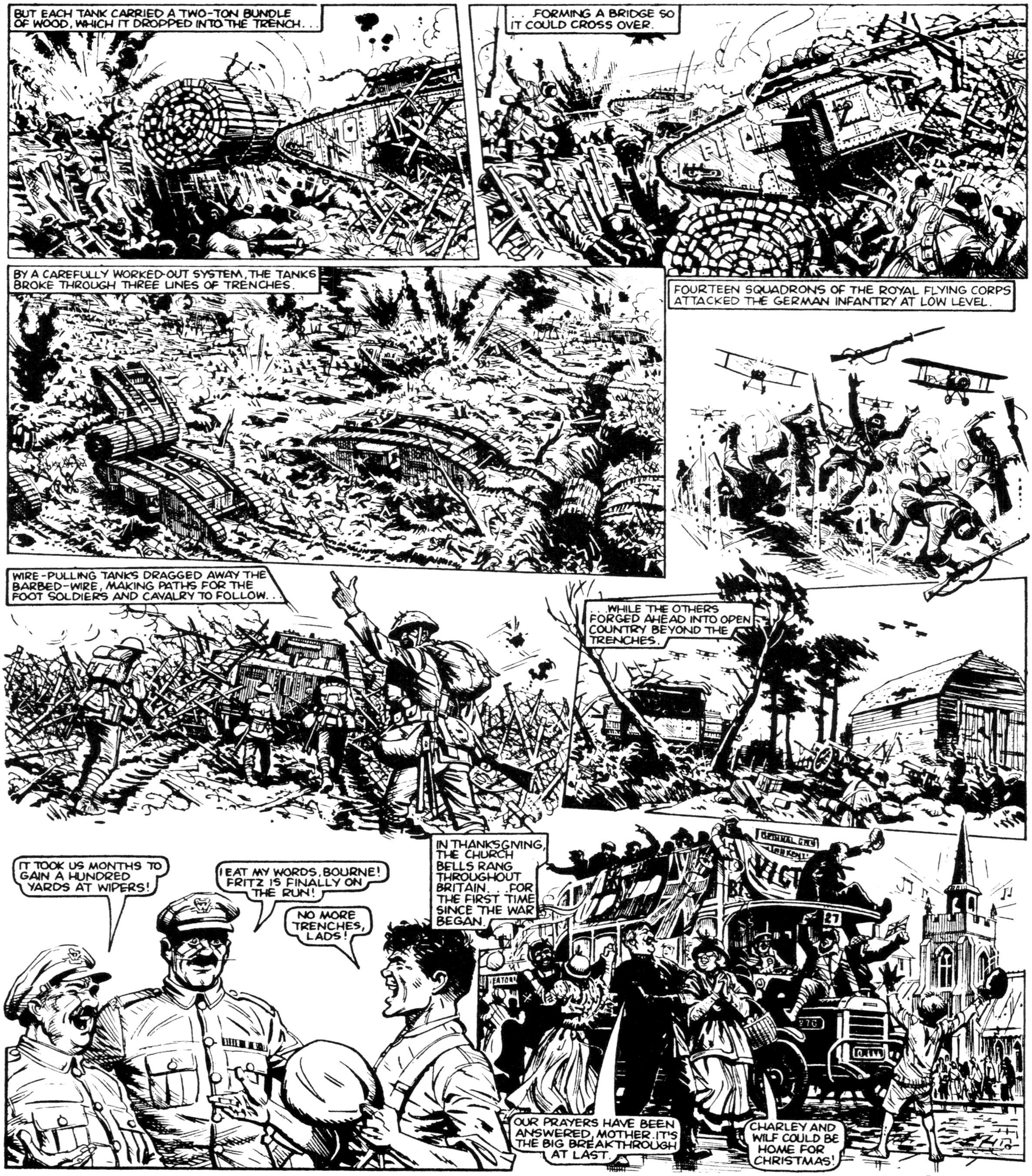

BUT EACH TANK CARRIED A TWO-TON BUNDLE OF WOOD, WHICH IT DROPPED INTO THE TRENCH. . .
. . FORMING A BRIDGE SO IT COULD CROSS OVER.
BY A CAREFULLY WORKED-OUT SYSTEM, THE TANKS BROKE THROUGH THREE LINES OF TRENCHES.
FOURTEEN SQUADRONS OF THE ROYAL FLYING CORPS ATTACKED THE GERMAN INFANTRY AT LOW LEVEL.
WIRE-PULLING TANKS DRAGGED AWAY THE BARBED-WIRE, MAKING PATHS FOR THE FOOT SOLDIERS AND CAVALRY TO FOLLOW. . .
. . WHILE THE OTHERS FORGED AHEAD INTO OPEN COUNTRY BEYOND THE TRENCHES.
IT TOOK US MONTHS TO GAIN A HUNDRED YARDS AT WIPERS!
I EAT MY WORDS, BOURNE! FRITZ IS FINALLY ON THE RUN!
NO MORE TRENCHES, LADS!
IN THANKSGIVING, THE CHURCH BELLS RANG THROUGHOUT BRITAIN. . . FOR THE FIRST TIME SINCE THE WAR BEGAN.
OUR PRAYERS HAVE BEEN ANSWERED, MOTHER. IT'S THE BIG BREAKTHROUGH AT LAST.
CHARLEY AND WILF COULD BE HOME FOR CHRISTMAS!

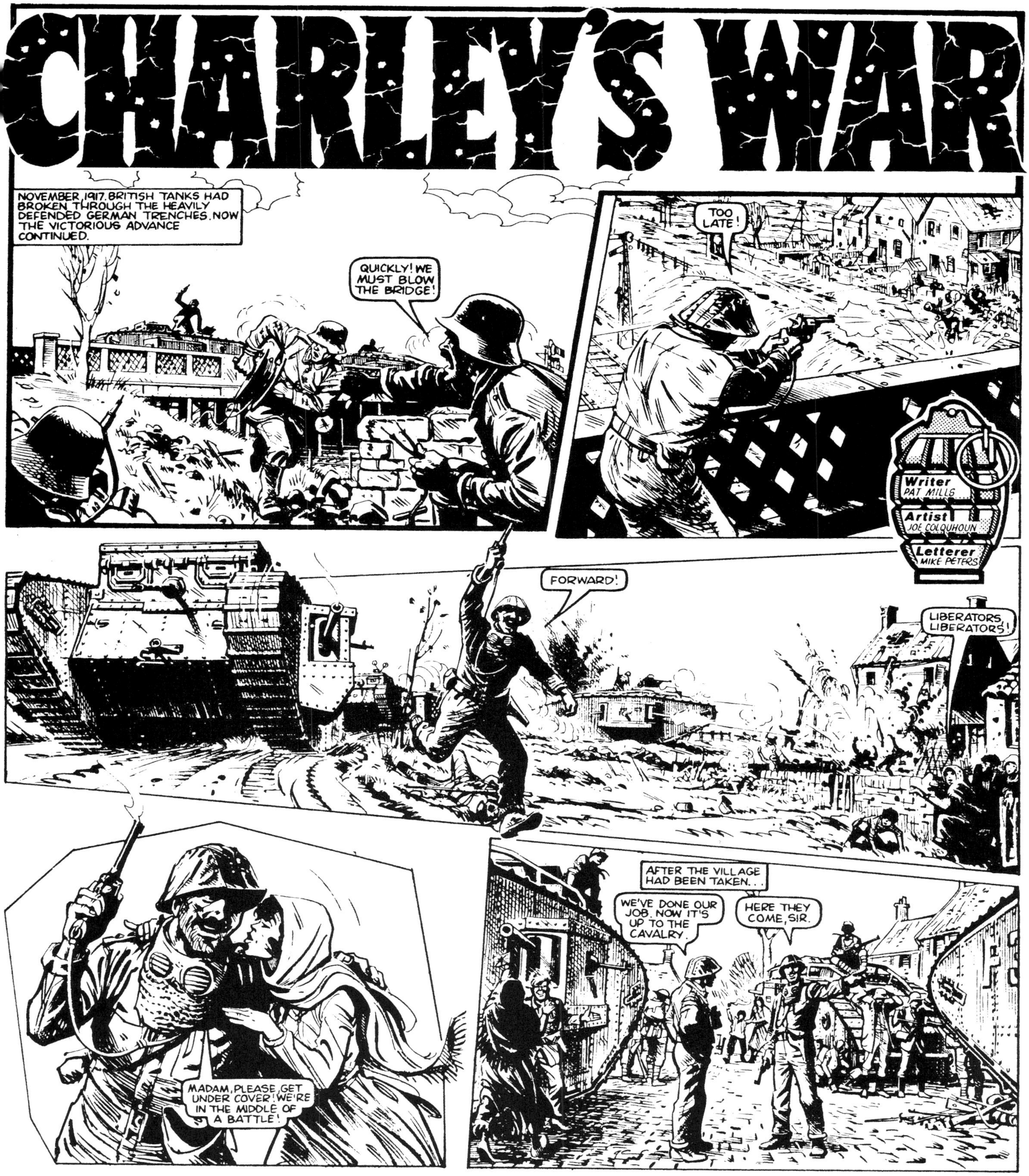
CHARLEY'S WAR
NOVEMBER, 1917. BRITISH TANKS HAD BROKEN THROUGH THE HEAVILY DEFENDED GERMAN TRENCHES. NOW THE VICTORIOUS ADVANCE CONTINUED.
QUICKLY! WE MUST BLOW THE BRIDGE!
TOO LATE!
Writer PAT MILLS
Artist JOE COLQUHOUN
Letterer MIKE PETERS
FORWARD!
LIBERATORS, LIBERATORS!
MADAM, PLEASE GET UNDER COVER! WE'RE IN THE MIDDLE OF A BATTLE!
AFTER THE VILLAGE HAD BEEN TAKEN...
WE'VE DONE OUR JOB. NOW IT'S UP TO THE CAVALRY.
HERE THEY COME, SIR.

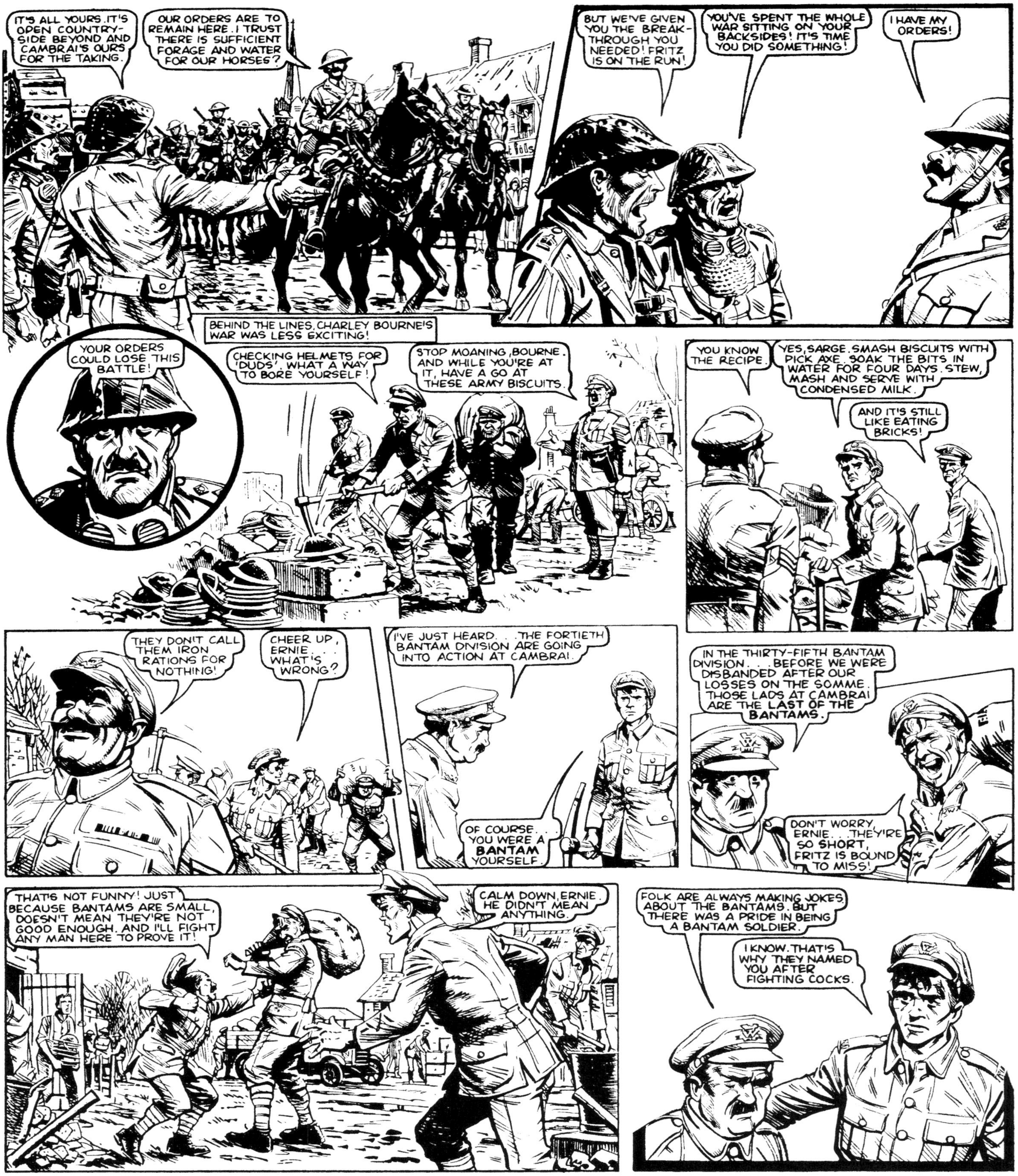
IT'S ALL YOURS. IT'S OPEN COUNTRY-SIDE BEYOND AND CAMBRAI'S OURS FOR THE TAKING.
OUR ORDERS ARE TO REMAIN HERE. I TRUST THERE IS SUFFICIENT FORAGE AND WATER FOR OUR HORSES?
BUT WE'VE GIVEN YOU THE BREAK-THROUGH YOU NEEDED! FRITZ IS ON THE RUN!
YOU'VE SPENT THE WHOLE WAR SITTING ON YOUR BACKSIDES! IT'S TIME YOU DID SOMETHING!
I HAVE MY ORDERS!
YOUR ORDERS COULD LOSE THIS BATTLE!
BEHIND THE LINES, CHARLEY BOURNE'S WAR WAS LESS EXCITING!
CHECKING HELMETS FOR 'DUDS'. WHAT A WAY TO BORE YOURSELF!
STOP MOANING, BOURNE. AND WHILE YOU'RE AT IT, HAVE A GO AT THESE ARMY BISCUITS.
YOU KNOW THE RECIPE.
YES, SARGE. SMASH BISCUITS WITH PICK AXE. SOAK THE BITS IN WATER FOR FOUR DAYS. STEW, MASH AND SERVE WITH CONDENSED MILK.
AND IT'S STILL LIKE EATING BRICKS!
THEY DON'T CALL THEM IRON RATIONS FOR NOTHING!
CHEER UP, ERNIE... WHAT'S WRONG?
I'VE JUST HEARD... THE FORTIETH BANTAM DIVISION ARE GOING INTO ACTION AT CAMBRAI.
OF COURSE. YOU WERE A BANTAM YOURSELF.
IN THE THIRTY-FIFTH BANTAM DIVISION... BEFORE WE WERE DISBANDED AFTER OUR LOSSES ON THE SOMME. THOSE LADS AT CAMBRAI ARE THE LAST OF THE BANTAMS.
DON'T WORRY, ERNIE... THEY'RE SO SHORT, FRITZ IS BOUND TO MISS!
THAT'S NOT FUNNY! JUST BECAUSE BANTAMS ARE SMALL, DOESN'T MEAN THEY'RE NOT GOOD ENOUGH. AND I'LL FIGHT ANY MAN HERE TO PROVE IT!
CALM DOWN, ERNIE. HE DIDN'T MEAN ANYTHING.
FOLK ARE ALWAYS MAKING JOKES ABOUT THE BANTAMS. BUT THERE WAS A PRIDE IN BEING A BANTAM SOLDIER.
I KNOW. THAT'S WHY THEY NAMED YOU AFTER FIGHTING COCKS.

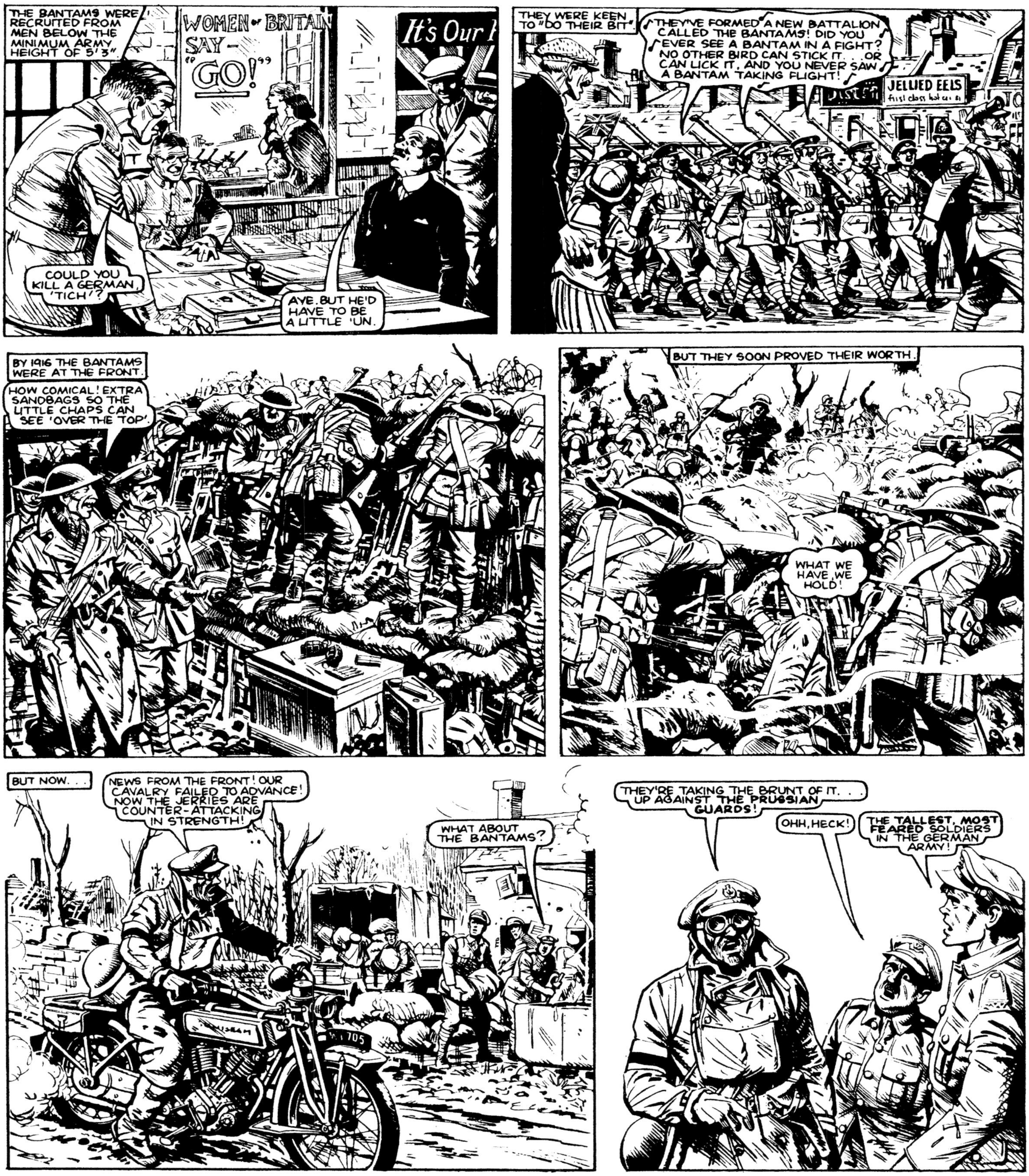
THE BANTAMS WERE RECRUITED FROM MEN BELOW THE MINIMUM ARMY HEIGHT OF 5' 3".
WOMEN OF BRITAIN SAY — "GO!"
It's Our
COULD YOU KILL A GERMAN, 'TICH'?
AYE. BUT HE'D HAVE TO BE A LITTLE 'UN.
THEY WERE KEEN TO "DO THEIR BIT".
THEY'VE FORMED A NEW BATTALION CALLED THE BANTAMS! DID YOU EVER SEE A BANTAM IN A FIGHT? NO OTHER BIRD CAN STICK IT. . . OR CAN LICK IT, AND YOU NEVER SAW A BANTAM TAKING FLIGHT!
JELLIED EELS
BY 1916 THE BANTAMS WERE AT THE FRONT.
HOW COMICAL! EXTRA SANDBAGS SO THE LITTLE CHAPS CAN SEE 'OVER THE TOP'.
BUT THEY SOON PROVED THEIR WORTH.
WHAT WE HAVE WE HOLD!
BUT NOW. . .
NEWS FROM THE FRONT! OUR CAVALRY FAILED TO ADVANCE! NOW THE JERRIES ARE COUNTER-ATTACKING IN STRENGTH!
WHAT ABOUT THE BANTAMS?
THEY'RE TAKING THE BRUNT OF IT. . . UP AGAINST THE PRUSSIAN GUARDS!
OHH, HECK!
THE TALLEST, MOST FEARED SOLDIERS IN THE GERMAN ARMY!

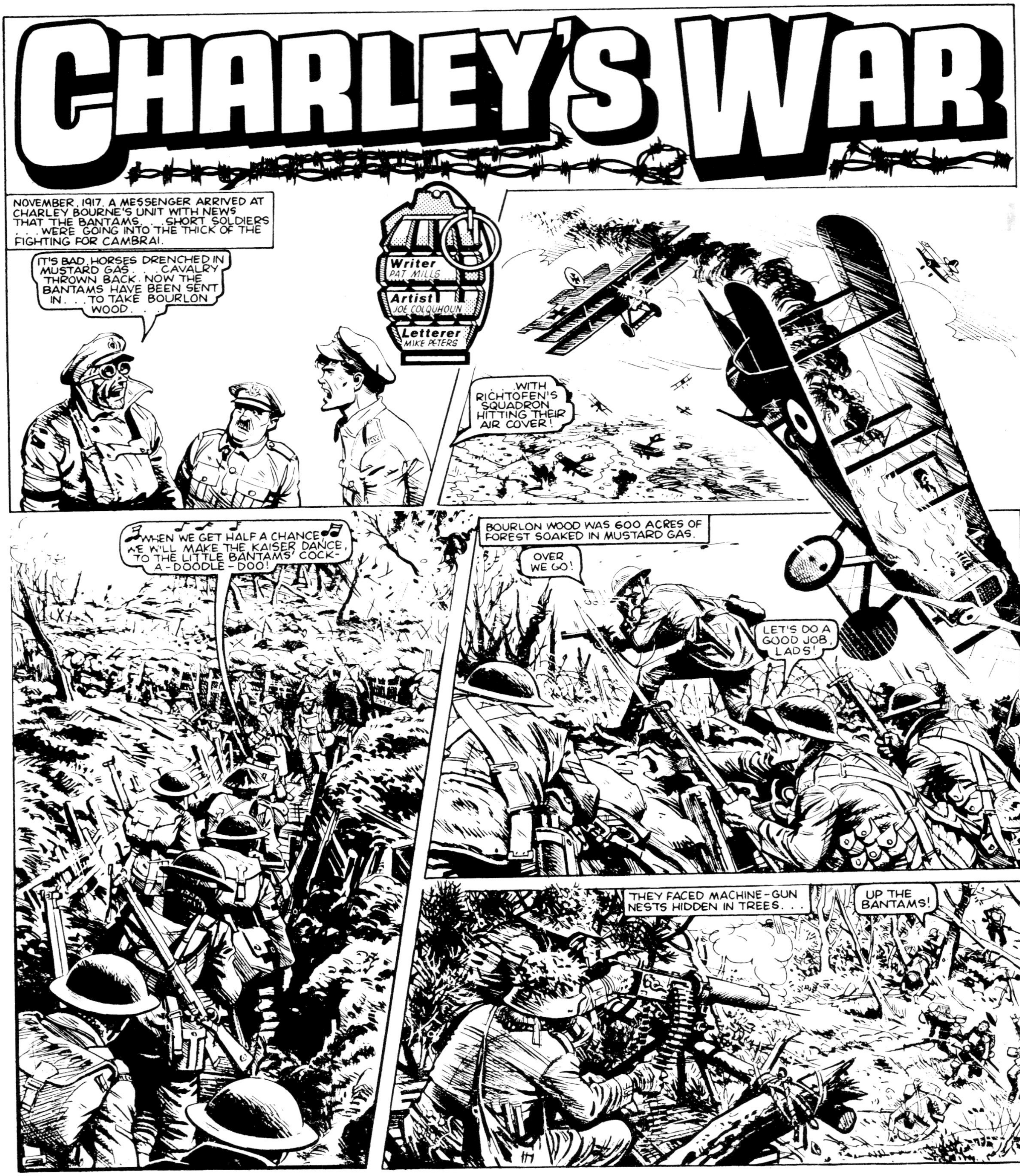
CHARLEY'S WAR
NOVEMBER, 1917. A MESSENGER ARRIVED AT CHARLEY BOURNE'S UNIT WITH NEWS THAT THE BANTAMS. . . SHORT SOLDIERS . . . WERE GOING INTO THE THICK OF THE FIGHTING FOR CAMBRAI.
IT'S BAD. HORSES DRENCHED IN MUSTARD GAS. . . . CAVALRY THROWN BACK. NOW THE BANTAMS HAVE BEEN SENT IN. . . TO TAKE BOURLON WOOD.
Writer PAT MILLS
Artist JOE COLQUHOUN
Letterer MIKE PETERS
. . . WITH RICHTOFEN'S SQUADRON HITTING THEIR AIR COVER!
WHEN WE GET HALF A CHANCE WE WILL MAKE THE KAISER DANCE, TO THE LITTLE BANTAMS' COCK-A-DOODLE-DOO!
BOURLON WOOD WAS 600 ACRES OF FOREST SOAKED IN MUSTARD GAS.
OVER WE GO!
LET'S DO A GOOD JOB, LADS!
THEY FACED MACHINE-GUN NESTS HIDDEN IN TREES. . .
UP THE BANTAMS!

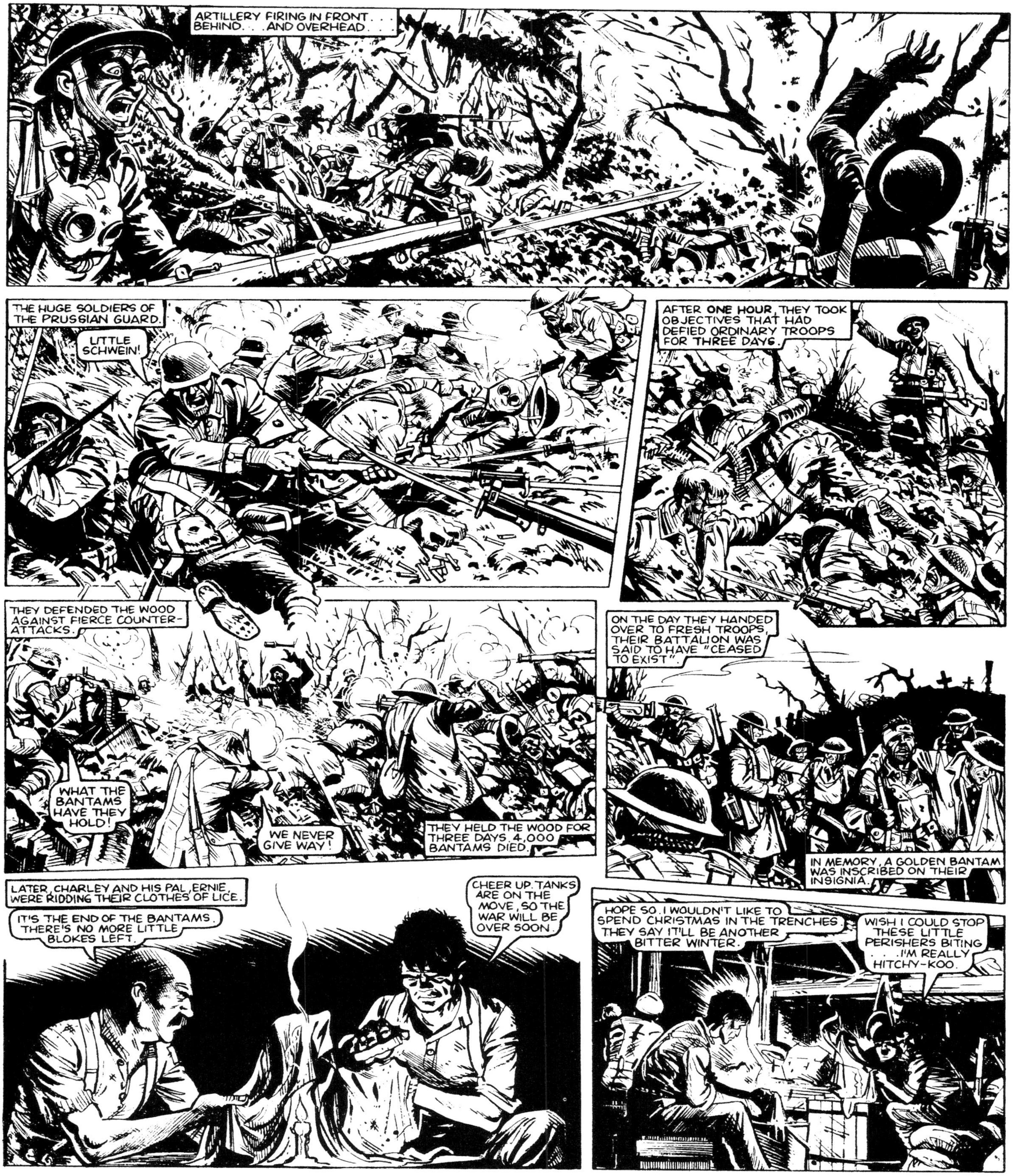
ARTILLERY FIRING IN FRONT . . . BEHIND . . . AND OVERHEAD . . .
THE HUGE SOLDIERS OF THE PRUSSIAN GUARD.
LITTLE SCHWEIN!
AFTER ONE HOUR, THEY TOOK OBJECTIVES THAT HAD DEFIED ORDINARY TROOPS FOR THREE DAYS.
THEY DEFENDED THE WOOD AGAINST FIERCE COUNTER-ATTACKS.
WHAT THE BANTAMS HAVE THEY HOLD!
WE NEVER GIVE WAY!
THEY HELD THE WOOD FOR THREE DAYS. 4,000 BANTAMS DIED.
ON THE DAY THEY HANDED OVER TO FRESH TROOPS, THEIR BATTALION WAS SAID TO HAVE "CEASED TO EXIST".
IN MEMORY, A GOLDEN BANTAM WAS INSCRIBED ON THEIR INSIGNIA.
LATER, CHARLEY AND HIS PAL, ERNIE, WERE RIDDING THEIR CLOTHES OF LICE.
IT'S THE END OF THE BANTAMS. THERE'S NO MORE LITTLE BLOKES LEFT.
CHEER UP. TANKS ARE ON THE MOVE, SO THE WAR WILL BE OVER SOON.
HOPE SO. I WOULDN'T LIKE TO SPEND CHRISTMAS IN THE TRENCHES. THEY SAY IT'LL BE ANOTHER BITTER WINTER.
WISH I COULD STOP THESE LITTLE PERISHERS BITING . . . I'M REALLY HITCHY-KOO.

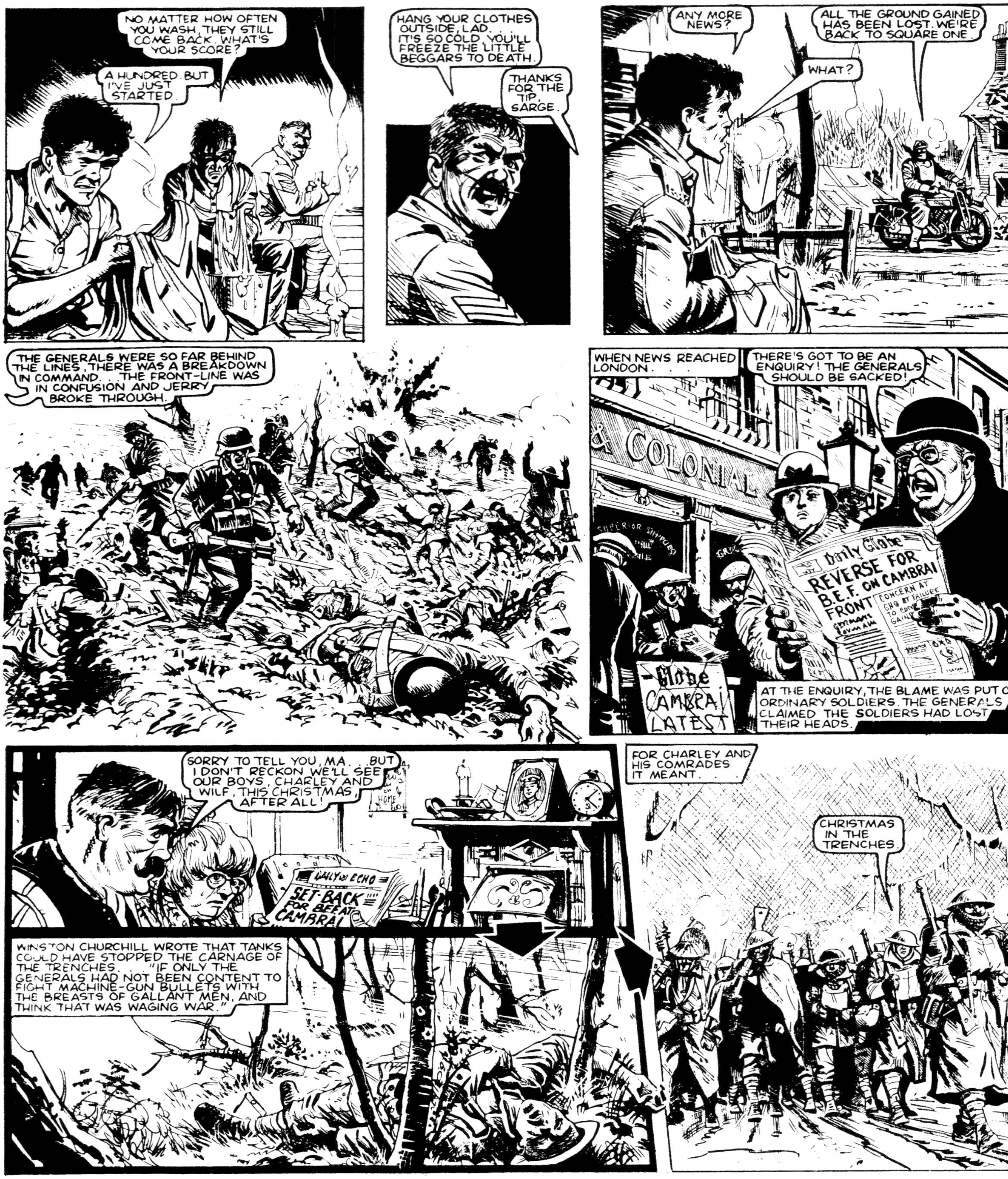

NO MATTER HOW OFTEN YOU WASH, THEY STILL COME BACK. WHAT'S YOUR SCORE?
A HUNDRED. BUT I'VE JUST STARTED.
HANG YOUR CLOTHES OUTSIDE, LAD. . . IT'S SO COLD, YOU'LL FREEZE THE LITTLE BEGGARS TO DEATH.
THANKS FOR THE TIP, SARGE.
ANY MORE NEWS?
ALL THE GROUND GAINED HAS BEEN LOST. WE'RE BACK TO SQUARE ONE.
WHAT?
THE GENERALS WERE SO FAR BEHIND THE LINES, THERE WAS A BREAKDOWN IN COMMAND. . . THE FRONT-LINE WAS IN CONFUSION AND JERRY BROKE THROUGH.
WHEN NEWS REACHED LONDON. . .
THERE'S GOT TO BE AN ENQUIRY! THE GENERALS SHOULD BE SACKED!
& COLONIAL
Daily Globe
REVERSE FOR B.E.F. ON CAMBRAI FRONT
Globe
CAMBRAI LATEST
AT THE ENQUIRY, THE BLAME WAS PUT ON ORDINARY SOLDIERS. THE GENERALS CLAIMED THE SOLDIERS HAD LOST THEIR HEADS.
SORRY TO TELL YOU, MA. . . BUT I DON'T RECKON WE'LL SEE OUR BOYS, CHARLEY AND WILF, THIS CHRISTMAS, AFTER ALL!
DAILY ECHO
SET-BACK FOR BEF AT CAMBRAI
WINSTON CHURCHILL WROTE THAT TANKS COULD HAVE STOPPED THE CARNAGE OF THE TRENCHES. . . . "IF ONLY THE GENERALS HAD NOT BEEN CONTENT TO FIGHT MACHINE-GUN BULLETS WITH THE BREASTS OF GALLANT MEN, AND THINK THAT WAS WAGING WAR."
FOR CHARLEY AND HIS COMRADES IT MEANT. . .
CHRISTMAS IN THE TRENCHES

CHARLEY'S WAR

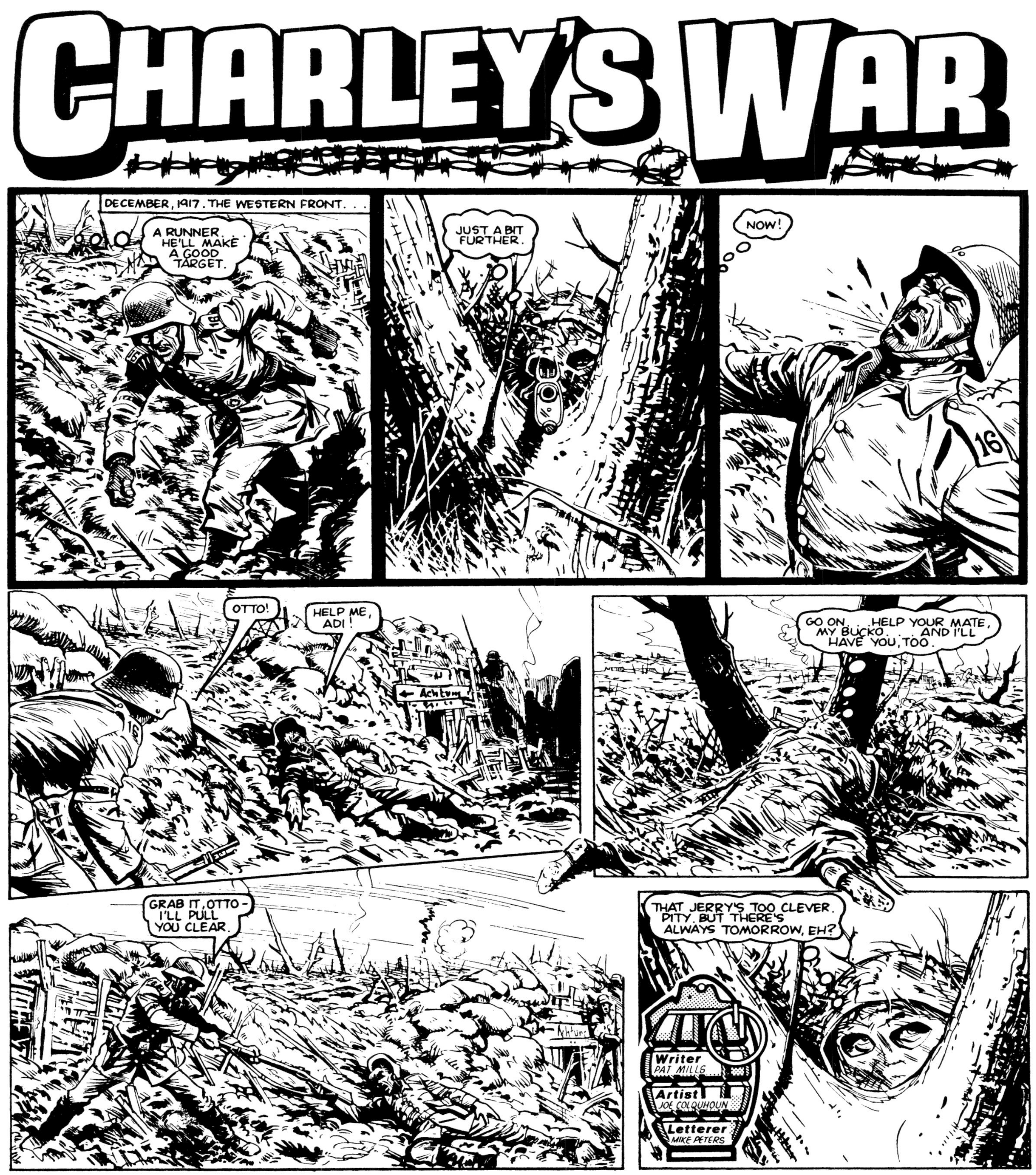

DECEMBER, 1917. THE WESTERN FRONT. . .
A RUNNER. HE'LL MAKE A GOOD TARGET.
JUST A BIT FURTHER.
NOW!
16
OTTO!
HELP ME, ADI!
Achtung
GO ON. . . HELP YOUR MATE, MY BUCKO. . . AND I'LL HAVE YOU, TOO.
GRAB IT, OTTO - I'LL PULL YOU CLEAR.
THAT JERRY'S TOO CLEVER. PITY. BUT THERE'S ALWAYS TOMORROW, EH?
Writer PAT MILLS
Artist JOE COLQUHOUN
Letterer MIKE PETERS

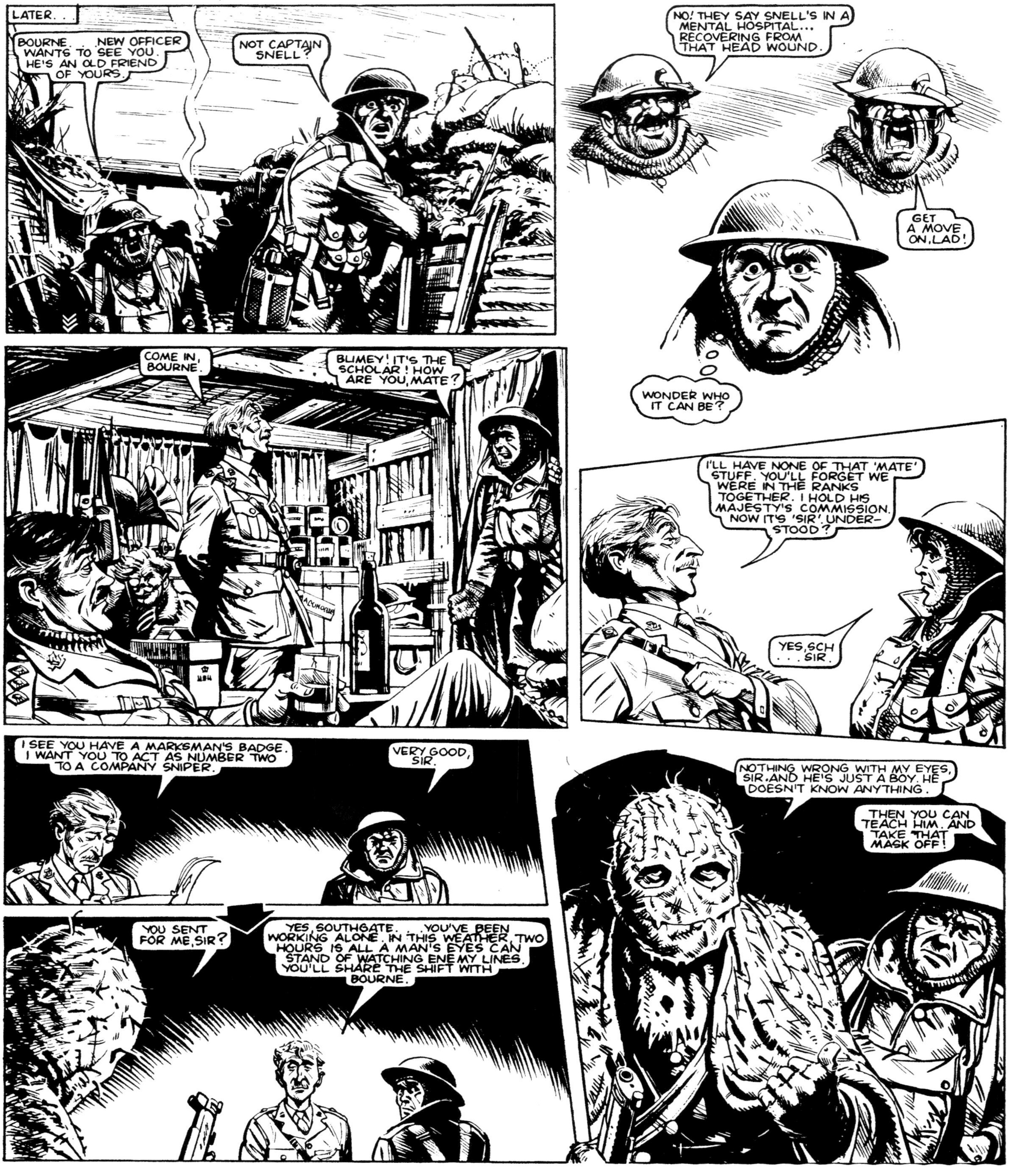

LATER. .
BOURNE. . .NEW OFFICER WANTS TO SEE YOU. HE'S AN OLD FRIEND OF YOURS.
NOT CAPTAIN SNELL?
NO! THEY SAY SNELL'S IN A MENTAL HOSPITAL... RECOVERING FROM THAT HEAD WOUND.
GET A MOVE ON, LAD!
WONDER WHO IT CAN BE?
COME IN, BOURNE.
BLIMEY! IT'S THE SCHOLAR! HOW ARE YOU, MATE?
I'LL HAVE NONE OF THAT 'MATE' STUFF. YOU'LL FORGET WE WERE IN THE RANKS TOGETHER. I HOLD HIS MAJESTY'S COMMISSION. NOW IT'S 'SIR'. UNDER-STOOD?
YES, SCH . . . SIR.
I SEE YOU HAVE A MARKSMAN'S BADGE. I WANT YOU TO ACT AS NUMBER TWO TO A COMPANY SNIPER.
VERY GOOD, SIR.
YOU SENT FOR ME, SIR?
YES, SOUTHGATE. . . YOU'VE BEEN WORKING ALONE. IN THIS WEATHER TWO HOURS IS ALL A MAN'S EYES CAN STAND OF WATCHING ENEMY LINES. YOU'LL SHARE THE SHIFT WITH BOURNE.
NOTHING WRONG WITH MY EYES, SIR, AND HE'S JUST A BOY. HE DOESN'T KNOW ANYTHING.
THEN YOU CAN TEACH HIM. AND TAKE THAT MASK OFF!

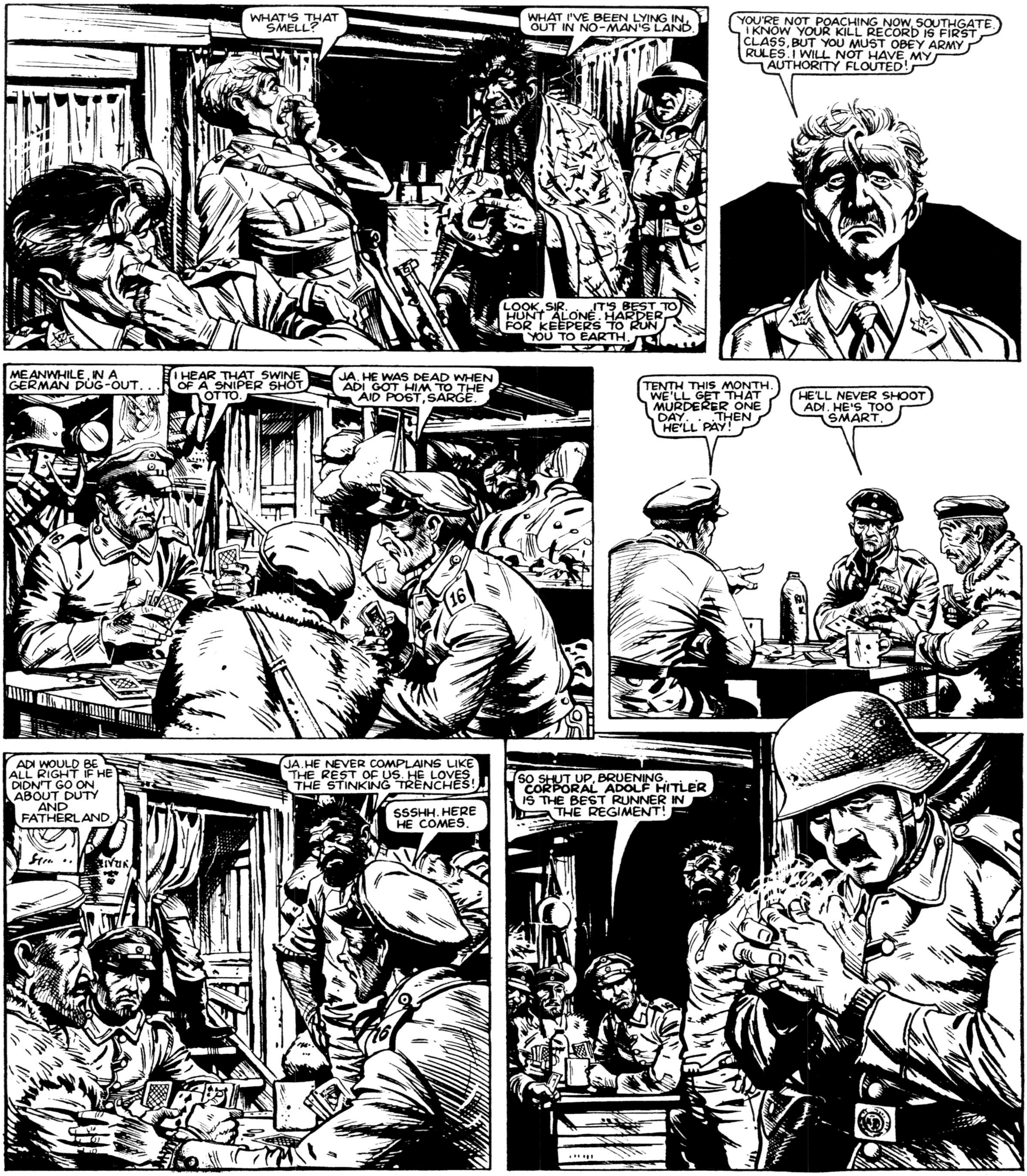
WHAT'S THAT SMELL?
WHAT I'VE BEEN LYING IN, OUT IN NO-MAN'S LAND.
LOOK, SIR. . . IT'S BEST TO HUNT ALONE. HARDER FOR KEEPERS TO RUN YOU TO EARTH.
YOU'RE NOT POACHING NOW, SOUTHGATE. I KNOW YOUR KILL RECORD IS FIRST CLASS, BUT YOU MUST OBEY ARMY RULES. I WILL NOT HAVE MY AUTHORITY FLOUTED!
MEANWHILE, IN A GERMAN DUG-OUT. . .
I HEAR THAT SWINE OF A SNIPER SHOT OTTO.
JA. HE WAS DEAD WHEN ADI GOT HIM TO THE AID POST, SARGE.
TENTH THIS MONTH. WE'LL GET THAT MURDERER ONE DAY. . . THEN HE'LL PAY!
HE'LL NEVER SHOOT ADI. HE'S TOO SMART.
ADI WOULD BE ALL RIGHT IF HE DIDN'T GO ON ABOUT DUTY AND FATHERLAND.
JA. HE NEVER COMPLAINS LIKE THE REST OF US. HE LOVES THE STINKING TRENCHES!
SSSHH. HERE HE COMES.
SO SHUT UP, BRUENING. CORPORAL ADOLF HITLER IS THE BEST RUNNER IN THE REGIMENT!

STRIP COMMENTARY

by Pat Mills

EPISODES ONE TO THREE

It's still incredible and very gratifying to see an army mutiny as the most popular story in a British war comic. It was inspired by the book and the TV series *The Monocled Mutineer,* and also by other accounts that confirm the mutiny at Etaples took place in September 1917. However, since the excellent TV version of *The Monocled Mutineer* by Alan Bleasdale (also writer of *Boys from the Black Stuff*) appeared, there have been desperate attempts by right-wing historians to challenge its authenticity. Any search on the web will now suggest to you it's a dubious work of fiction. Even the BBC DVD states the drama, "based on supposedly true events", is adapted from "the novel" and notes that the "the BAFTA award winning series provoked intense political controversy on its broadcast in 1986 and, after an initial repeat, has not been shown since on British television."

I've read the source book carefully many times and whilst there are sections that are legitimately speculative, as in a novel, they are relatively few. Nowhere does it state it is a work of fiction. Also, contrary to what some otherwise distinguished historians claim, their subjective views repeated as fact *ad nauseam* on the web, the authors of the book *do* quote their sources, even giving the full names and addresses of the soldiers who described their encounters with Percy Toplis, the Monocled Mutineer, who led the revolt. Edwin Thomas Woodhall, the British secret service agent who arrested Toplis at Etaples also relates the story in his 1936 autobiography *Secrets of Scotland Yard*, quoted in the book. So there is no question as to its authenticity or to similar events described here in *Charley's War.*

Which leaves me wondering just why establishment historians should go so far out of their way to play their part in burying such a fine drama series. Alongside *Charley's War,* it is the only popular record we have of our grandfathers' and great grandfathers' courageous revolt against the British officer class who treated them so disgracefully.

I fear the truth – that Toplis, a working class borstal boy, made a mockery of his 'betters' and ordinary soldiers fought a cruel, mindless authority and *won* – still threatens, still chokes the British establishment to this day.

Supposedly, a full account of what happened at Etaples will be released by the Ministry of Defence in 2017, one hundred years after the events. So there's seven years to go – but don't hold your breath. As the *Daily Record* noted only last year, the British government did not even concede there had been a mutiny at Etaples until 1978.

However, there is one comforting thought from these events. The *Guardian* stated after the recent Tory victory that it might persuade Alan Bleasdale to write more anti-establishment dramas like the *Monocled Mutineer.* Every cloud…

EPISODE FOUR

Charley's friend Blue, a deserter from the French Foreign Legion, features here. Already established in an earlier *Charley's War* story, he is a natural for a similar role to Toplis. Paul McGann was superb as Toplis in the

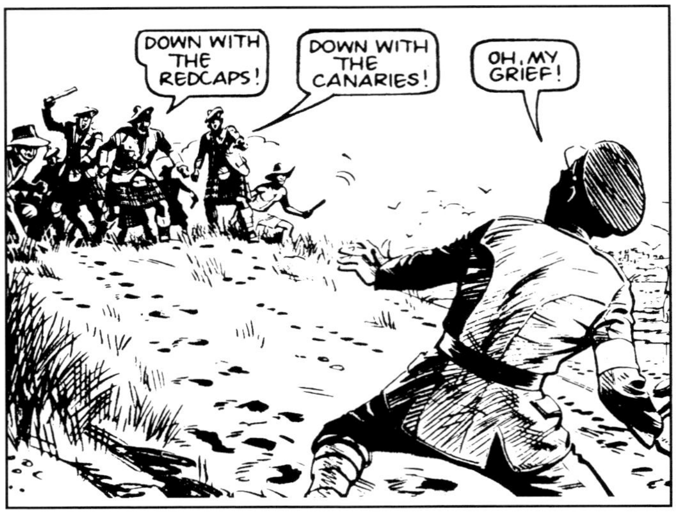
DOWN WITH THE REDCAPS!
DOWN WITH THE CANARIES!
OH, MY GRIEF!

TV drama, but I recall at the time there was some talk of Roger Daltrey playing the role – although I can find nothing on the web now to confirm this. He would also have been superb, perhaps with a tougher working class look than McGann. I based Blue partly on a young Jack Nicholson.

EPISODE FIVE

The relevance of these episodes to modern times, and why the establishment is still so desperate to hide the truth about the mutiny, was brought home to me recently by the case in March 2010 of Lance Corporal Joe Glenton who went absent without leave rather than serve a second tour in Afghanistan. He was jailed for nine months.

His defender, Mr Wrack said: "He was told that the troops' presence in Afghanistan would improve the country, that democracy would be bought and that the position of women would improve. This motivated him to go.

"His experience and reality conflicted with what he had been told. He questioned the morality and legality of the war, and spoke publicly about it when he returned."

A spokesman for the Stop The War Coalition said: "Joe Glenton is not the person who should be facing a jail sentence. It should be the politicians who have led us into disastrous wars in Iraq and Afghanistan. The fact that they are not brings shame to justice in this country."

EPISODE SIX

The episode begins with a cover reprise on the French mutiny. I would love to see some modern films on this momentous event or similar stories that describe the truth of war. Channel 4 did an excellent drama about British soldiers in Iraq with *The Mark of Cain.* But I share John Pilger's

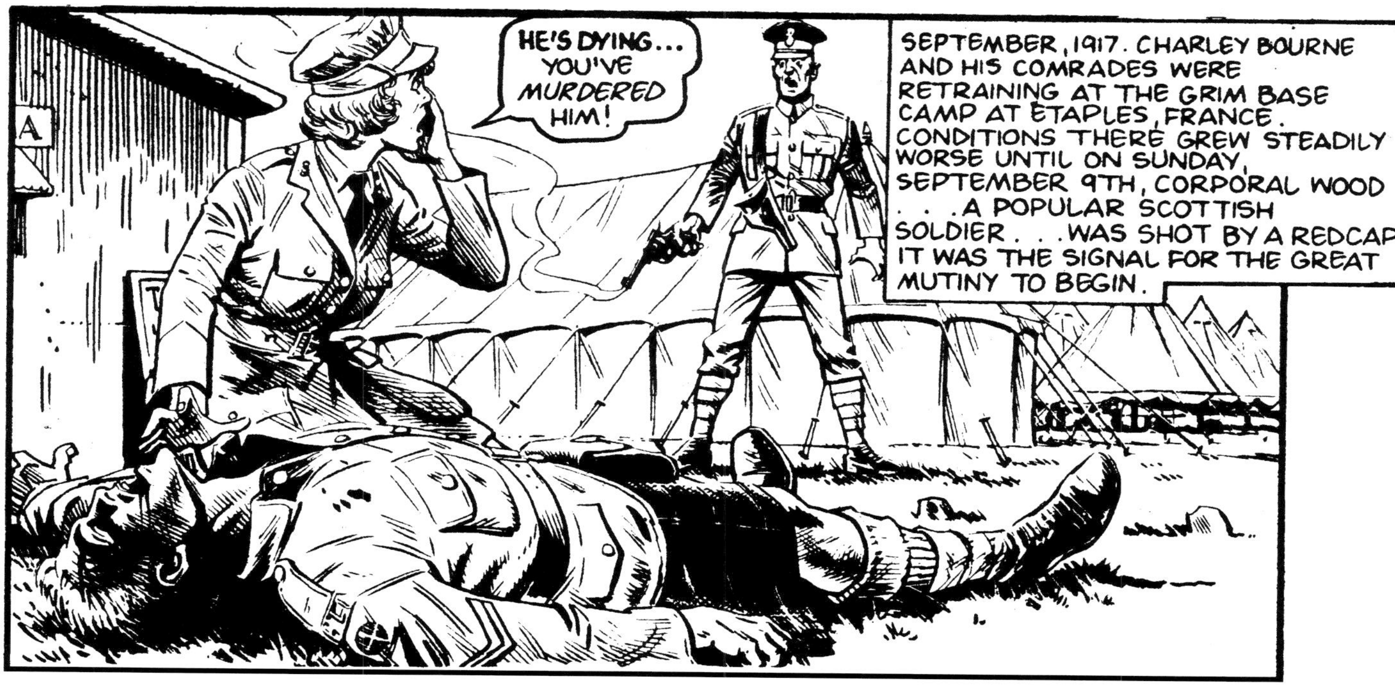
HE'S DYING... YOU'VE MURDERED HIM!
SEPTEMBER, 1917. CHARLEY BOURNE AND HIS COMRADES WERE RETRAINING AT THE GRIM BASE CAMP AT ETAPLES, FRANCE. CONDITIONS THERE GREW STEADILY WORSE UNTIL ON SUNDAY, SEPTEMBER 9TH, CORPORAL WOOD . . . A POPULAR SCOTTISH SOLDIER . . . WAS SHOT BY A REDCAP. IT WAS THE SIGNAL FOR THE GREAT MUTINY TO BEGIN.

views on Hollywood's treatment of war. Writing in the *New Statesman* about the Oscars he says, "the dominant theme is as old as Hollywood: America's divine right to invade other societies, steal their history and occupy our memory… (*The Hurt Locker)* offers a vicarious thrill through yet another standard-issue psychopath, high on violence in somebody else's country where the deaths of a million people are consigned to cinematic oblivion."

EPISODE SEVEN

I'm relieved this episode will appear in black and white. The colour on the original is pretty wretched and does nothing for Joe's wonderful artwork. Believe me, you're not missing anything.

EPISODE EIGHT

The end of the mutiny. I would have loved to have written about what happened to Blue next. His real-life counterpart, Toplis, escaped the British secret service but was ambushed and shot dead by police in 1920. I like to think Blue didn't share his fate and lived to a prosperous ripe old age.

All too often, working class anti-heroes who buck the system are shown receiving a finger-wagging comeuppance and, sadly, Toplis is no exception. It's probably the only reason it was ever allowed to be screened. But I won't have this happen in my stories. Thus, when I wrote a TV film treatment recently about a drug-taking prostitute involved in scandalous real-life events in the 1920s, she doesn't end up dead in the gutter or in the workhouse. That would be the expected fate for those who 'break the rules'. In my final reel she rises above her dubious past and ends her days running a tea-shop. To hell with 'learning your lesson' and 'knowing your place'. It's important to show that ordinary people can rebel and *win.*

EPISODE NINE

With this story set back in the trenches, I'm reminded of the drama potential of *Charley's War* in other media. I could really see *Charley's* working as an audio play and last year, together with director Dirk Maggs (who directed radio versions of *Hitchiker's Guide, Batman*, and other excellent dramas) we submitted the story as a classic serial for Radio Four. On that occasion we didn't get it through. But you never know…

EPISODE TEN

A great cover by Joe, but wow! Did editorial know how to screw it up? First there are still those awful captions 'Continued on Next Page' – as if the readers hadn't the intellectual capacity to figure it out for themselves. Then there's a huge flash caption stuck on the sombre artwork: 'Can you solve the fruit gums secret? Free poster inside!' Subtle it was not. Mercifully, you have been spared this on the Titan edition!

EPISODE ELEVEN

Charley as stretcher bearer at Passchendaele. Once again the serial was breaking the rules by having a non-combatant as a hero. It's a tribute to the readers and to Joe's powerful art that it worked and the saga remained as popular as ever. On the Titan edition you are also spared the original topline 'Stretcher bearers had a tough time during World War One!' *Duhhhh!* Talk about stating the (literally) bleeding obvious.

EPISODE TWELVE

Some shocking truths here about the reality of war and being a stretcher bearer. I was told recently that when *Charley* was first reprinted in *Battle* it was censored and toned down without my knowledge. I had absolutely no idea! I haven't studied the changes in detail because they would just make me too angry. Shame on whoever was responsible. However, rest assured the version you are reading here is the real McCoy.

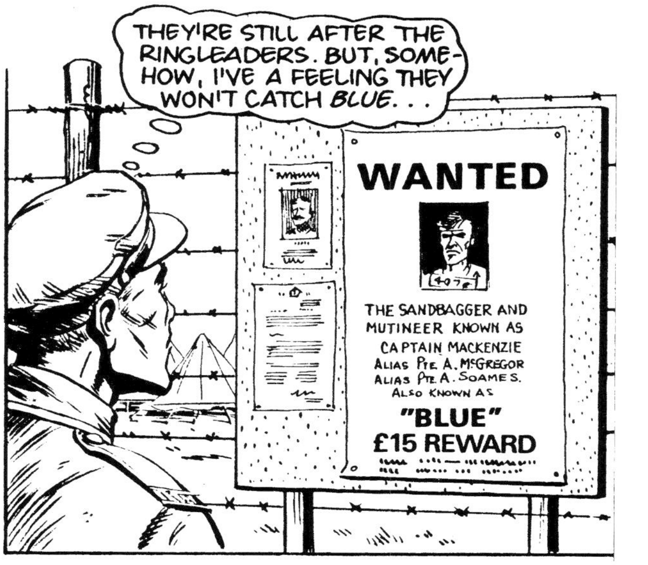
THEY'RE STILL AFTER THE RINGLEADERS. BUT, SOMEHOW, I'VE A FEELING THEY WON'T CATCH BLUE. . .
WANTED
THE SANDBAGGER AND MUTINEER KNOWN AS CAPTAIN MACKENZIE
ALIAS PTE A. McGREGOR
ALIAS PTE A. SOAMES.
ALSO KNOWN AS
"BLUE"
£15 REWARD

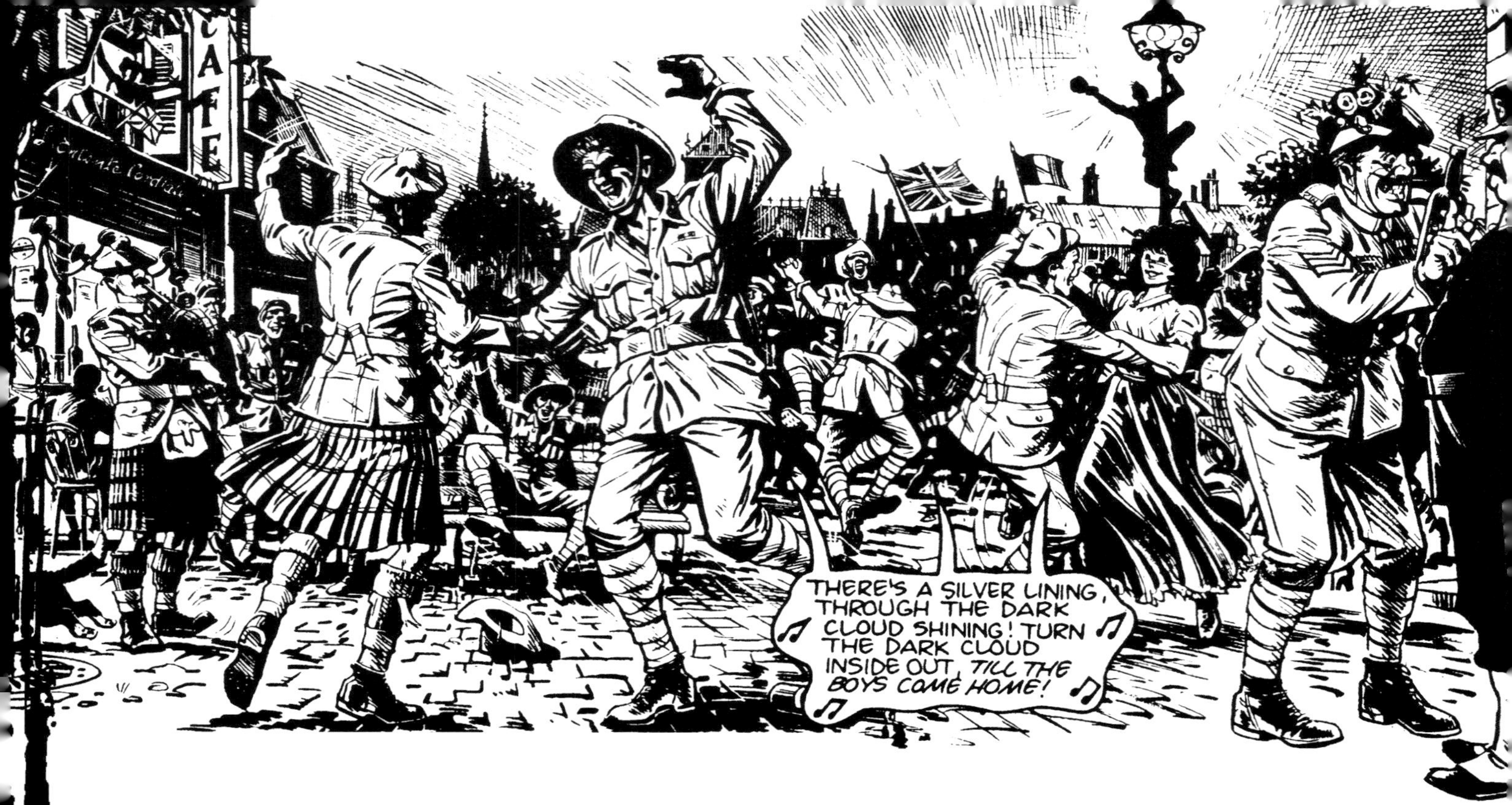
THERE'S A SILVER LINING, THROUGH THE DARK CLOUD SHINING! TURN THE DARK CLOUD INSIDE OUT, TILL THE BOYS COME HOME!

EPISODE THIRTEEN

It was around this time that Joe was taken ill and there was a gap in the story. To fill it, by popular request, editorial reprinted the first three episodes of *Charley's*. As editor John Freeman told me, 'To the *Battle* editor's credit, virtually every other editorial during the gap refers to Joe either in hospital or getting better.' With this episode we are back on track.

EPISODES FOURTEEN TO SIXTEEN

Difficult decisions for Charley and a drama involving poison gas. It's interesting to consider that in the year this story first appeared – 1982 – the Falklands War, the Russian invasion of Afghanistan and the Iran–Iraq war were raging. Poison gas was used extensively in this war against the Iranians and also the Kurds. The latter first had an experience of such a 'weapon of mass destruction' when it was dropped on them by the British in the 1920s, acting on Churchill's orders.

EPISODE SEVENTEEN AND EIGHTEEN

The nightmare of Passchendaele continues. I was using original source material from books wherever possible, but I wish I'd been geared up to collect my own eye-witness accounts from veterans who were still alive at that time. This is an approach I prefer these days.

For instance, I recently wrote *The Ayatollah's Son* featuring the riots in Tehran. Published by Ctrl.Alt.Shift in their anthology *Unmasks Corruption* and superbly drawn by Lee O'Connor, it's the account of how a young man turns against his father, an Ayatollah, and becomes a revolutionary. His story was told to me by an Iranian journalist I met in Paris. If you come across it, you will recognise the modern day counterparts of Charley and his comrades and similar 'trench humour'. For example, an Iranian student is taken before an Inquisitor because he has been drinking – a crime punishable by thirty lashes. He had the presence of mind to chew cigarettes first. The Inquisitor smelt his breath, "Ugh! It doesn't smell of beer at all. It smells of shit!" and let him go. That's pure *Charley's War*! This actually happened to my Iranian contact when he was a student. The stories of such 'ordinary' heroes fascinate me. Marjane Satrapi's autobiographical graphic novel *Persepolis* has also proved that 'political' stories don't have to be boring and can be more entertaining than the meaningless adventures of men in tights.

I've put up *Ayatollah's Son* on a dedicated Facebook site. I hope to add to it with images from *Charley's War* and other political stories I've written. For example, the *Inspector Ryan* stories by myself and Alan Mitchell, drawn by the late John Hicklenton and my *You are Maggie Thatcher* book, drawn by Hunt Emerson. I'm hoping it will create a possible forum for politically-orientated comic stories like *Charley's War*. It's under the heading *PatMillsPoliticalComics*. I welcome your feedback.

EPISODE NINETEEN

The blood transfusion episode. It seems unbelievable that blood should be pumped straight out of one soldier into another – and yet it's all horribly true.

EPISODE TWENTY

Fabulous artwork by Joe. The incident where General Haig only sees soldiers who have acceptable wounds is authentic. "Nothing gruesome or upsetting. Like faces blown off…. He can't bear to look at the really

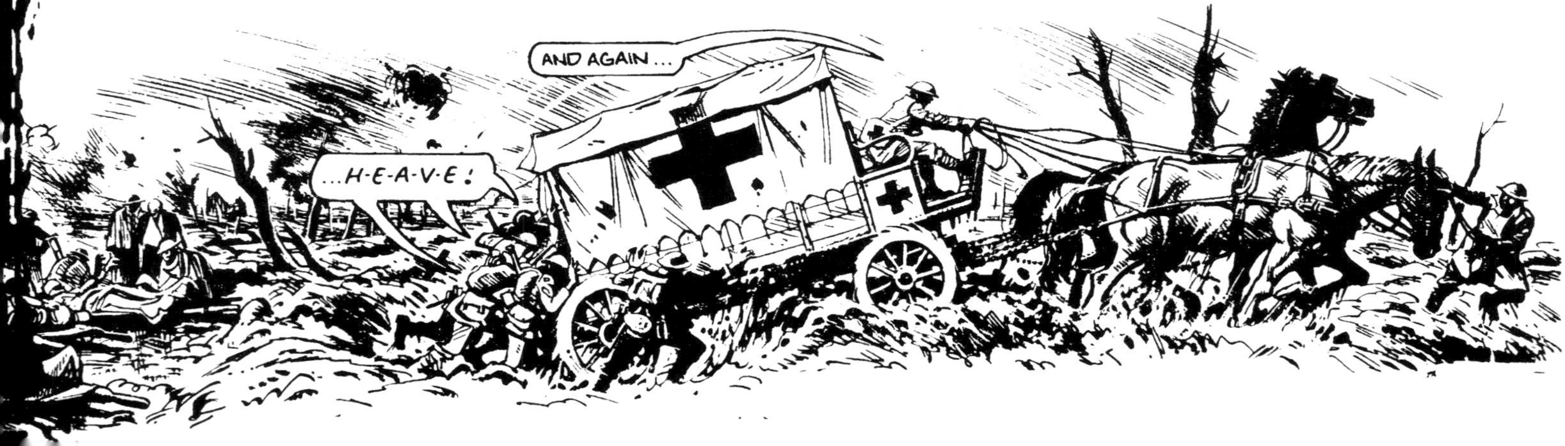
AND AGAIN…
…H-E-A-V-E!

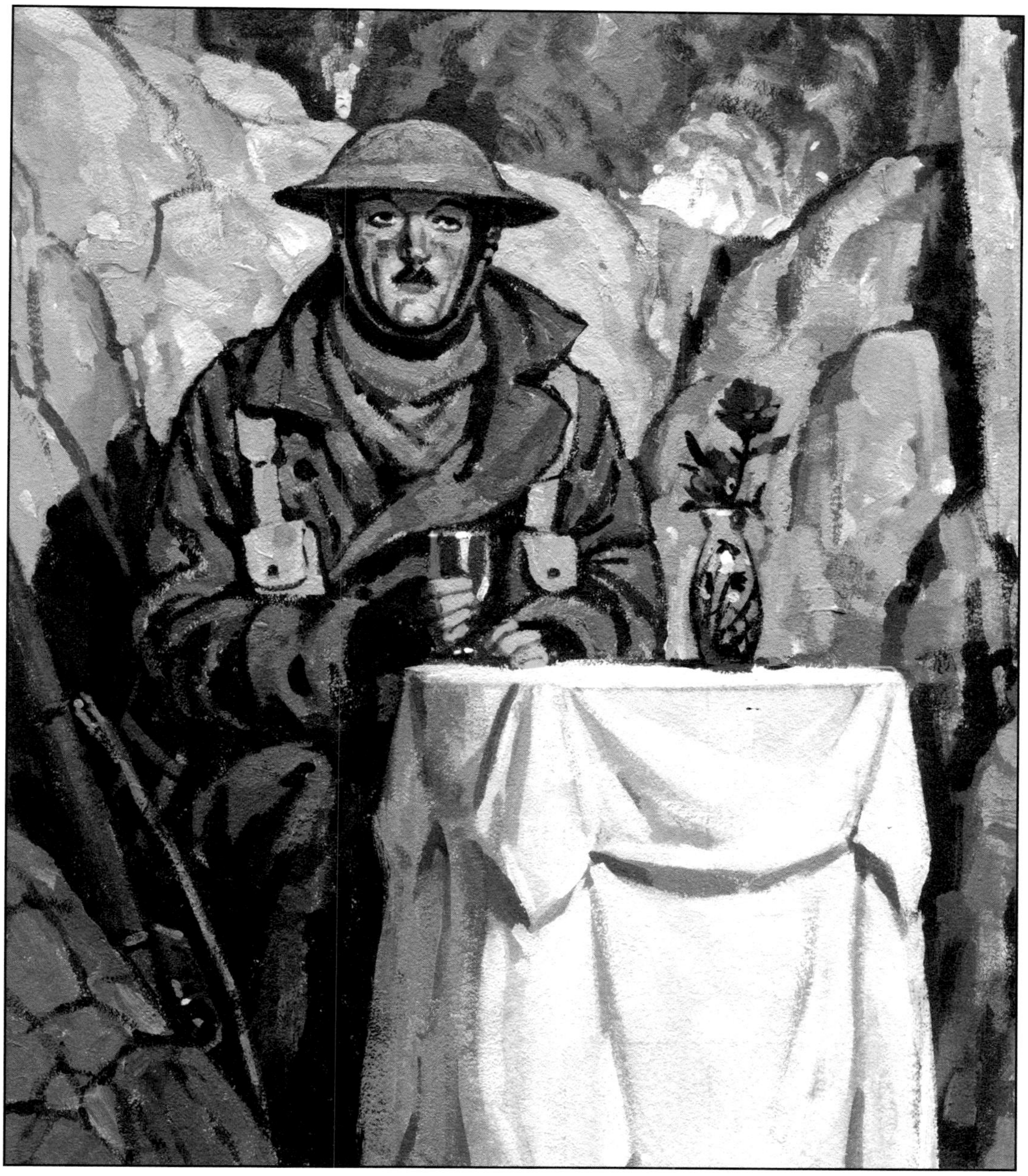

LEFT: ***Gourmet Rifles*** **by Paul Slater, from his collection,** ***Fried Eggs in Brine*****, reproduced here by kind permission of Paul and Atlantic Press.**

horrible cases. They make him feel ill." It's good that it's appearing at this time where there is an odious attempt by historians to rehabilitate Haig as some kind of misunderstood 'hero'. Although I doubt modern politicians visiting the war wounded from the Iraq and Afghanistan wars are any different to and only share 'photo opportunities' with soldiers who have 'suitable' wounds.

EPISODE TWENTY ONE

Joe's art continues to knock me out, particularly the last page and his view of the cattle trucks. I never thought any other artist would capture the combination of nightmare imbued with surreal comedy that is so often World War One. But recently I came across a book by artist Paul Slater: *Fried Eggs in Brine*. It is absolutely stunning. It contains surreal paintings with a very satirical view of British militarism. Do check it out.

EPISODES TWENTY TWO TO TWENTY THREE

The story of Charley's Last Carry. This adventure leads us up to the 'modern day' story of the tour of the war memorials. It reminded me of various attempts to have the *Charley's War* artwork exhibited in British war museums, including the Imperial War Museum, but so far without success. We have, however, been more fortunate in France and I'm told *Charley's War* was included in an exhibition at the Historial de la Grande Guerre museum earlier this year.

France has always taken its comic books more seriously than Britain. I have fond memories of looking at a lush graphic novel, the 300-page *Le Cri du peuple*, set in 1871's Paris Commune by Tardi. This brilliant artist also produces superb stories on the French war in the trenches. I guess the Etaples Mutiny had much in common with the Commune; certainly red flags were carried by the mutineers. Then, and in the 1919

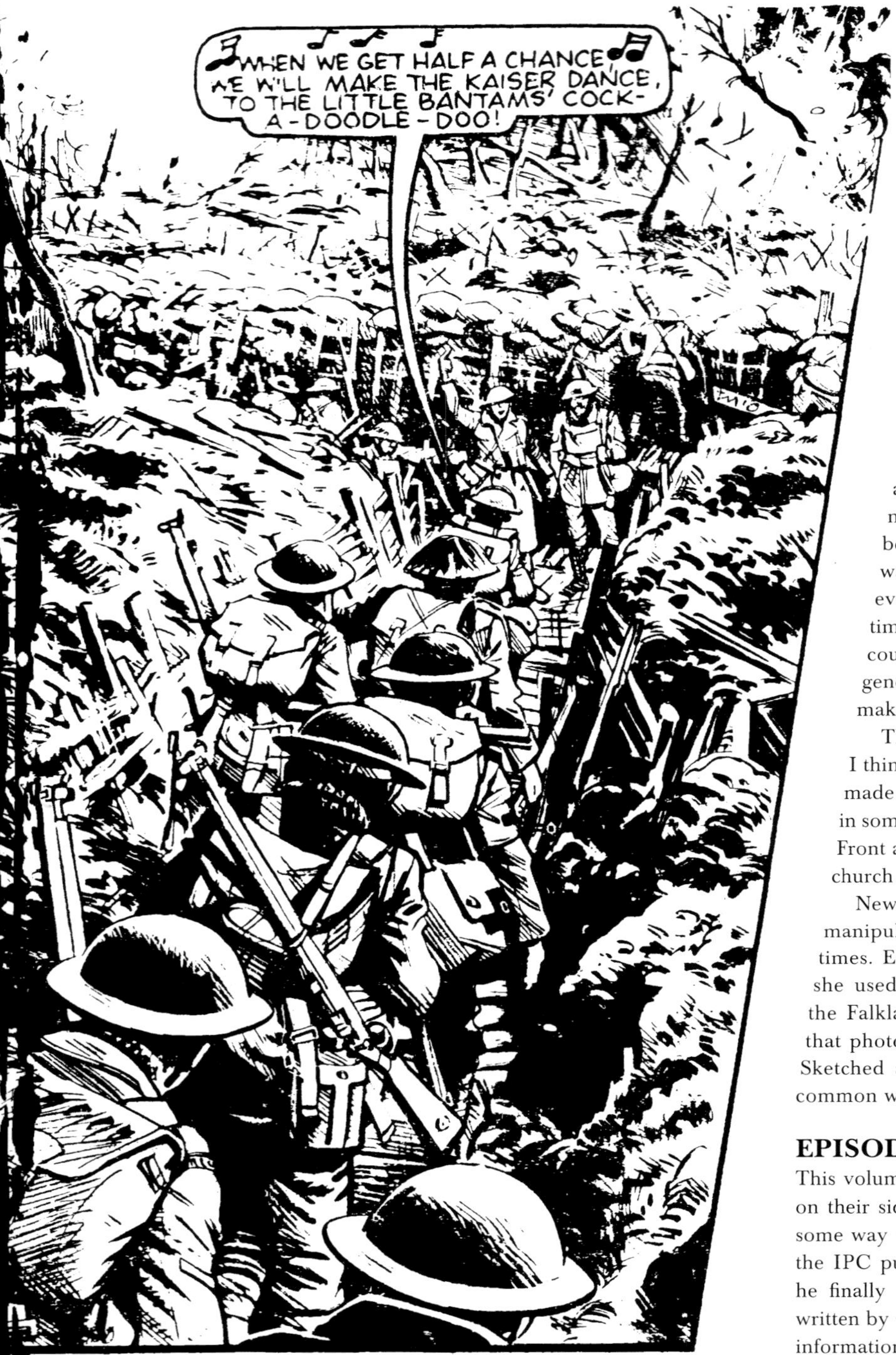
WHEN WE GET HALF A CHANCE WE WILL MAKE THE KAISER DANCE, TO THE LITTLE BANTAMS' COCK-A-DOODLE-DOO!

mutinies when British soldiers refused to invade Soviet Russia, there was serious talk of revolution.

It would be impossible today to produce British equivalents in comic book form – on the 1926 General Strike, for example – for the Anglo-American comic market where fantasy rules. These days, I have to sneak my interest in history and politics into my stories, but never too much in case a small but vocal section of my audience starts complaining once again that history and politics are 'not entertainment'. Sigh! Thus in *2000AD's Defoe*, a science fantasy clockpunk adventure set in the 17th Century, Titus Defoe is the last Leveller and is guilt-ridden that he has sold out to become the King's Zombie Hunter. This allowed me to explore the belief systems of the Levellers, the first socialists, and how they were betrayed by Cromwell. My critics haven't noticed. Don't tell them.

EPISODES TWENTY FOUR TO TWENTY FIVE

I think these two episodes of the veteran returning to Ypres in 1982 are probably amongst the most powerful and emotional episodes of the entire *Charley's War* saga. Joe has surpassed himself with his characterisation and authentic detail.

EPISODES TWENTY SIX TO TWENTY EIGHT

The Battle of Cambrai. Charley doesn't feature in the action and I think this was deliberate – to show that major events do not always involve my central character, because that would be contrived and unrealistic. It was a reaction to traditional war hero stories – like Captain Hurricane – who featured in every major theatre in Europe and the Far East. At the same time, it was important to feature these momentous events, the courage of the Bantams and the criminal incompetence of the generals. Not to mention that ludicrous dummy tank which still makes me laugh.

That said, I doubt I would write the story in this way today. I think I would have created a stronger sub-plot for Charley that made him more pro-active and engaged him in the central events in some other way. Perhaps with a stronger emphasis on the Home Front and how people really believed victory was in sight and the church bells rang in triumph.

News of events at the front was highly controlled and manipulated by the authorities and this continues into our own times. Excellent girls comic artist Charlotte Fawley told me how she used to draw images of battle for BBC2's *Newsnight* during the Falklands conflict and the first Gulf War. There was a ruling that photos could not be used but drawn images were acceptable. Sketched at *very* short notice, they are superb and have much in common with Joe's depictions of war.

EPISODE TWENTY NINE

This volume concludes with a sympathetic depiction of the Germans on their side of the trenches. With *Battle* and *Action* comics we went some way to showing Germans were heroes, too. I had pleaded with the IPC publisher to let me run a serial with a 'good German' and he finally agreed. This became *Hellman of Hammer Force*, superbly written by Gerry Finley-Day and illustrated by Mike Dorey. However, information which shows the Germans in a positive light is still thin on the ground. For instance, I only recently discovered the story of the Edelweiss Pirates and the Roving Dudes – German teenagers who courageously fought back against the Nazis in the Second World War. These young heroes have never been recognised as a resistance movement, perhaps because they also fought against the British and Americans during the brutal first years of the Allied occupation of Germany (another largely untold story). They were regarded as 'a serious menace' by the Allies.

Although there will be many 'good Germans' in this next *Charley's War* story, the episode ends with one of my all-time favourite cliff-hangers: the appearance of the young Adolf Hitler! ✛

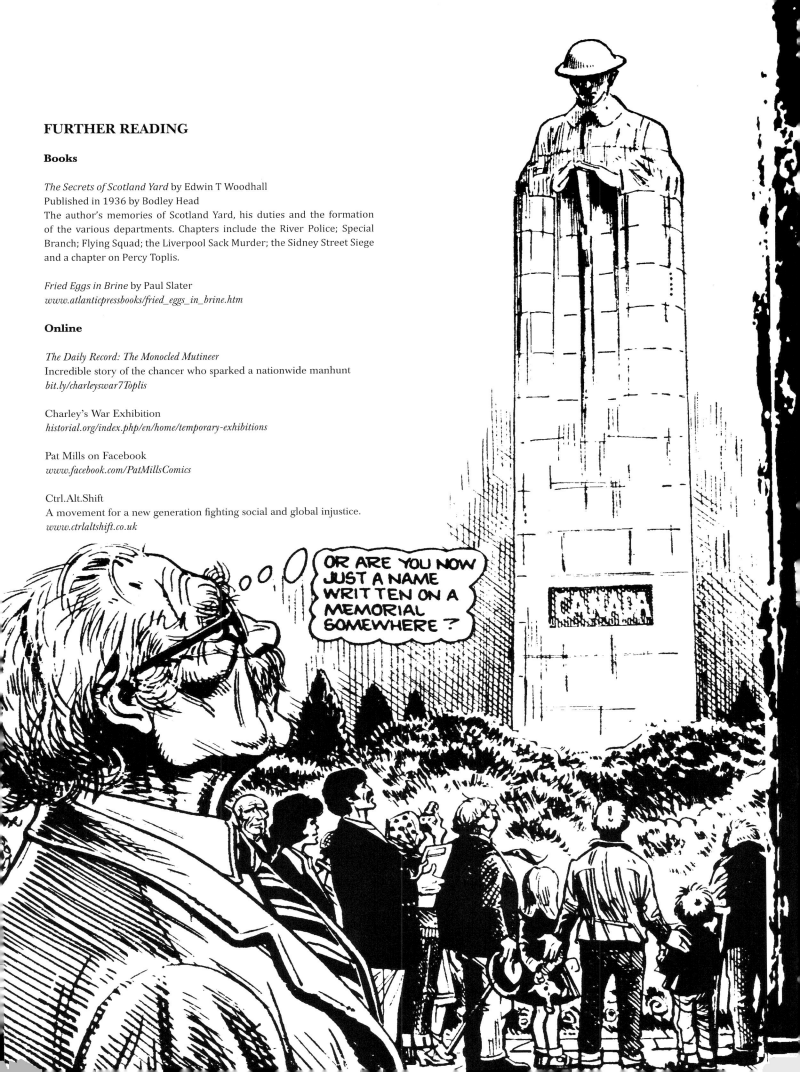

FURTHER READING

Books

The Secrets of Scotland Yard by Edwin T Woodhall
Published in 1936 by Bodley Head
The author's memories of Scotland Yard, his duties and the formation of the various departments. Chapters include the River Police; Special Branch; Flying Squad; the Liverpool Sack Murder; the Sidney Street Siege and a chapter on Percy Toplis.

Fried Eggs in Brine by Paul Slater
www.atlanticpressbooks/fried_eggs_in_brine.htm

Online

The Daily Record: The Monocled Mutineer
Incredible story of the chancer who sparked a nationwide manhunt
bit.ly/charleyswar7Toplis

Charley's War Exhibition
historial.org/index.php/en/home/temporary-exhibitions

Pat Mills on Facebook
www.facebook.com/PatMillsComics

Ctrl.Alt.Shift
A movement for a new generation fighting social and global injustice.
www.ctrlaltshift.co.uk

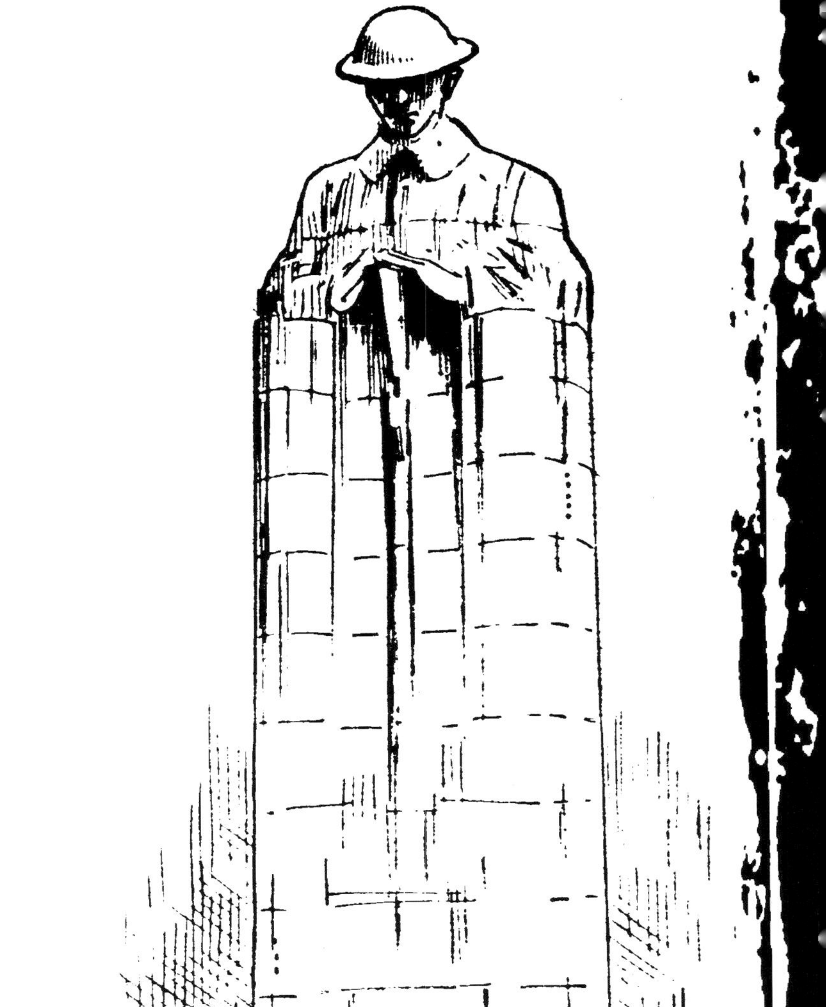

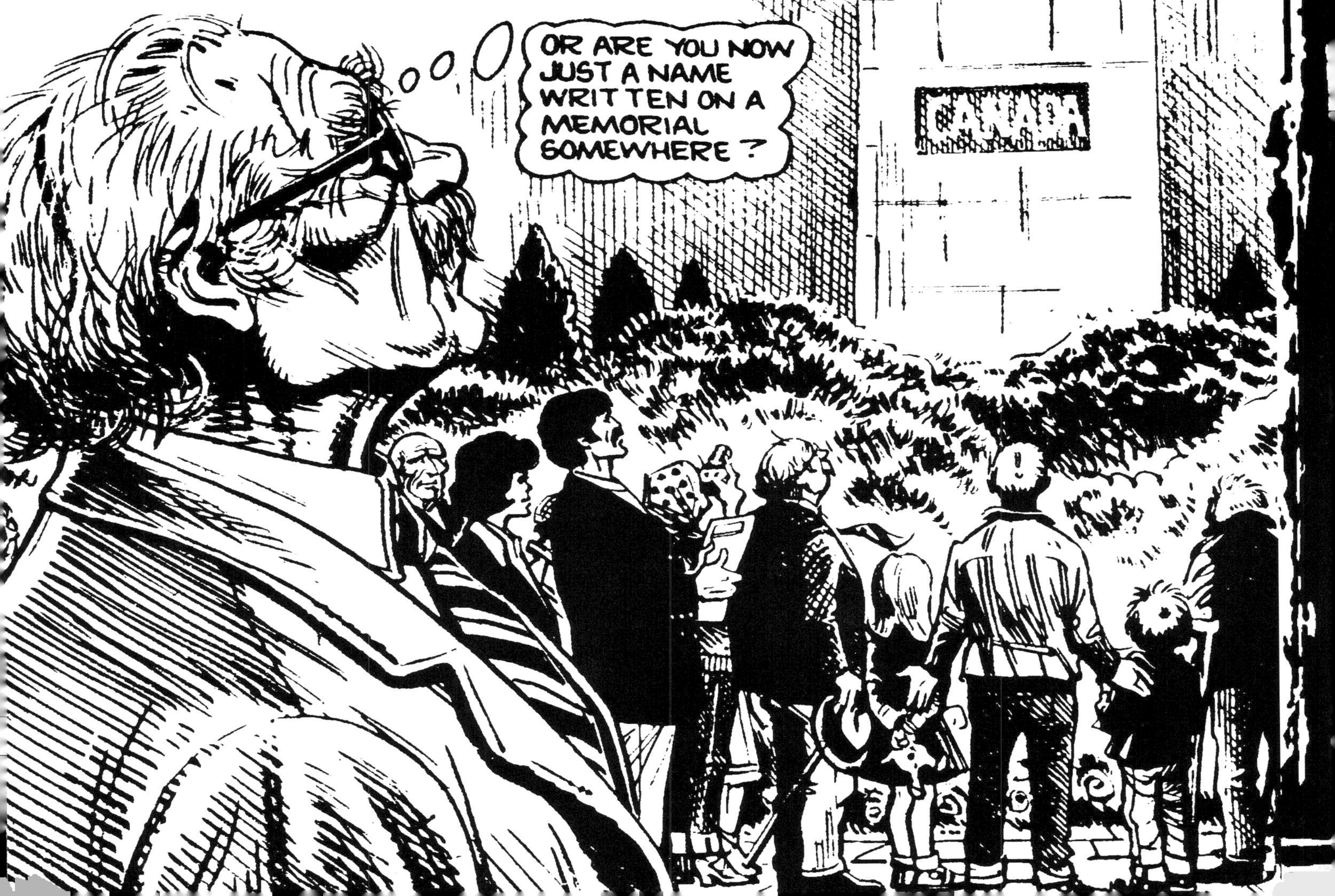
OR ARE YOU NOW JUST A NAME WRITTEN ON A MEMORIAL SOMEWHERE?
CANADA

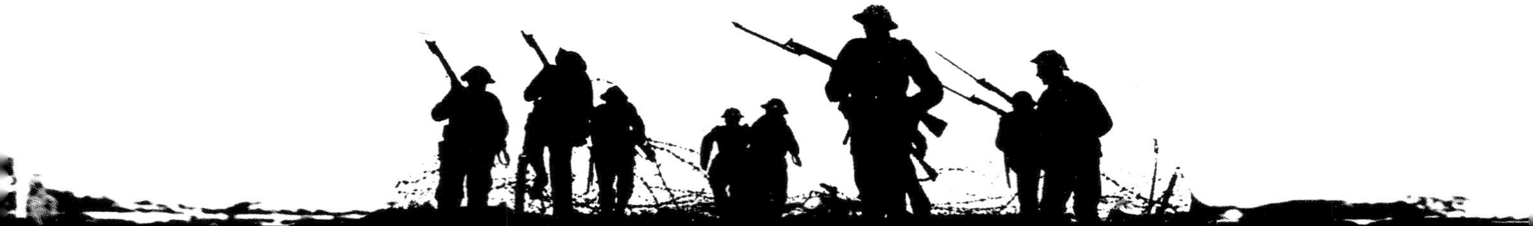

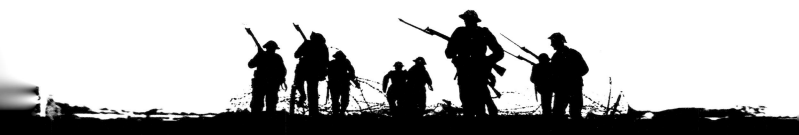

ALSO AVAILABLE FROM TITAN BOOKS

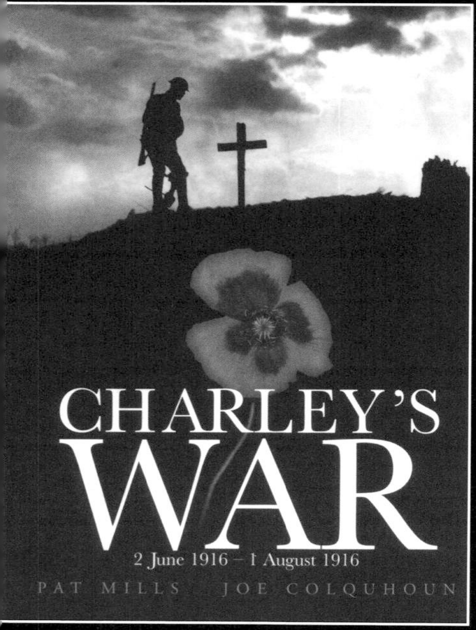
CHARLEY'S
WAR
2 June 1916 – 1 August 1916
PAT MILLS JOE COLQUHOUN

ISBN: 9781840236279

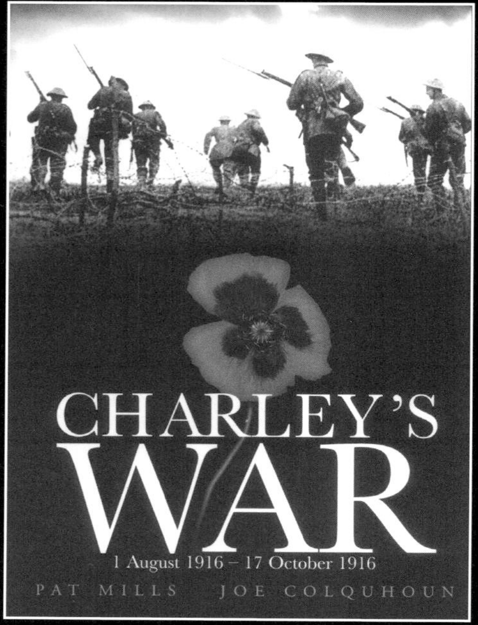
CHARLEY'S
WAR
1 August 1916 – 17 October 1916
PAT MILLS JOE COLQUHOUN

ISBN: 9781840239294

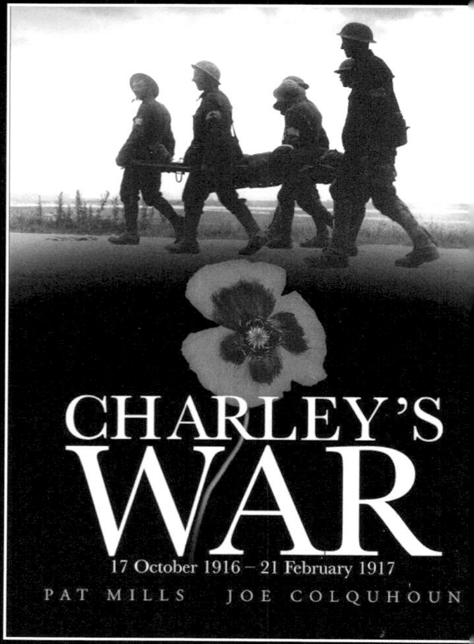
CHARLEY'S
WAR
17 October 1916 – 21 February 1917
PAT MILLS JOE COLQUHOUN

ISBN: 9781845762704

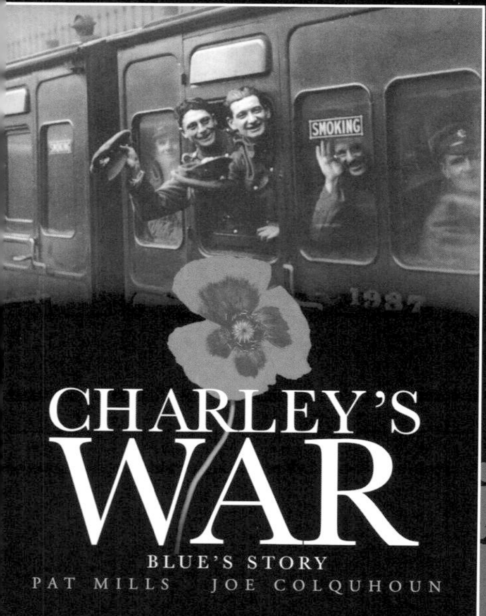
SMOKING
CHARLEY'S
WAR
BLUE'S STORY
PAT MILLS JOE COLQUHOUN

ISBN: 9781845763237

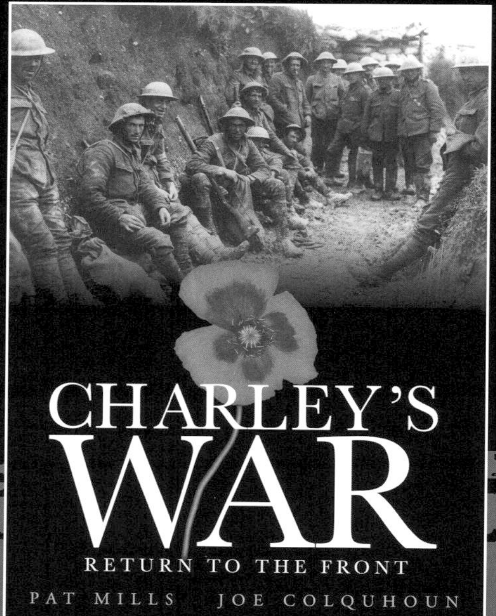
CHARLEY'S
WAR
RETURN TO THE FRONT
PAT MILLS JOE COLQUHOUN

ISBN: 9781845767969

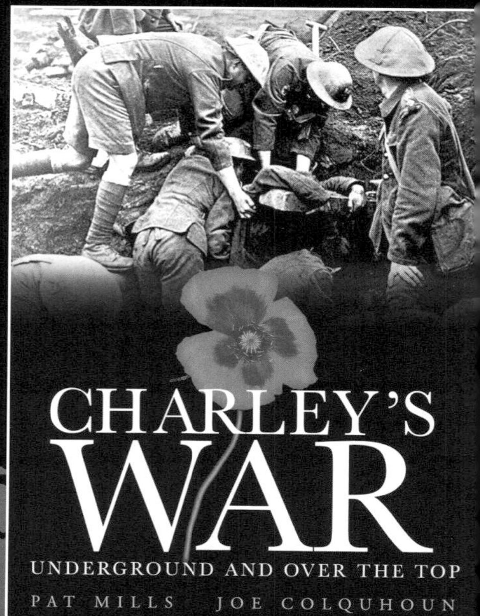
CHARLEY'S
WAR
UNDERGROUND AND OVER THE TOP
PAT MILLS JOE COLQUHOUN

ISBN: 9781845767976

www.titanbooks.com